To: Marian
From: Bobby

MW00613184

A roast for **COACH** dan **SPEAR**

small town football dreams from the florida fifties

by robert **BOWIE**

Robert Bowie
Nov. 9, 1997

ogee **Zakamora** publications
Hamilton ohio

A Roast for Coach Dan Spear
Small Town Football Dreams from the Florida Fifties

By Robert Bowie

Published by:
Ogee Zakamora Publications
P.O. Box 7207
Hamilton, OH 45013

Bowie, Robert Lee
A Roast for Coach Dan Spear: Small Town Football Dreams from the Florida Fifties / by Robert Bowie. —1st ed.
p. cm.
ISBN 0-9658258-7-6

1.Memoirs–United States
2.Biography
3.Sports

....

Dedications

This book is dedicated to:

Nana T. Laney who taught me how to write.

Dan Spear who taught me how to block.

D.D. Roseborough who tried to teach me to be kind.

....

Acknowledgements

Special thanks to my Central Florida sales rep and P.R. man: Lawrence Calvin Smith. Also to Rob Bowie for the proof reading and to L. Berl Willimas. I am grateful to Rondi Tschopp for the excellent work on page layout and cover design, to Elizabeth Runyon for technical advice and encouragement, and to Charlotte Wharton, who is never too busy to help. Finally, I would like to thank my publisher and editor, O.G. Zakamora, whose persistence and unfailing high spirits kept this project on the rails. None of the above persons, however, is responsible for opinions expressed in the book. That responsibility is mine and mine alone.

This is a true story. Of course, when you recall things thirty-seven years later your memory gets creative. So people who were around then may have different recollections. All I can do is tell it the way I remember it. Most of the names are real, but I have altered some, to avoid embarrassment to the living and the dead. I apologize in advance for misspellings of names or for the angle from which real events are viewed. No maliciousness or malice aforethought is intended, in regard to any private person or any institution.

Book design by: *Five* Visual Communication *& Design*
7544 *Lakewood Circle*
West Chester, Ohio *45069*
five@*eos.net*

....

A Roast for Coach Dan Spear

To Be Read at the Dan Spear Festivities,
Mt. Dora, Fla., *Apr. 30, 1994*

"Living through a life is not like walking through a field."
...Russian proverb

Contents

MOUNT DORA HIGH SCHOOL
700 North Highland Street • Mount Dora, Florida 32757

HURRICANES- "The Year of The SPEAR"

We're having a ROAST !!!

You're invited. Come join the FUN
to help celebrate Dan Spear's 30+
years at Mt. Dora High School.
Coaches, teachers, students and friends:
Plan to be part of the evening's
festivities for a lot of fun in
honoring a true legend.

Date: Saturday, April 30, 1994
Time: 6:00-7:00 Cocktails;
7:00-8:30 Roast (followed by dinner)
Place: Downtown Mt. Dora - Top of the Lamppost"
The Old Charlie's Bar & Grill

If you have a
funny or interesting
story about Dan
and would like to
share it during the
roast → PLEASE →
Let us know !!!

Hope to see you there,
The Dan Spear Roast Committee

$ 25.00 per person...
Proceeds to benefit
The MDHS football
program.

Limited
Space
Available

Make your reservation
EARLY — at least
by March 30.
"Achieving today for success tomorrow"

....

Note to the reader:

Dear Dommy Hartson,

I'm sending this note out Federal Express, and I hope you get it in time. Rhoda told me you're the one who'll be reading my letter at the roast tonight. I want to apologize: I got carried away and wrote too much. I know that after the cocktail party you've only got two hours for the actual "roasting" and the awards. There'll be lots of people with stories to tell about Dan Spear and Mt. Dora football. Why, just the great '51 and '59 teams could take up all the time, and they deserve it, I'm sure y'all don't want to hear much about that piddling '57 team of ours, so, anyway, just pick out the best parts of my thing.

Come to think of it, you can omit the whole bit called "Halftime." Nothing much really happened during the half of that game. Well, the band marched, and Nancy Eichhorn twirled her baton, and they ran the mosquito fogging trucks around the field again, little kids trailing behind, romping through the pesticides, and then those same kids got up a game of tackle football, joined by a mongrel who trotted sideways onto the field, folks in the stands getting a good laugh out of that bedraggled mutt, meek smile on his dogged face, tail at half mast, eyes pleading (Can I play too?). But I wasn't there to see any of that, since we, the team, were back in the gym. It's just the way things always went. So, anyway, I'm afraid the part called "Halftime" might just put people to sleep, being as it's a long digression about things that have no bearing on that football game. Leave it out.

Oh, yeah, one other thing. My sense of humor is kind of raunchy, and there could be some folks at the roast get offended. Look out into the audience as you're reading along, and if you come to something ticklish about somebody sitting there, well, just skip that. Like the part about Joe Raff in Chapter Five, well, I always liked Joe Raff, and though what I'm telling is God's truth, and Joe was young and wild then, and nobody would hold that against him now. Still, thirty-seven years later I doubt he'd want that told on him.

And maybe that thing in Chapter Four about Waiford Bedford and Lonnie, the night Lonnie caught up with him in the parking lot over at that bar in Leesburg, and Lonnie being just a skinny mountain man from the foothills of West Virginia, nothing left of his teeth at age twenty-five but a few rotten tobacco stains, and Waiford big and brawny as he was, whoever would have thought he'd end up with his nose rubbed in the gravel, but then it wasn't really surprising if you knew Lonnie, who was the most easy-going fellow on earth until you riled him, I remember once seeing him whip up on Ephraim Carlotti, who after all, was from New York and had boxing lessons and thought he was hot crap, one day I saw Ephraim punch poor David Coffield's face like a punching bag for twenty minutes straight, out on the football field during recess, and David not giving up, tears running down his Elvis sideburns, keeping on coming, taking wild swings and missing and Ephraim, with his reddish hair and white Yankee skin, up on his toes, dancing around like a prize fighter and just peppering away at David's face raising reams of bumps and welts, I always liked Janice and Joyce and David Coffield, wonder where they are now, but when Ephraim gave some lip to Lonnie down at the hardware one day, why, Lonnie just proceeded, in a matter of seconds, to literally kick the living bejesus out of Ephraim Carlotti, and he ends up cold conked in the lumber room on his back. Well, anyway, people in a small town can be sensitive, even forty years later, so leave that out about Waiford panting after Lonnie's wife, and how Lonnie caught up with him that night over on 441 near Leesburg.

Come to think of it, there might could be other things you better just skip. The army and the Russian adventures. Maybe the stuff about Bobby Rodmon, how they ran him out of town, and the story of math teacher

....

Renjy Mottle, when he grabbed the butt of Sadie, my friend Jake's girl friend, in the cloakroom one day, and she threatened to turn him in, had him in tears, what Renjy didn't know was that Sadie, at age seventeen, had probably ten times more the sexual experience that he ever did, even him being thirty years older. And the revelation about who shot out the Christmas lights at Holler's Point, that year (was it 1956?) when the whole town had vengeance steaming out its ears, swearing they'd crucify the bastard when they caught him, though I suppose the statute of limitations has run out on that by now.

So, anyway, you're the reader, you decide what to read. Hmm. I just had an idea. Conjure up "The Walking Jesus." Imagine him perched on a chair out there in the audience at the roast, in his white satin pants. With his calloused bare feet and that fluff of soft grey hair drooping down his back, pink and purple and chartreuse silk scarfs wrapped around his body. You look out there at The Walking Jesus, looking back at you with the glint of God-ordained rectitude in his crazed dark eyes, and then you just omit anything you believe might offend him.

You remember The Walking Jesus, don't you, Dom? Sure you do. Anybody who grew up in Mt. Dora remembers The Walking Jesus. Well, I guess that's all. Thanks for being my reader, and enjoy the party!

Bobby

P.S.

Actually, I was surprised the roast committee would want to use any of this mishmash. I wrote it fast, trying to get it done by the end of April, finished it just two days ago and got it off overnight mail. Then, yesterday morning a female voice calls me on the phone, and first off it says, "Bobby

Bowie, I love you." Well, I knew right away it must be from Mt. Dora, Florida, because nobody's called me 'Bobby' for thirty years. But I didn't know why she loved me.

When she told me her name, Rhoda Manson, I said, "Let me guess, which Manson are you married to, Ivan or Donny Gene?" She said "Ivan." Turns out she's from Orlando originally, where I hear that you are living now, Dom, of course, I wouldn't give a rat's whisker for Orlando any more, not since they trucked in all that Mickey Mouse chickenshit and ruined what was a nice town, why, I remember we used to play football down at St. Cloud back before it and Kissimmee and the whole area got swallowed up by this jackass "fun culture" America, and then, after that, I asked Rhoda why it was she happened to love me, us never having met.

She said she read my letter right after they got it, and it was a wonderful thing and they wanted you, the master of ceremonies, to read it to the audience at the roast. It surprised me that Rhoda, who didn't come from Mt. Dora, it was strange that the letter would be of interest to her, but then, of course, she is married to a Manson, whose brother is in the story, yet still, another thing she told me really amazed me. She said, "I liked it so much after I read it the first time, that I sat down and read the whole thing through again. Then, last night, I went to bed, and I couldn't get to sleep, and I got up and started reading it the third time. I was sitting at the kitchen table, reading, it was three a.m., and I was wiping away the tears with a dish towel."

Now, you tell me, Dom, what is there in my story for the roast that could make somebody from Orlando, Florida, cry? It's a funny story, full of joy and good humor. It's about the happiest day of my life: Nov. 1, 1957.

1

P R E G A M E

Rapid Robert/ A statue in the flesh that laughed/ '57 team/ Gringy Bahls/ Arrested in Tijuana, although innocent/ Speaking Russian in a drunk tank/ Frederick Gosnell/ Robbed by gypsies/ Mulberries steaming in Samarkand/ Ty Barker kicked in the backside, while doing his best/ Naked on a ping-pong table/ Our butts stomped in Groveland/ C.M. Jones—two black eyes and a broken nose/ Laughter in the woebegone school bus/ Barry Keitel/ Dan Spear makes a threat/ Nobody but nobody thought we could win/ Except Earle Williams/ Pre-game pep talk (not)/ Racking like Bobby Correll/ The splendor of "Right 32"/ Coach Spear, grieving in the fumes of the analgesic balm/ Austin Simpson was surely laughing/ "Cain't never could, Bobbie Jean"/ The yellow hibiscus/ Flame vine on the fence/ Our dog Danny/ A big nose, on a face from Eastern Europe/ Your favorite song, "Good Night, Irene"/ You called the girls "Abigail"/ "Seven Months of Boyhood Adventures"/ My sister wanted a pony/ George White's seegar/ Give 'em hell, Hurricanes!/ Beautiful, moist, subtropical Mt. Dora, Florida/ The Walking Jesus

Remember me, Dan Spear? My name was Bobby Bowie (rhymes with 'Booby'). I played tailback and wingback on some of the truly wonderful teams in the annals of the "Golden Hurricanes." I was number Nine in my senior year. You called me "Rapid Robert." Or "Twinkle Toes." I was fast, I was great! Well, maybe not as fast or great as Jerry Dake, or Billy Odom, Harry Wise. But they've probably got statues of those folks up at MDHS these days. Standing with a football under one arm, wearing oversized hip pads and the old leather helmet, gazing off soulfully into the distance, toward Lake Franklin.

I'm sorry I didn't make it to the roast tonight, but since I couldn't come I decided to send you this story, which describes one particular game, on one particular night—Nov. 1, 1957. I was a statue myself before that game. A statue in the flesh that laughed. See if you remember this anything like I do.

The '57 team. We didn't have much size or strength, but we won a lot of games on sheer guts. Captain Billy Moon was at center, middle line-backer on defense, weighing 125. We had the great Lew Earle Williams, Jr., right guard at 143, and then there was Gary Potter (147) at the other. We nicknamed him "Muff," after the derelict character in *Tom Sawyer*. That is, Larry Smith did. He was the nicknaming specialist in our class. He came up with "Ace" for Ronnie Aldrich and "Jack" for Donald Alexander. He called Judy Sadler "The Holy One." The name somebody (C.M. Jones, Senior) tacked on Larry himself was "Goofy." But it didn't stick.

"Muff" Potter was playing football on his last legs that fall; he died of nephritis a month after we graduated the following spring. I'll never forget how he got sick in the Groveland game. Remember when he vomited all over the field? But then, we all felt like throwing up that night, didn't we?

Our largest players were the tackles: C.M. (Bub) Jones, who weighed 164, and Willie Vanzant, who may have even hit 185. In the backfield there was another Vanzant, Robbie (145), there was Rick Gardner (140), Neil Stoothoff (155). And me, I weighed 150. Who else was on that team? John

Lavin, Joe Graf, Ken Bliss, Fred Thibault, Owen McCallister, Herbert Flavell. Future stars Frank Peck, Charles Kinsey, Arthur Norris, Donny Dake. And then there was Gringy Bahls. I apologize to those I've forgotten. It has been a long time.

God, the things that have happened in yours and mine and everybody's life since then! I can only speak for myself. After high school I attended the University of Florida, graduated in '62. Then I went in the army, and things started getting wild. For example, in 1964 I was arrested in Tijuana, Mexico, and thrown in a military prison in San Diego. They put us in the drunk tank, my two army buddies and me, though we hadn't been drinking. There was a sailor passed out on the floor, drooling right into the drain, and we kept on speaking Russian until they reamed us out. Later, in the summer of '64, I lived in a G.I. tent in a wheat field, overlooking the barbed wire of the East German border. On the other side of the fences and plowed mine fields the Russians were doing tank exercises. To protect us up on our hill, in our wheat field (in case the Russian tanks came across), the U.S. Army sent us a German shepherd guard dog and one M-14 rifle. They didn't send any cartridges for the rifle, though, and the dog bit everybody in our camp.

What else? Well, for example, I learned the Russian language in the army and chased a lot of women. Never learned to chase women till I left Florida. I've always preferred foreign types—ended up marrying a girl from England. Later I spent time in the Soviet Union. I was in The Botkins Hospital in Moscow (with dysentery) in 1972, same place they took Lee Oswald after he attempted suicide. Back in the USSR a lot more times after that. In January, 1986, I watched oblique sunrays reflecting off snow banks, playing games on the pastel pinks and light greens of the baroque palaces of Leningrad. There's no Leningrad any more. I was around for the Reagan Summit meeting in 1988 (met Tom Brokaw and Peter Jennings at the

Rossiya Hotel on Red Square). In 1991 I stayed at the "Horse Race Hotel," overlooking the Moscow Hippodrome. Watched the horses running from my window sill, sitting in sunshine, drinking vodka, fending off the advances of a huge Estonian chambermaid. That same summer my Russian friend Volodya drank too much (I was with him) and got mugged, beaten unconscious. The name of that story is, "The Day They Kicked the Crap out of Volodya and It Could Have Been Me." Also that summer I went on tour with a Russian bluegrass group, "The Red River Valley Boys," serving as their translator and lyricist. They sang all their songs in English but could only speak Russian. I helped them with the twang, which I recalled from my Southern boyhood.

Since the early seventies I've been a professor of Russian at a college in Ohio. On Nov. 1, 1957, could I have imagined spending my birthday thirty-five years later sleeping under a stairwell at the nightmare airport of all the earth, Domodedovo, in Moscow? That was in 1992, when I was working for the Red Cross as a 'freight courier', transporting a copy machine to Alma Ata, Kazakhstan, Central Asia. Starting in 1988, I was group leader for student groups studying Russian in the Soviet Union. After the country began coming apart we were robbed (among other places) in the Moscow Puppet Theater (1990). In 1993 our suitcases were rifled while our plane sat on the ground, at the airport in Lvov (now Lviv), New Ukraine. A year earlier marked the infamous midnight flight on Air Azerbaijan, when the drunk Azeri fruit pedlars went after our women. I flew Aeroflot four more times that summer, after my student group went back to the States. Each of those flights was an adventure.

You ever hear about the gypsies of Eastern Europe? You're a foreigner, sightseeing away, trundling down the streets of the un-Soviet Union, and they send their little kids to hang on your legs and hold your arms, while the women grab your wallet. When you've got the time to listen, Dan Spear, let me know. I'll tell you all these stories, and more! Like how I was stranded in the deserts of Samarkand, Uzbekistan, where they've got Tamerlane's mausoleum, where it's so hot that the fresh mulberries in the open-air markets are breathing mist. You walk through the bazaar and the hucksters babble at you in Uzbek, Russian, Sanskrit, Persian, and they wink and beckon, pulling at their Saadam Hussein moustaches, holding out free samples of steaming mulberries on a soup spoon, okay, okay, that's enough. Time to get back to 1957.

Our football team was limping through the fall. Someone was always hurt. We didn't even practice hard for fear we'd lose another body. But we won games. We beat Eustis that year, 12-7, and beating Useless always made our season. Does Mt. Dora still play the mighty Panthers? I hear they've got black kids over there now who weigh in at 280 and go on to big time college football at Florida or F.S.U. Is that true? Our old Mid-Lakes Conference wasn't like that. Schools were segregated, and we didn't have weight rooms for bulking up. We were runts and Caucasians. Neil Stoothoff's father, Herbert, hired a bunch of us to pick corn at Zellwin Farms in the summer of 1956, and after that ordeal he swore he'd be damned if he'd ever hire another white boy on a harvesting crew.

You will, of course, recall, Coach Spear, that Mt. Dora football in the mid fifties was none too spectacular. The teams with Bobby Alderman, Roland Lane, Jeff Ray, with Donald Gregg and Billy Simpson, those weren't big winners. Not that I'm criticizing anybody. I was on those teams too (we went 2-7 my junior year). After we lost you could be very hard to get along with. Shanks Hansel, line coach, would try to act mad too, but he wasn't really mad. He was the head basketball coach, and his mind was thinking ahead to important things, like the coming roundball season.

But you were, Dan Spear. Mad. Really. You were small, but mean. I remember how once, in practice, you got around behind Tyrone Barker, because you were displeased with the way he blocked on one play, and you told him that if he didn't do it right the next time that you would kick him right smack in the large backside, and he didn't, and you did. I always liked Tyrone, that ample good-natured way he had about him.

But, anyway, what I want to talk about today is just one home game, on All Saints Day, in 1957. It was against Bishop Moore, the Catholic school from Orlando. Our story begins in the old Mt. Dora gymnasium, down at what is now Roseborough Elementary School. It was an hour before the game, and our team was in the locker room, putting on the pads and suiting up. I was out on the gym floor, standing naked on a ping-pong table.

We had big problems that night, as you surely remember. We had played the powerhouse of the conference, Groveland, the week before, and they had turned us every way but loose: 40-0.

I can recollect riding bleakly along in that yellow school bus, heading home, through the orange groves of Clermont, over the hills of Howey-in-the-Hills, with my face so thoroughly rubbed in the turf that I could still smell the grasses of Groveland in my nostrils. But C.M. couldn't. I looked over at C.M.(Bub) Jones III, hunkering down in his seat with his broken nose and his two black eyes, and I laughed. As we ambled through the humidity down State Highway 19, past the live oaks with their dangling moss, the scrub pines and palmettoes, that bus was oh so quiet. Approaching Tavares, crossing the bridge over Little Lake Harris, where my father and I used to fish for bass. Very quiet, reeking of the damp thick silence that you don't hear anywhere but in Lake County, Florida. Then I glanced at C.M. and I couldn't help laughing. God, he did look funny. And when you get beat that bad, there's not much else you can do but laugh. Or cry.

Of course, nobody laughed in front of Coach Spear. He was on that bus too, he was driving it, and when you got beat, you didn't laugh out loud on the ride back home. But I was looking at C.M.'s mournful face and chuckling under my breath, and he smiled and snorted laughter through his swollen nose, and maybe that's when the whole laughing business got started.

So here we were a week later playing the Bishop Moore Hornets, and we knew in advance we were beat. It seemed like half the team didn't dress out. He wasn't saying so, but even Dan Spear conceded that it was hopeless. Still walking wounded after Groveland, we had to play an undefeated team that was averaging thirty points a game. A team that had linemen who weighed two hundred pounds. The laughing spirit was roiling inside me, Dan Spear, as you wrapped my leg on the ping-pong table. I had a bad right leg that year, so we had to restrain it before every game, but only this one time did you have me climb up on a table. That could be the central fact in this whole story. If not for the ping-pong table things might have turned out altogether different. I remember standing up there in the old Mt. Dora gym, wearing only a jock strap. You were down below, wrapping my leg, Coach Spear, and you were mad. I was posed with arms crossed over my chest, looking into the distance, in the guise of a famous statue, and my team mates kept walking by and grinning. I thought it was funny too; everything was hysterical that night. But I didn't laugh out loud—I just played like a statue. Because Dan Spear was mad. He didn't like to lose, and he knew, sure as Spanish moss hangs on Florida oak trees, faintly coughing in the humidity, that Bishop Moore High was about to regally kick our butts.

You didn't say anything. You just wrapped, Coach Spear. You were sweating. Where else but Florida could it be this hot in November? I stood there like a statue, with my arms crossed and my bottom bare, and later on I heard that a couple of MDHS cheerleaders had walked past the doors outside and got a good giggle out of that scene (they may be here at the roast tonight, so I won't mention any names). Everything was funny, Shorty Johnson, Judy Sadler, not just to me, but to the whole team, to the cheerleaders, maybe even to the fans. As if that suppressed chuckle on the bus back from Groveland had grown to enormous proportions in one week, had spread a cloud of wild laughter over all of lovely, sun-drenched, moist, sub-tropical Mt. Dora, Florida. But not over Dan Spear.

I'll never forget Barry Keitel, the athletic director of Bishop Moore, the way he walked into our gym right in the middle of that leg wrapping. How in the world can I still remember his name after thirty-seven years? But that was it: Barry Keitel. What did he look like? All I can conjure up is a semi-bald head with a few long hairs wrapped over the top. Mr. Keitel spotted Coach Spear over by the ping-pong table; with a smile of good will he headed our way, holding out his hand. As you reluctantly took and shook that hand, I stood looking down on Barry Keitel's congenial semi-bald head and the angry bald head of Dan Spear beside it.

The Bishop Moore bus had just arrived, and Barry must have assumed it the proper thing to do: come by before the game and pay his respects to our a.d. and coach. That was a mistake, Barry Keitel. Dan Spear was in no mood to hear polite respects paid by the athletic director of a team that had come to thoroughly tramp our emaciated bottoms, then drive back, singing B.M. fight songs in the bus, laughing derisively, to Orlando.

Of course, Mr. Keitel knew we didn't stand a chance in that game. There wasn't a soul on earth thought we stood a chance. Except Earle Williams. Right, Earle, Jr.? Are you out there in the audience tonight? Sure you are. You wouldn't miss the Dan Spear Roast. Yes, only Lew Earle Williams, Jr. thought we could beat Bishop Moore.

Well, you held your temper, Coach Spear; you tried to be polite with Barry. You kept your eyes down and talked to him out of the side of your mouth, while you went on viciously tearing tape and wrapping leg. But then, suddenly, you lost it. You said, and you said it loud, in that voice out of Martin's Ferry, Ohio, looking right at him with those beady black eyes, you said, "I'm going to tell you one thing, Barry. If you run the score up, I'm pulling this team off the field. You understand me? I hope you're listening. Because I've got a bunch of gutsy small boys, and they don't deserve that. We're beat up, we're hurt. I won't stand there and watch these boys humiliated."

Mr. Keitel didn't know what to say. I don't remember him saying anything. He just turned red in the face and on top of his head, he mumbled something, and then he backed away and got the hell out of our gym fast. You went back to wrapping even more furiously, Dan Spear, and I stood up there bare-butted, laughing to myself. Then you finished the leg, and I climbed down off that ping-pong table and put my pads on.

Everything was different that night, and everything was funny. You didn't even give us your pre-game pep talk. After you finished wrapping ankles and knees, you went down to your little office, beside the front entrance to the gym, and you sat there in the fumes of the analgesic balm, alone, stewing in your sorrow, Dan Spear. Meanwhile, we were laughing. Gary Potter would say, "You know what? We're *really* going to get our butts kicked tonight!" And everybody would laugh. Then Neil Stoothoff would say, "No. We're *really, really* going to get our butts kicked tonight!" And everybody laughed still harder. Me, I was radiating wild hysteria. John Lavin only had to look at my face and he burst out laughing. Then a bunch of others looked over at me and they laughed too. The fact that we were about to be pulverized, for the second week in a row, was hilarious.

The usual pre-game talk would feature one of your prize players from the past, Coach Spear: Bobby Correll (pronounced Co-ral). You'd try to stir us up by telling us how Bobby Co-ral used to play. You'd talk about racking. That was your favorite word. "I want to see all y'all get out there tonight and rack somebody. You hear? Rack the other team, rack your own team mates. You can even rack the referee, but I mean I want to see you *rack* somebody! Back when Co-ral played I remember one time watching him knock a man down, and that man got back up, and Co-ral knocked him down again, and then he got back up again and Co-ral knocked him down *again*! Now, that's what I call *racking*!"

But on the night of the Bishop Moore game there was no pep talk. You sat down in your office, grieving in advance. You didn't know your team was out there on the gym floor, lacing up hip pads, pulling each others' bright orange jerseys down over shoulder pads, putting on the high-top cleats, laughing. You wouldn't have stood for that, Dan Spear. Laughing and losing just don't go together. Not in your play book.

Speaking of play books, let me take this opportunity to thank you for the wonderful single wing formation, unbalanced line to the right, and the plays we had: Right 27 around end, which was great when I carried the ball from tailback, or even better when I played wingback and got to ambush the enemy left end. Right 26, off tackle, was almost as good, and then there was that thing of beauty, the reverse, Right 32, both guards pulling, and me taking the handoff and seeing lots of clear space. Cut back and find the day-light, Bobby Booby. Then turn on the afterburners and breeze.

The time came for us to take the field. I went through my final pre-game ritual: putting on my magic low-top game shoes—Kangaroo brand. Then silently telling the toes in those shoes how fast they would be tonight. You didn't come out of that office, Dan Spear. We kept looking down there, but you didn't come out. Where was Assistant Coach Shanks Hansel? I don't remember him being there at that game at all. Was he off sick that night? The referees emerged from the locker room where they dressed and headed for the field. You didn't come out. Mt. Dora School principal D.D. ("Prof") Roseborough, waiting in the stands with his wife Precious beside him, Prof in his shock of white hair, rimless glasses glinting in the arc lights, sent somebody (I think it was Ronald E. Aldrich, his second in command at MDHS) to find out what was going on. The Bishop Moore team was on the field, Dan, warmed up, getting antsy, said Mr. Aldrich.

You didn't answer him, or deign to look at him. You sat there staring at the walls, wondering why you ever took up coaching as a career. He left to report back to Prof, though he had only your lugubrious glare to report. You didn't come out.

Finally, Billy Moon, our team captain, figured we couldn't wait any longer. He told us to get lined up outside the gym. Out there in the rear alleyway. Remember? With the flame vine on the fence? We had a rah-rah ritual back then. I wonder if the Mt. Dora Golden Hurricanes of today do this. Are they still "golden," by the way? Our school colors were orange and white, and, besides that, I never could figure out how the color of a hurricane could be golden. Anyway, we would line up to run out to the field, and the captain, at the head of the line, would yell, "What's the good word?" And we would yell back in unison, "Give 'em hell, Hurricanes!" Then we'd break into our pre-game trot and go raging, like the storms we were named for, out onto the playing grounds.

But tonight everything was different. Everything was funny. Billy Moon, with his skinny body and his gaunt face, black-haired Billy Moon put on his white Riddell helmet, smiled, and yelled, "What's the good word?" We screamed, "Give 'em HELL-LL-LL, Hurricanes!" But then we all burst out laughing. Billy Moon took off running, laughing, with the long line of us laughing and running behind him, and we laughed our way all the way out onto the football field, which was right there on Seventh Avenue, across from the stucco house where I used to live (820 E. 7th). We ran laughing, single file through the gate, passing beneath the goal posts with those strips of orange and white crepe paper dangling down from the cross-bar. When we appeared beneath the arc lights, that humongous hometown crowd whooped out its greeting.

Was the crowd laughing too? I often wonder about that. Certainly those good faithful Mt. Dora fans realized, like everyone on earth (except Earle Williams), that we were about to get macerated and swallowed whole. I wonder if any of those fans are at the roast tonight. Maybe Austin

Simpson? I know your son Billy graduated the year before, but you must have been in the crowd that night, Austin. You were at Groveland the week before. I remember because you and my daddy were talking about how the only thing worth watching down there were those spectacular outfits on the Groveland majorettes. So if you saw the Groveland game you must have been there for Bishop Moore. Now, I realize that much of the crowd from that night is presently residing where my parents are, at the far end of Donnelly St., but you're still around, God bless you, Austin Simpson, so you can tell me: were the Mt. Dora fans laughing on the night the mighty Hornets came to town to sting our bottoms?

D.D. (Prof) Roseborough, principal of MDHS, never missed a football game, and I only wish he were here at the roast tonight. There's somebody who deserves having not one, but three or four schools named after him. God, how I loved that man. And then there was Ronald Aldrich, assistant principal, a person who was kind to me at times when I didn't deserve the kindness. He's off in a different dimension now too, but maybe his son is in the audience. I'm trying to think who else might be listening to this story tonight. I mean, besides all the ghosts. Are you out there, Mary Lou Davidson? Jo Brown? Larry Smith? (Yeah, Smith, yeah, Smith). Bud Bliss? Kenny Atkins? J.W. Shaw? My favorite teachers are gone: Evelyn Cassady, Nana T. Laney. What about Eudell Sutley? Are you still walking God's green earth? If you are, let me just tell you now what I should have said thirty years ago: you were a great Spanish teacher. When Barbara Jean Carson would get discouraged with the *hablo espanol* and say, "I just can't do it, Mr. Sutley. I can't," you always answered, with that distinctive Southern chirp, "Cain't never could, Bobbie Jean. Cain't never could."

More teachers potentially in the stands that night: Alexandra Birkbeck, Doris Camp, Argel Rittenhouse, George and Bobbie Clements, Rhoda Todd Horton, E.B. Shotts and his wife Will Laceye Shotts.

Anybody not from Mt. Dora wouldn't believe some of those unusual names, but y'all at the roast remember them—they were/are real people.

So we ran out from the alleyway and clattered with our cleats across Seventh Avenue, stepping on hunks of pumpkin and frayed bits of erstwhile firecrackers (last night was Halloween), we ran past the little white stucco house where I used to live, with the yellow hibiscus blooming out front, we ran onto the playing field, knowing we didn't have a prayer, laughing.

Our family wasn't living in that house any more. We had moved farther up Seventh Ave., first to 616, then to 522, the pink house with the orange grove, where we lived when my sister Jacqi died of leukemia in 1956.

It's funny how isolated memories stick in your mind. Here's one. I must have been seven years old, and I was sitting in sunshine, out in front of that stucco house across from the football field. The Spanish moss on the oak trees was quavering in the breeze, and I was pushing to and fro one of those enormous old-fashioned perambulators, feeling grown up and important, watching after the new kid, soothing her to sleep while my mother worked inside. And being proud. I had a new baby sister! And just then Dan Spear walked by, smiled and said hello, and it felt great that he could see how big I was, and how good I felt.

You used to walk past our house at 820 E. Seventh on the way to work in those days, Coach Spear. Do you remember our dog, the small brown one? Looked like what folks called a "dash hound"? He used to charge out after you every day, snarling and barking, and we wondered if you thought we named him Danny just for spite. Because he was always trying to bite Dan Spear. But it wasn't true. He was named Danny after the Daniels family, the people who gave him to us. What year did we get him? Probably about 1946. My God, you were only twenty-nine years old, Dan Spear, on the day we got our Danny! What year did you come to Mt. Dora? How old were you? Was this your first job, right out of college?

I know so little about you, Coach Spear. I just learned recently that your home town was Martin's Ferry, Ohio. I know you went to college at Chattanooga. You were a quarterback there, weren't you? During our phys ed classes you always played touch football with us—you were the passer. You could have passed for any of the teams I played on for you; you were still in shape and still that good. What else can I remember about you? A short man (maybe 5'7"), prematurely bald, a big nose on a face from Eastern Europe, a voice like Joe Namath's. You weighed probably one sixty in 1957, the last year I played for you. You were forty years old that year, a lot younger man than I am now. Your predominant emotion was anger. But you had a light side too. In the summers you worked in the recreational programs. You drove the kids in the school bus out to the city beach on Lake Gertrude. You joked a lot and sang as you drove. You wanted all the kids to sing along. Your favorite tune was "Good Night, Irene." Your favorite expression was, "My grandma was slow, but she had a wooden leg."

Everybody was so young in 1957! My father was only forty-five. When he was just out of school Robert N. Bowie, from Seneca, South Carolina, had hitch-hiked all over America with his buddy, Pick. It was the time of the Great Economic Depression. I still have a copy of the handwritten journal that he compiled after that trip. Entitled "Seven Months of Boyhood Adventures," it starts out like this:

"In a small town near the Blue Ridge Mountains of South Carolina lived two young lads of nineteen years of age. They had finished high school together the year before but had not attended college... They were two adventure seekers, very eager to see the country in which they lived; to see the things of which they had read... On one cold February morning they were sitting around a coal heater in a filling station discussing the possibilities of going places, as usual.

"They decided to make a short trip to Central Florida to see Bob's brother, this being a distance of approximately 600 miles. They were to leave the next morning very early as it happened since they were lucky enough to get a ride on an orange hauling truck to Sanford, Florida, only 18 miles from their destination, Mt. Dora. They packed their outfit and spent the night at Pick's house, setting the alarm for 2 o'clock. They were scheduled to leave at 3:00. Here is their story:"

That was my father's first trip to the town that later (in 1943) became his permanent home. His early travels also took him to Oklahoma, and a job in the oil fields. Then he ended up in New Jersey, where he worked on the railroad and married my mother, Myrtle L. Handerhan, an Irish Catholic, in 1936. Two kids came along, my sister June, then me, three years later, on her birthday. I think she really wanted a pony. After that the war started. Daddy got a draft exemption by working in an airplane factory, building fighter planes. He had lived in New Jersey for years by then, and he was hating it more and more. During the cold winters he longed for the sunny South, especially for Mt. Dora, Florida, where his brother Cecil had relocated from South Carolina, and where he, Daddy, had worked that one winter as a bellhop at the Lakeside Inn, back when President Calvin Coolidge vacationed there.

In a word, we moved. Right in the middle of the war. Daddy stuffed us into a '38 Chevy: wife, two kids, huge old radio, two cats. My sister June, who's a storyteller, swears we couldn't get a moving van on account of wartime. So we packed our furniture in an army truck carrying explosives and followed the dynamite all the way to Florida. Somewhere in Georgia, crazed by the long drive, the cats ran off into the woods during a urination break. The two kids cried, grieved over the lost cats, while Daddy drove doggedly on. I remember pulling up, at the end of that long trip, in front of the house across from the football field. I was three years old, and that is the first clear memory of my life. Spanish moss on live oak trees. Poinsettias, sandspurs, hibiscus. Palms. Heat. And soil that was dirty white on top. The white soil amazed us, June and me. We sat on the ground, in our new front yard, and we dug and dug. And just then the man everybody called "The Walking Jesus" came strolling, muttering to himself, on his bare feet down the sidewalk.

I still have the note for $1200 that Daddy wrote out to my Uncle Cecil when he borrowed the money from him to buy that stucco house. It's dated May 1, 1943. He started off by going down to see George White at the First National Bank (on the corner of Donnelly and Fifth) and asked him for a loan. Later on he often told the story of his visit, in a spirit of high indignation. He was seen into the office, where portly bald-headed Mr. White sat behind a desk, smoking a cigar (pronounced see-gar). When he told George what he wanted, George said, "Fine. Now what kind of collateral have you got to offer?" And Daddy flared up and said, "Collateral? The only collateral I've got is my own good name!" And George puffed once on his big Havana and said, "Sorry." After that my father borrowed the money from his brother Cecil and hated George White for the rest of his days on earth.

2

The good old days/ Kids breathing pesticides—no problem/ Bomb shelters (roaches and mildew)/ The Walking Jesus/ Myth of the lost generation/ See Dick, Jane, and Spot/ Run/ Cathy Land skips first grade/ Charlene is an elephant/ Parson Browns/ Mrs. Bennett's rhythm band/ Waymon Snell/ Rayvell Wigwell died last week/ Mrs. TeStrake, hibiscus bloom in her hair/ Guavas and oranges/ Levi gets a charge/ Prof makes us kind/ Billy Waldridge gets a whipping/Joe Stalin is dead/ Robbed by the gypsies/ I'm too big for polliwogs/ Talking talk at the Dixie Drive-In/ "The Class of '57 Had Its Dreams"/ Bishop Moore is special/ Roland stomping in the honky tonks/ Uh-oh, Coach Spear finds out/ Little girls squat to pee/ Broken leg/ Ninety yard run/ Musante, Stuart, and the Ellis boys/ Racking at St. Cloud/ Blast that Herschel Stone/ "We're going to cream yals'es ass"/ Catholic vs. Protestant/ How you doing, Jackie Woodall?/ "Frank Peck, he's our man"/ The Groveland majorettes put on a fine show

So we ran out laughing, past my old house, through the gate by the scoreboard, under the center bar with its crepe paper streamers, onto the field. Smudges of black and gold were congregated by the goal posts on the other end, in front of the Press and Florence Atkins residence. Through the adrenalin rush in my brain it didn't dawn on me what those blurs of color were: Bishop Moore's football team. The thick Florida air smelled of flowers and DDT. It was already November, but mosquito trucks still fumigated the grounds before every game, rolling around the sidelines, then up and down the playing field, blowing out pesticides from the rear. Little kids were frolicking through the billowing smoke of the poisons, whooping and screeching, just like I used to do when I was a boy.

Nowadays kids who romp behind mosquito trucks are probably fitted with special gas masks. Nobody worried back then about getting horrible diseases. Children didn't even wear helmets when they rode their bikes—it had not yet occurred to people that if you fell off your bike and cracked your noggin, well that could be bad! We ate anything we wanted to; the word 'cholesterol' had not been invented. Besides that, smokers didn't smoke two packs a day for thirty years and then sue R.J. Reynolds when they got cancer. One of the fictions by which we live: the "Them was the good times" myth. "Folks in a small town just basically down to earth, why back in those days nobody in Mt. Dora, Florida, even bothered locking their doors, wasn't no perverts wandering the streets, just good God-fearing country people."

Well, that's the story any generation propagates when it looks back at its childhood. Sure, things in our small town appeared to be simple. But we didn't live the "Happy Days" of the t.v. program. What are days made for? To be happy in! So said the British poet Larkin, but he knew it wasn't that easy. We had happy days and days not so happy and some miserable days too, just like the days of human lives throughout the history of the world.

34

After all, in the 1950's some birdbrain also came up with the myth of impending Armageddon. The Walking Jesus was maundering about our town, preaching hell fire and damnation under his breath. People were expecting a nuclear war with the Russians momentarily, and all over Mt. Dora they were excavating for bomb shelters. These consisted, usually, of one stifling little underground room, where, after the mushroom cloud, your family could hunker down and subsist on canned pork and beans, with *The Reader's Digest* for entertainment.

The town probably still has a few holes in the ground, where these ridiculous structures once proudly crouched. Pat Frank, a local author, wrote a best seller called *Alas, Babylon*, about how some people came through a nuclear war and made a new life out on Lake Beauclair. He made big money out of that book, and everyone in Mt. Dora respected him for that. Meanwhile, the national press of the fifties pontificated gloomily, grieving over a younger generation (us) that was doomed to destruction. Consequently, we youth were supposed to be humorless and morose, contemplating our imminent demise and feeling resentful for the mess our elders had got us into. We were too feckless, thank God, to pick up on that message. We were tooling around in cars with fins, in what would now be called "classic" '57 Chevies, Thunderbirds, beat-up Model A's (Judy Sadler drove a '29 Ford), drinking "Miller High Life" beer and listening to Ricky Nelson whine out teenage lamentations about lost love. Don't get me wrong. We certainly weren't all that carefree, but I didn't know anybody at MDHS who mulled over the nuclear war or what would come next (life with the roaches, irradiated lizards and mildew of a bomb shelter). The American media loves fabricating myths about how a certain generation thinks and behaves, while, in reality, every generation goes on thinking and behaving unpredictably, erratically, as human beings always have.

What is now Roseborough Elementary was just Mt. Dora School back then. A row of white stucco buildings, typical Spanish style architecture. Twelve grades worth. You started in the first grade classroom down on Seventh Avenue, and you worked your way toward Fifth Avenue, where you graduated twelve years later. They didn't have enough teachers or classrooms, so some of the grades were doubled: Mrs. Gary's first and second grades, Mrs. White's second and third. I never got into any of those split classes though. I was in Mrs. Nichols' straight first grade and Mrs. Bennett's straight second.

We learned to read in 1946 from the old Dick and Jane picture books. First page: "Dick." With picture of a happy boy in shorts. He was a little behind the times since he still had long hair; for us the crew cut age had dawned. Second page: "Jane." Picture of happy, smiling girl. Third page: "Dick and Jane." Fourth page: "See Dick." Fifth page: "See Jane." Sixth page: "See Dick and Jane." Then things started getting complicated. Verbs. Seventh page: "See Dick run." Eighth page: "See Jane run." Ninth page: "See Dick and Jane run."

Sweating in those hot classrooms, we read, laboriously, aloud, under the tutelage of Mrs. Nichols. This was the Time Before Air Conditioning, and the best they could do were the big fans on the ceilings, which spread the sweating humidity around. You sat and waited your turn, while, for example, Margaret Rigdon would read: "See..... Dick....and...... Jane .... run!" I forget when the plot got interesting, that is, when the dog Spot came into the story. But the best and longest line in that book, and the ultimate challenge for the neophyte reader, was: "See Dick and Jane and Spot run."

All of this was child's play for people with natural verbal talents: Louis Bedell, Cathy Land, Mary Kay Rehbaum, the three denizens of the top reading group. Cathy made such mincemeat of Dick and Jane that they soon took her out of our class altogether and upped her to Mrs. Bennett's second grade. She's probably a rocket scientist by now. Of course, even back in our unenlightened times, before stickers with little smiley faces took over the American educational system, even back then they didn't want the inferior readers to feel bad. So they gave the reading groups animal names instead of numbers or letters. As if this would deceive anyone. What's more, the lower level groups always seemed to be named after big, lumbering animals. I heard my mother talking to Charlene Rodenfeld's mother, who told her indignantly, in her deepest deep South accent, about where they had placed her daughter: "And you know what Charlene is? Charlene's a *elephant!*"

When Mrs. Nichols walked into our classroom first thing in the morning, we had to stand up beside our desks and sing together: "Good morning to you, good morning to you, good morning, dear teacher, good morning to you." Besides that there was a broad repertoire of other songs, but the one I remember best had to do with the glories of life in the Sunshine State: about awakening every morning where the orange blossoms grow, and where the sun would come creeping into where you were sleeping and the blue jays chirped 'Hello!' The fresh cracker air, and the cracker sunshine, how good it was for you, you know? So you'd make your home in Florida, where the orange blossoms grow!

The thing about the orange blossoms was no exaggeration. My family had citrus trees growing behind every house we lived in. The little white stucco house had mostly satsumas, but later on, at 616 E. Seventh (the green house) and 522 E. Seventh (the pink), we had big groves with any kind of citrus you could want: tangerines, grapefruit, navels, parson browns, rubies, pineapples, temples, valencias. At one time that city block, bounded by Fifth Ave., Seventh Ave., Clayton and Grandview, was a solid orange grove (called, originally, the old Gullers Homestead). Then they started bulldozing the outer trees and putting houses along the streets. Our family built two of them in the fifties. We planted palm trees in the front yards, we ate fresh oranges out back. In March we sat on the side porch and smelled the orange blossoms. Wonderful! Like living with a gardenia stuffed perpetually up your nostrils.

The streets were lined with huge live oaks, trailing wisps of Spanish moss. Azaleas bloomed all over, and the very air was steeped in serenity. God, what a beautiful place! Living in Mt. Dora, Florida, was living in paradise, wasn't it, Dan Spear? Maybe still is.

I was reminded of that first grade song recently in the office of an Ohio dermatologist, who asked me, "Where did you grow up?" When I told him Florida, he said, "Oh, well, that explains it then. I've never seen so many basal cell carcinomas on the body of any one person!" Of course, back when I was young they still thought the sun was beneficial. Ignorance is bliss. They had us gulping salt pills after football practice too.

Did all elementary schools have "rhythm bands" back then, with kids clicking spoons together, banging on chunks of wood and shaking tambourines? Don't know, but I do know that in Mrs. Bennett's second grade we had one hell of a rhythm band. We performed for our parents, who dutifully applauded while Charlotte Bennett beamed. We were good and we knew it!

When it came time for third grade everybody hoped to avoid Esther Maglathlin, who had the reputation as the meanest teacher in the Mt. Dora School. At least that's what I always heard. Didn't you too, Sara Jo Land, Joyce Moon, Kris Boring, Hazel Ann Avery, Jimmy Malone, Bobbie Moots, Delores Billette, Grady Sills, Margaret Sadler, Max Bulske, June Bowie, Henry Haas, Mardie Bardwell, H.B. Howell, Corda Burns, L.G. Simpson, Ann Whittington, Waymon Snell, Linda Lee Lane, Wheeler McDonald, John Haddock, Verline Hughes, Daisy Eaton, Wiley Hobdy, Bobby Partridge, Anita Stedronsky, Billy Pat Harding, Dunn Stovall? I lucked out and got Mrs. TeStrake for my third grade teacher.

Can't resist throwing in the names of my fellow pupils at Mt. Dora

School, just for the sheer poetry of it all. Take another look at those familiar names, Dan Spear. They are poetic, aren't they? Rayvell Wigwell, from
Sorrento. How's that for a name? I often wondered what happened to
Rayvell, and just recently I found out. My sister June was telling me about
how her husband Don got a kick out of hearing the names of people she
went to school with. He's from Pennsylvania, where the names are ordinary,
Pennsylvania Dutch, like the name of my army buddy from Bethlehem:
Frederick Schoellhumper. Don always thought "Rayvell Wigwell" was the
best name he ever heard. Not long ago, when June and Don were back in
Lake County for a visit, they ran into another old classmate, Remy Bonner.
June brought up the issue of the poetry of the names, and of course it all
ended up with Rayvell Wigwell, and they laughed, and then Remy kind of
stopped talking, put this serious look on his freckled face, and said,

"It's funny you happened to mention Rayvell Wigwell. You know what
happened to Rayvell last week?"

"No, what?"

"Well, he died."

Few solid memories are left of elementary school fifty years later. I do
remember the first day of first grade, in Sept., 1946, when at least half of
the kiddies were sitting around in despair, weeping and wailing, after their
mothers let go of their hands and went home. I was proud of myself for not
crying, and even cocky enough to get into trouble. My most vivid memory
of that first day was how I (I, little Bobby Bowie, who always did what the
teachers told me!) was locked away in a dark cloakroom for some infringe-
ment of the rules. Nowadays parents would sue the school, on grounds of
cruel and unusual punishment.

What else? Well, not much. Mrs. Batton (Fourth Grade) had a little
red paddle. She hit people with it. Hibiscus was blooming all over town

(still is), and Mrs. TeStrake would wear a bright red blossom, with the speckled stamen and the long hibiscus stem, in her hair. Judy Sadler picked some Japanese plums and brought them to school in a cigar box. Kids today are deprived. We kept everything we collected in cigar boxes, and kids today don't even know what a cigar box looks like! Up here in Ohio kids are really deprived; they've never tasted a Japanese plum. Only oranges and fresh guavas can compare. Even now, when I smell the pungency of guayaba, all of my childhood in Mt. Dora, Florida, comes flooding back over my soul. What a privilege! How many Americans have the luck to grow up with guavas?

Later on came the not so good years, the traumas of adolescence. The feeling, at age thirteen, that a big tiger had suddenly jumped on my back. That big tiger was Sex. I was innocent. My daddy's Daddy had never had a talk with him, so he didn't see any reason to have a talk with me. But that wasn't really fair. He, Daddy, had grown up on a farm in South Carolina, watching the pigs. I didn't have any pigs to watch, all we had was an orange grove. So when the hormones raged about in the night, all I knew was that some great big something was going on in my insides. Of course, I didn't talk to my parents. Do boys ever ask their parents about anything as embarrassing as why their middle leg swells up?

A few things from the junior high years stand out in my mind. That pornographic comic book, brought to school by, I think it was (I apologize if I'm wrong), no, I better not say who, but it was a she. We took turns looking at those grotesque depictions of human sexuality; we examined them with great joy and lust. Levi Compton got even more of a sensual thrill in the seventh grade from the bra strap he could see on Miss Jordan's back, through her translucent blouse. Levi kept pointing out that bra strap every time she turned to write something on the board. He would point and giggle, truly inspired by the sight. How little it takes to make a boy happy.

Then there was the day Rhoda Todd Horton lost control of our class.

It started when somebody threw a piece of chalk and somebody else threw it back. Soon there was a full-blown chalk war going on, laughter and shrieking and missles flying all over the room. Nobody paid any attention to Miss Horton's frantic attempts to stop us. She finally broke into tears and rushed out into the corridor. After that happened we figured maybe things had gone too far, and a few minutes later, when school principal Prof Roseborough walked in, the class was hanging its collective head, dead silent. Prof didn't get mad. He didn't bother mentioning how badly we had behaved; that was taken for granted. He just told us in that soft voice of his that Miss Horton was a young teacher, and it was hard for her just starting out, and from then on we were to be kind to her.

We were ashamed. Prof left us and Rhoda Todd Horton walked back into that classroom, and for the rest of the school year we were kind. That's what the world needs most of all—more Prof Roseboroughs to remind us that if we hope to be genuine human beings, we better stop acting like animals. Drop our "uncouth" ways (one of your favorite words, Dan Spear).

As for you, I have one recollection of something you did when I was in the eighth grade. You took over our class one day as a substitute; some other teacher suddenly got sick and you had no time to prepare a lesson. You talked for a while about how boys had to be tough to get along in life. About how you grew up in the coal mines of Eastern Ohio, with degenerates and hoodlums. About how all the men in your family had tough genes and lived long lives. About one uncle from Croatia who attempted suicide at age 116, but failed (he was too tough even for suicide). Then you announced that you would now paddle every boy in the class. This would make us tougher. So, amidst uproarious laughter, we each went up to the front of the room, leaned over the desk, and took our licks. The bigger boys (and I was big for my age) got a really solid whomp, but they (I) grinned and bore it.

Everyone waited in vicious expectation for Billy Waldridge's turn. Blonde-haired Billy was the model student of our class. Over the course of

41

eight years of schooling, he had never done anything wrong. You saved him
for last, Dan Spear, so as to prolong the expectation and the fun. Everybody
was chanting and pointing, "Now, Billy! Now, Billy!" Meanwhile, Billy sat
quaking at his front row desk, sheer terror clomped onto every pore of his
white face, every thin hair on his head. Finally you said, smiling, "Okay,
Billy, your turn now." He arose, bewildered and pale, amidst the howls of
the wolves all around him, and staggered forth. He leaned over the desk,
looking like he might vomit on the math books there. But then you laughed
and gave him just a light tap, and all we wolves moaned in disappointment.

One of the assistant football coaches in those, our junior high days,
was burly Asher Codom. With his square bulldog face and powerful
physique, Mr. Codom was the most feared teacher in all of the school. I had
him for a study hall. He would throw erasers at anyone who even looked up
from a textbook. Or he would walk around the room with a huge stick, and
suddenly bang it down on a desk if he saw someone illegally batting an eye.
Once he caught Russell Russell with a grin on his face. He hauled Russell
by the scruff of his neck to the front of the room. He drew a circle up on
the blackboard, put Russell up on his tiptoes until his nose was in that
circle, and the nose had to stay there for the rest of the hour. Russell
deserves a lot of credit though. Even with his nose up against the wall, he
never took the grin off his face.

Everybody liked Russell Russell. He was from Pistolville, what was
called the "white trash" end of town. Russell quit school in the ninth grade,
and, maybe two years later, we saw him on the campus of MDHS, over by
the cafeteria, digging a ditch for some construction company. He was
smiling. Everybody said, "Look, it's Russell! Hey, Russell, how you doing?"
Russell was doing fine. I wonder what he's up to these days. Still digging
ditches? No matter where he is, I bet he's smiling. Like Bill Lynch. I can't
imagine Bill Lynch any way but smiling.

What are the chances of running into two Russell Russells (no kin) in the course of a lifetime? Well, when I taught ninth-grade English in 1967, at Maynard Evans High School in Orlando, I had a totally different Russell Russell in my class. Wonder what part of this earth he's wandering in 1994? What about all the other great kids at Evans? My favorites: Frank Register, Marcia Calley, Sammy Palo, Ann Benson, and the greatest of all, Ronnie Netto. Are you all grandmothers and grandfathers by now?

I remember sitting in our seventh grade classroom, on the day that I now know was Mar. 5, 1953. The teacher, it may have been Miss Horton again, walked in with an air of joyous exhilaration and said: "People, I have an announcement to make to you. The worst dictator in the history of the world, Joe Stalin, died today, over in Russia." As soon as she said that our whole class stood up spontaneously and began whooping in unison, screeching, laughing. Someone, I think it was Bobby Joe Cook, performed a series of Rebel yells. We didn't read newspapers, but we knew from what our parents said that Joe Stalin represented all that was evil on earth. What a joy it was that he was dead!

Now, what would little Bobby Bowie have said, if you told him that day that he would learn to speak the Russian language like a native, or that exactly forty years later he would be using his football stiff arm on the gypsies of Russia, ex-USSR? Here's how it works. If the gypsies see you're a foreigner they come up and try to beg money off you. Usually it's a four-year-old kid, or a young woman with a baby. If you give them anything, you're done. They make some kind of hidden sign to all the other gypsies, and a mob of them descends upon you, babbling gypsy language, hanging on your legs, poking you in the ribs, big kids, little kids, women with babies (not men though—the men, apparently, are back at the gypsy camp taking a nap). This huge gibbering mass gets entangled in your arms, and then one tiny hand picks off your wallet. After that they skeedaddle in a thousand

43

different directions, cockroaches dumped out of a gunny sack. Meanwhile, the Russians stand around watching the show, laughing.

All through his school days Bobby Bowie was a good little boy. His parents appreciated him, the darling first-born son, while his main rival for their love, his sister June, three years older, was often in their doghouse. I'm not sure she has ever forgiven me for being born on her birthday, in the same bed three years later, on Chestnut Ave., Metuchen, N.J. When June started smoking, at about age fifteen, she kept her cigarettes in a Sucrets box, disguised as throat lozenges. She would sneak out of the house and go up to the corner of Seventh and Clayton, to visit Patsy Wells. Berry Wells, Pat's mother, would be at work, so they could puff away at their leisure. Of course, Daddy eventually discovered the Sucrets box.

Our father was an angry man. When we were little kids, if we did something wrong during the day, we knew what to expect when he got home from work. While we cowered in the back bedrooms of the white stucco house, Mommy would make her report. Then he would whip off his belt and fold it in two:

Daddy: "All right, bend over the chair. How many licks you think you deserve for what you did?"

Me (whining): "I won't do it any more! I didn't mean to!"

Daddy: "You get ten this time. Lean over."

Me (whining louder) "I didn't really do anything. It was a accident! I won't do it again, ahhhhhhhhhh!"

Daddy: "Now, be quiet. You only get ten. But if you yell, you get extra."

He was nervous. He didn't like loud noises, such as kids yelling while he was hitting them. But, actually, when it came to his children, he was pretty soft-hearted. He didn't hit as hard as he could have, and being belted occasionally didn't do any harm. After all, everybody beat their kids in those days, back before the Progressive Era. I've been accused of being whacko, but if I am it wasn't the belt that did it. I just came out of some kind of foul-up in the gene pool! Or maybe what happened was that when God's little elves were passing out brains I was up near the head of the line, but then I wandered off somewhere to use my new brains and showed up late at the counter labeled "Nervous System Base Stability."

When the ninth grade came along, I ended up on the varsity football team. That was an unpleasant surprise. I wanted to be on the polliwog (junior high) team one more year, but I was five pounds over the weight limit. I was gaining ten pounds a year through junior and senior high, and Dan Spear was doing the math in his head. He had me figured for 175-180 by my senior year. He started calling me "J.C. Caroline," after one of the great NFL players of the fifties. Billy Vanzant was the only other freshman too big for polliwog football. He and I sat on the varsity bench all season. But you provided my baptism of fire, Coach Spear. After we made a touchdown I went in at tailback against Lyman of Longwood, ran the ball around end, and scored an extra point. My first point. November, 1954.

Now, as I look back on the main focus of this story, 1955, '56, '57, '58, I see that my high school years had mixed blessings, good times and bad. There are memories awash in the dreary viscous Florida air, with the acrid smell of pesticides, lugubrious coos of the mourning doves, in the ominous shadow of The Walking Jesus. I was one for whom Prof Roseborough reserved his highest compliment. He looked at me in his civics class one day, and he said, with that typical Prof chuckle, he said, "Bowie's a thinker. You know that, people? He's a thinker." Of course, the non-thinkers of the world may have an easier time of it. In the late fifties I thought a lot about death.

This business got intense in 1956. We'll come back to that later, because that was the year that turned my life inside out. Skipping ahead, for

45

now, one year, to 1957, Ronnie Gardner, Richard's brother, the most popular boy in the Mt. Dora School, tanned and handsome, thick black hair, with the long sideburns of the times, was a few weeks short of graduation. He might have gone into crop dusting, just as my friend Gary Potter would have. Their parents ran the Gardner-Potter Dusting Service over in Zellwood.

It happened on a perfectly innocuous Friday night, May 24, with no hint of anything amiss. He was on a date with his girlfriend, Ima Burns. On the way home they stopped off, as everyone did in those days, at the Dixie Drive-In, the hamburger joint out at the fork in the road—where, driving from Mt. Dora, you took the left turning to Tavares or the right to Eustis. People sat around there drinking milk shakes and eating burgers, talking with fellow students from all over the "Golden Triangle." I'm not sure what Ronnie Gardner talked about at the Dixie that night, the last of his life, but isn't it a shame that he didn't spend, say, two more minutes there? Why couldn't he have opened up his hood for a couple of onlookers and discussed the merits of his engine? Dale Craigmiles, 25, had just left the American Legion Dance in Mt. Dora and was driving drunk, heading out Highway Nineteen. Just Ronnie's raising the hood would have allowed enough time for Dale to run off the road, or to make it past the Dixie Drive-In fork, weaving his way on along to Tavares or Eustis.

C.M. Jones, Gary Potter and I went out to the junk yard a few days later. We looked at the broken glass and the smashed-in door, and we imagined the dying Ronnie Gardner, pinned there in the wreckage. The funeral, at the Zellwood Methodist Church, was a wild, wailing affair. The girls of Mt. Dora High School loved him, and they were shrieking through it all, while Ronald Gardner, Class of '57, lay in the open coffin, with his pompadour hair and his Elvis sideburns.

"The Class of '57 Had Its Dreams." That was an old rock song that came out in the seventies. It was about what happens to the fantasies twenty years later: the business failures, personal imbroglios, divorces. The people who can't face the reunion because they don't want their classmates to see what a mess they've made of their lives. And the deaths. Ronnie Gardner, who didn't even live to graduate. Billy Simpson, Norma Jeanne Wise, Charlie Reid, dead of cancer before they reached fifty. Patsy Wells, whose love in Texas left her bereft of hope, blond Pat Wells, an excellent student and a great cornet player in the MDHS marching band. Who else by now from the '57 bunch? Probably a few more. I was Class of '58, and we've had our share of vicissitudes too. Am I complaining? No. I'm just telling a story, Dan Spear. My story's about, primarily, the happiest day of my life: Nov. 1, 1957.

Ronnie Gardner, part of our team the previous year, had been dead five months, but his brother, hard-nosed, competitive, but amiable Richard, was in that line of orange jerseys that ran out laughing onto the field. Our cheerleaders waved their arms and yelled, "Yaaaaayy!" The home crowd roared its greeting to the mighty Golden Hurricanes. We stretched out, jogged around lifting up our knees, fell into formation for the warm-up drills. Captain Billy Moon, standing out in front of the rows of white pants with orange stripes, led the calisthenics. Billy Moon, clapping his hands, psyching us up ("Come on, y'all, let's get some spirit going!"), but still smiling.

"All right, then. Jumping jacks. Ready? Exercise!.. One, two, three, four, one, two, three, four!" Did you think we had a chance that night, Billy Moon? I doubt it. But you weren't about to give up, whether we had a chance or not. You and Rick Gardner were the aggressive spirit of the Hurricanes. Your guts were hanging out in the open, for everyone to see, and both of you had an amplitude of guts. What people didn't realize (maybe you didn't either, Coach Spear) was that there was also a quiet kind of gutsiness on our team. Young players like Owen McCallister had it. So did the great Earle Williams. Earle didn't say much, didn't go around slapping butts and hollering rah-rahs. But Earle Williams planned on winning every game he played.

Out there on the dew-shine of the fresh grass, doing jumping jacks and squat jumps, counting cadence and laughing, I felt wonderful. Why? God knows, but I can't remember a night before or since when I felt as good as I did on All Saints Day, 1957. I'm thinking, 'Okay, Bobby Booby. So we get beat. That's all right. You're going to have fun. We can lose 60-0, but you're going to have fun. This is Bishop Moore. Remember Bishop Moore a year ago? When you flew in your magic Kangaroos? You gonna run fast and wild, tonight, Rapid Robert, and you gonna do you some racking!'

I had a special feeling for Bishop Moore High School. The year before, when my life was wrung dry, the Bishop Moore game was the first one I played in, after staying out of school for a week and missing Groveland on Oct. 26. We played B.M. in Winter Park, on Nov. 2, 1956, and I scored both our touchdowns in a 13-12 loss. As I recall, you were mad before that game too, Mr. Spear. We were mired in a horrible losing season, but that particular evening's mad had to do with linebacker Roland Cane. Roland was (is?) a good guy. I'm not saying anything against Roland. But he had been stomping away on the dance floors, in the honky tonk bars up at Salt Springs, and somehow you found out about that.

I watched as you raged around, right after we got off the bus you had driven, at Harper-Shepherd Field, "Home of the Hornets." Using very strong language. At one point poor Roland was on the verge of being physically assaulted. I was watching all this in a spirit of utter passive detachment. Frankly speaking, I didn't care who won the game against

Bishop Moore that night, Dan Spear; I couldn't care less whether I even played. Laughter had departed the earth and football was irrelevant.

My memory of that game, and my favorite memory of any game, has to do with the second touchdown I scored. We were a weak team. Bishop Moore was outplaying us all night, pushing us around the field. They were on a long drive and had reached our fifteen yard line. I was at defensive left halfback. They should have stayed with the running game, since we weren't having much luck stopping it. But they tried a short pass over the middle. From his linebacker position Roland got a hand on that ball. The write-up in the *Sentinel* said it was B.M.'s Ellis who touched it, but no, it was Roland. He tipped it up in my direction, and I caught it from a running start and went ninety yards with the interception. The reason I remember it so well was because I felt as if I had never run faster in my life, as if no one on earth ever had.

When I was a small kid, living in that stucco house across from the football field, I went out every afternoon after school to watch the MDHS team practice: the great players of the early fifties—Billy Odom, Pinckney Turner, Harry Wise, Bobby Correll, George Keen, Frank Keller. Other little boys would always show up (Clarence Sims, Billy Simpson, Peanut Hughes, etc.), and we'd get a tackle football game going, using one of the spare balls lying around. You, Dan Spear, never minded our borrowing those fat balls, which looked more like rugby balls than today's slimmed-down footballs, because out of the corner of your eye you were always looking for future prospects.

When did you first notice the pure speed of little Bobby Bowie? When he was eight, nine years old? By the seventh grade you were pressuring my mother to get me on the junior high team. I wasn't sure I wanted to play; I didn't have a whole lot of confidence. But every time you saw Mommy you'd say, "Listen, you got to get that boy out for football. That boy can *run!*"

He was right. From the first grade on there was never anybody faster in my class. And when we chose up sides for those afternoon football games I was the first one picked. So I did end up finally going out for polliwog football, in the eighth grade. Can't remember much about it now except the halftime pep talks of Coach Boo Landridge. His favorite motivating tool was to question our sexual identity. He'd say, "You know what you boys look like out there? You look like little girls! Why, any minute I expect all y'all to squat down and pee! Cause that's what you look like: a bunch of little girls who squat to pee!" I always had a puritanical streak, and I remember being shocked, at age twelve, by that vivid image.

But it didn't make me angry, like it was supposed to do. Football coaches think that the main thing about coaching is to make players mad. Take you, Dan Spear, you used to insult me all the time when I played for you. But you didn't get much reaction out of me, and I remember you telling me after my last season, "You know, you were a player who was totally uncoachable." Thanks! What a compliment! I'd like to believe I've lived my whole life uncoachable.

My junior high career was brief and not remarkable It ended during a game against Eustis. I was running the ball around end on Right 27 and something just popped in my leg. Nobody tackled me but I fell at the sideline and writhed around in pain. You weren't coaching that team, Dan Spear, but you were there by the bench, and I remember you telling me to shut up and lie still. It was a charley horse in my thigh muscle and you had to work it out. So I was lying there and you were pounding on my right leg, getting mad, because I wasn't taking the pain like a man. Only four years later did we find out it hadn't been a charley horse at all. The sheer power of that thigh muscle had ripped it off its attachment at the right hip as I ran, slightly fracturing the bone in the process.

I wondered what the lump was that formed under the hip bone after the injury, but I didn't bother asking anybody about it. What it was was a mass of scar tissue that provided the thigh muscle with a spot to reattach itself. I soon recovered, and through my freshman, sophomore and junior years the pure speed remained. But then, in the summer practices of 1957, the leg started hurting and we had it x-rayed down at Doc Montgomery's office, and Doc just looked at that x-ray and shook his head and said, "Whew!"

But that was August of 1957. On All Souls Day, Nov. 2, 1956, on Harper-Shepherd Field in Winter Park, against Bishop Moore, the leg was fine. The lump of scar tissue was hanging in there, doing a great job of anchoring the muscle. They threw that pass and Roland Cane tipped it up in the air. I grabbed the ball on the run, headed for the right sideline, and took off. John Ellis, the fastest man on their team, was behind me from the start; I think he was the one the pass was intended for. Some of those in pursuit were John Hormuth, Paul Baccarney, Dick Beausejour, Stuart Stuart, Bernie Baumann, Paul Musante. Who threw a block for me? Fred Kurras? Bones Lofroos? Thomas Norris? Or nobody? I got to the sideline quick, and after that I was ahead of all my blockers. Three or four Hornets had a shot at me, but none of them touched me. Each time one of the B.M. players got close I turned on a little more speed. It was eerie. I thought I was running as fast as I could, but whenever I needed to pick it up I found a higher gear. It was the time of the pure speed. The last man I had to beat was the quarterback who threw the pass, Mike DeVoe. He had a good angle on me, but I pulled out one more burst of power and breezed past him, and by that time I felt like I was flying. No one on earth could have caught me, not Billy Odom, not Harry Wise, not J.C. Caroline, and as I crossed the goal line it felt as if my dead sister were with me.

Now it was one year later, and the leg was hurt. Bishop Moore had a better team than last year. We were about to get tramped on and scraped raw, like the dance floors at Salt Springs, on the nights when Roland was stomping there, in his gator skin cowboy boots with taps on the heels.

The game started. In looking back on it now, thirty-seven years later, I realize that I don't have a lot of clear detail to recall. Listen, all y'all out there in the audience tonight. Feel free to shout out corrections at any point that you hear something wrong. Especially you, Dan Spear.

Who kicked off to who? Can't recall. But the game began, and we started having fun. We were happy. We weren't laughing out loud, but the laughter was still roiling around in our insides. At the beginning Bishop Moore, with its potent offensive attack, ran wild. They didn't have much of a passing game, but those big Irish and Italian boys on the line could make space for their backs. Halfback Jimmy Ellis was good already, though just a skinny sophomore or junior that year. His brother John, a senior, was the biggest star: a fast powerful runner. Then there was the fullback, Paul Musante, slower but persistent, good for three to four yards a carry.

It became apparent early in the game that they were going to run for a lot of yardage. They scored a quick touchdown, Jim Ellis on a short rush to cap off a forty-five yard drive. At this point our cheerleaders and our fans and Dan Spear must have thought, 'Uh-oh, here we go. It's Katy, bar the door time.' Maybe we felt that way too. But our insides didn't stop laughing.

We couldn't generate much offense when we got the ball in the early going. They'd stop Richard Gardner, or me, or Neil Stoothoff for short gains, and Neil would punt the ball back to them. Then the Ellis brothers and Musante would come at us again. No passes. Rush after rush, building up the yardage. But not scoring again. Somehow we'd get every drive stopped short of our goal line.

At this point in the season I wasn't even working out in pads; we were saving all strength in the gimpy leg for the games. I'd take hand-offs at practices, just to keep our timing right in the backfield. I'd jog around in shorts, lifting knees high, at the Thursday evening tune-up. Then I'd play on Friday.

Back in August, after Doc Montgomery's x-ray had revealed the extent of the injury, my father took me to an orthopedic specialist in Orlando. He said I needed an operation on the leg, to cut out the scar tissue and reattach the muscle to the hip. He wanted to do it right away, but I was desperate to play my senior year of football. That's when the taping began, Dan Spear's way of restraining the thigh muscle so as to keep the damage down. Where did you learn to wrap a leg like that, Mr. Spear? It's amazing the things a high school football coach could do in the fifties.

In the first game of the '57 season, against St. Cloud, I was on the bench. Nobody was sure how much I could play, including me. But I kept itching to get in the game, and when Dan finally put me in, in the second half, I got the winning touchdown on a forty-seven yard run. The score ended up 13-7, and the next morning, when Dan Spear came by the pink house to pick me up, he was happy. Nothing like a win to put him in a good mood.

His picking me up on a Saturday morning was unusual. What happened was that Ken Bliss, playing on the line against St. Cloud, had taken a severe blow to the spleen. Transported by ambulance to Orange Memorial Hospital in Orlando, he was lost for the season. Dan Spear had invited me to drive over to visit him. On the way to Orlando we exulted in the win of the previous evening, and at one point Dan said, "Wow, did you see that hit Dake put on Godwin, when he had the ball and was running loose?"

I said, "Are you talking about over on the far sideline? The body block into his legs from behind?"

He said, "Yeah. Brutal!"

I said, "That wasn't Dake. That was me."

And Mr. Spear looked at me as if to say, "You mean you can be that vicious?" I don't think he, or many others, ever figured that one out. Your basic emotion, Dan Spear, was mad. What you didn't know was that after Oct. 22, 1956, anger was running my life too.

At the beginning of the '57 season somehow I believed I was still invincibly fast, even with the gimpy leg. It was a state of mind; I knew the pure speed was there. I was a believer for only one game, though. After St. Cloud came Tavares, and that damned Herschel Stone made a non-believer out of me. We won that game too, 13-6. John Lavin, playing end for us, caught a pass from Stoothoff for the winning touchdown, bringing down on his brother Bee the ire of all of Tavares. Why? Because John had transferred to Mt. Dora High School from Tavares just the year before and Bee was still going to THS. So Bee had to listen to people calling his brother "traitor" for the whole next week. Kinne Pearce, Joe Jenkins, Roger Gibson. All the Purcells.

As for Herschel Stone, he delivered a blow to my image from which I thought I'd never recover. You see, when I played football I always knew how much space I needed. No way nobody would catch me, from side or back, once I got my space. All fast running backs have this sixth sense. Ask O.J. Simpson, John Ellis, Emmitt Smith. Anyway, we were on maybe the fifty yard line. I got the ball from wingback on the reverse, Right 32. The hand-offs and fakeries in our single wing offense were deceptive. We ran that play so smoothly that nobody on the Tavares defense could follow it. I was bent over with both arms around the football, and when I glanced up I saw: (1) a huge hole, and (2) a Tavares defensive halfback looking frantically around, wondering where the ball was. I went through the hole, raised up, and headed for the left sideline. That's when I knew I had my space. Easily outrunning that halfback (after he finally figured out it was me), I set myself up right beside the chalk line, turned on the afterburners, and headed straight down field. I was gone. Touchdown. I thought.

Then, suddenly, Herschel Stone. Where the hell did he come from? He must have been playing safety in the middle of the field. He didn't catch me directly from behind, he had a slight angle on me. He knocked me down, and I lay there in a daze. It was impossible. Okay, so the leg was wrapped, restrained. But I knew when I had my space. Even with a gimpy leg I was the best, the fastest around. That's what I always believed. Until Herschel Stone proved to me that times had changed. I looked down at my toes in my magic low-top Kangaroos, and my toes couldn't look me in the eye.

Bee Lavin told John Lavin who told me the next week: at Tavares High they were saying, "Yeah, they think Bowie's so great, but did you see the way Herschel caught him from behind? Just plain outran him. Bowie's not such a big deal after all." I knew they were right. This wasn't 1956 anymore. The era of the pure speed was over.

There was a lot of flu around in the fall of fifty-seven. We postponed a game against Umatilla at their request. We had to make it up on a Tuesday night and then play another game, against mighty Groveland, on the Friday of that same week. Remember the pass play we used when the other team played double safeties, Coach Spear? From our wing-tee formation, with Stoothoff at quarterback, we flared each of our ends out to pull the respective safeties toward the sidelines, while I, playing wingback, fiddled around for a minute ("posted") and then sprinted straight down the empty corridor in the middle of the field.

I caught that pass from Stoothoff against Umatilla (Jack Austin, Billy Jenkins, Elliot Seabrook) for a fifty-two yard touchdown. We won, 31-0. Late in the game we tried the other big pass play in our repertoire (46 long). I angled out toward the sideline on a little curl, and after that maneuver drew in the defensive halfback, I turned down field and ran past him. That would have been another touchdown, but Neil led me a little too far. Trouble was, I pulled up lame again trying to get to the ball.

The whole puissant, cocky undefeated Groveland team had come to Mt. Dora to watch us play Umatilla that Tuesday. They were swaggering around in their crew cut heads and pea green letter jackets, talking big talk in the stands. Jan Potter, who was sitting near them, said later that they crowed like roosters when they saw me limping back to the huddle. Jake Wolker, their star lineman, sneered: "Bowie's hurt, but even if he wasn't y'all wouldn't stand a chance against us on Friday. We're going to cream yals'es ass."

Of course, Jan and the other Mt. Dora students tried to counter that with sneering repartee of their own, but their sneers lacked conviction. Wolker turned out to be right. What a team Groveland had that year. Very well coached too. Next to Dan Spear, that Groveland coach, what was his name?, Buck Something, must have been the best in the conference. I never saw a team that could block like that. Jay Polk, Billy McMurphy, Charlie Roberts, Gano, Sloan, Moody, Charles Howard. Why, they would send Wendell Bridges out to knock me down at defensive halfback when the play was run clear to the other side of the field! And Wendell would knock me down. And if I got up he'd knock me down again. Like Bobby Correll!

This leads us back to where we began: the bus ride home through the humidity, the grass of Groveland in our nostrils, C.M.'s broken nose, the laughter.

At least on Nov. 1, 1957, I was playing all the time, offense and
defense. The leg felt good, I was running fine, even without the pure speed.
Tonight, on the happiest day of my life, I was having fun playing football.
Blocking, carrying the ball, making tackles on John Ellis. There were a lot
of tackles to be made in the secondary, because Bishop Moore was ripping
big holes in our line and coming out after our linebackers.

The Mt. Dora crowd was quiet. The cheerleaders were trying desperately to get some spirit going. They would do a cheer and then appeal,
exasperated, to the fans: "Come on! Y'all aren't *yelling!*" But the Mt. Dora
crowd wasn't getting into it. I don't think they were laughing any more. If
they ever had been. They were subdued, expecting the worst and just
waiting for it to happen.

My parents were in the crowd that night: Robert and Myrtle Bowie,
sitting side by side. Now they're side by side at the far end of Donnelly St.,
and their perpetual quarrel over religion and race is done. There was poten-
tial for argument even on the evening of All Saints Day. After all, Bishop
Moore was a Catholic high school, the only parochial school on our schedule. Despite her allegiance to the Mt. Dora team, my mother must have felt
a lot of sympathy for that school. She always cheered for Notre Dame, for
example, and Daddy hated Notre Dame. I remember watching a t.v. game
with him some time in the seventies, when I was home for a visit. Notre
Dame kicked a field goal in the final seconds to win it, and Daddy
screamed, "The luck of the black folks and the God damn Irish!" Mommy
just smiled.

You see, she was a vehement Catholic and he an inveterate Protestant.
She was raised in an Irish family in New Jersey, and she grew up believing

that if you don't do everything the priest and nuns and bishops tell you to do, then you're one hundred per cent sure to burn in Hell. She believed that all her life. Raised in South Carolina, in a Catholic-hating and racist family, he was brought up on the idea that white and Southern was beloved of the Lord. How could they, my parents, think they could calmly join themselves in holy matrimony, putting huge unresolved problems on the back burner? God knows. I guess they were young and in love.

Their marriage certificate, which I have here on the desk as I write, informs us that Robert Norton Bowie and Myrtle Lucille Handerhan were lawfully married on the first day of March, 1936 (my father's twenty-fourth birthday), in Our Lady of Peace Church, Fords, New Jersey.

Our Lady didn't send a lot of peace to the marriage. At least, not after the kids came along. Remember that story in the Bible, where two women are both claiming the same child? They come to Jesus, or King Solomon, and they ask him to arbitrate their dispute, and he says, "Well how about if one of you takes him by the left arm and one by the right, then you have a, like, tug of war, and you split the child asunder, and each of you gets half?" Well, naturally, the real mother of the child says, "My God, I mean, Lord Jesus, what kind of advice is that? We'll end up killing the poor kid!" But the other mother, the fake one, said that it sounded like a good idea to her. So Jesus (or was it Solomon?) replies, "Aha, I know you're an imposter mother, 'cause a real loving mother wouldn't want to rip her child apart! So get thee hence, you shrew!" Then the true mother tearfully embraced the urchin, and all was well.

Of course, that always seemed to me like a stupid story. I mean, not even the phony mother would be willing to murder a child she wanted for her own. But if we ponder this thing more deeply, maybe Jesus had some-thing there. Because the ways parents can metaphorically rip their children apart are fully as insane as that idea that the fake mother agreed to. When my sisters and I were kids, we were the rope in an infernal tug of war.

Each of our parents was dragging us toward his or her version of religious truth, and each knew that God was on his/her side. To this very day I can't stomach people who tell you what God wants: Southern fundamentalists, hard-line Catholics, loony Islamic jihadists who blow up innocent Jews in a bus, loony Jewish West Bank settlers who shoot up innocent Palestinians in a mosque. All those who are sure that God is on their side.

On Sundays, even today, I feel that old pull again, only now it's two dead people pulling me. But I don't hate those two people the same way I hate religious fanatics. Those people are my parents, and feelings for parents are complicated things. I may still be angry at them, but I love them anyway. And I'm not blaming them for anything that got screwed up in my own insides. There's far too much of that sort of whining in today's America. We need to take responsibility for our lives. Don't sue Jack Daniels for your cirrhosis of the liver, which you spent all those relentless years of self-destructive drinking to achieve. Quit going to psychiatrists with your petty neuroses. If we've got long-term demons roiling in our souls (and yes, sir, we do), we better grit our teeth and face up to them on our own. Line up opposite them and then hit them hard. Knock 'em down. And if they get up, well, you knock them down again! Then, at the end of the game (no matter who wins), shake their hand and tell them they played a good one.

One thing I will say for the hard-line Catholic spirit, though. It brought my two little sisters, Jacqi and Peggy, out of nonbeing and into my world. Late in his life, long after my mother was dead, Daddy told me that he had never wanted more kids after the first two. But Mommy considered any kind of birth control a mortal sin. "It's like the God damn Pope was running me all my life!" said Daddy. But me, I'm happy the Pope was around: his strictures on condoms got my baby sisters born!

So what were they thinking, Mommy and Daddy, sitting in the stands that night, watching their son play football? They were still pretty young back then. They had half a lifetime in front of them. Were they making

59

plans for the future? Were they hoping their own private hopes? Well, certainly they were planning and hoping. As long as we're alive we go on making grandiose plans for what could be a very brief future. But precisely what hopes were they hoping and what plans planning? I'd give a lot for a tape recording of everything that ran through my parents' heads as they watched us play, on the night redoubtable Bishop Moore came to town.

The game continued. The fans were listless. The black and gold Hornets were buzzing on, piling up the yards, but somehow they couldn't score again. We kept stopping them short, or they fumbled. When time ran out at the end of the first quarter they had only that one touchdown. It was six to nothing. As we changed sides for the second quarter, we walked past the Bishop Moore players. Nobody looked at anybody, and not a word was said. That was standard etiquette for the side-changing ritual. But when we played the nearby schools, Tavares or Eustis, we would walk by people we knew, fellow frequenters of the Dixie Drive-In, so there could be a few fervent, and none too friendly, remarks exchanged in the heat of passion as we passed.

There were exceptions, though, folks who were blessedly free of the hotheaded ways of the competitive young male. Tavares had some good sports. I remember Harry Pearce, as we walked past once, changing at the quarter, Harry in his red and white Tavares colors, holding his sweaty helmet in his hand, smiling upon the Mt. Dora team and saying, "Hey, y'all are playing a great game tonight!" What a human being Harry Pearce was (is?). Joe Jenkins, son of the Lake County Superintendent of Schools, was another good guy. All the Purcells. And, of course, Jerry Woodall, the quarterback, a fine passer and a wonderful person, who later became a Marine officer and ended his earthly sojourn in a place even more swampy and humid than Lake County, Florida: Vietnam. I wonder what his twin sister, Jackie Woodall, is doing now? I dated her for a while in the sixties.

What did people talk about while they sat parked at the Dixie Drive-In, eating burgers and drinking shakes? Well, I'm not sure what the girls said to one another, but the boys talked about cars and sex.

Sex: "Who you out with tonight?... I hear she puts out. Getting any?" Then came all the lies. I remember once seeing John Laughtery, Bill's brother, respond to that last question. Four boys were perched on the hood of somebody's wide-finned car, while John's girl was in the passenger seat of his Olds 88, demurely sipping on a milkshake. John didn't use any words for his answer; he just put on a wink and a leer. Then whoever asked him said, "Don't give me that shit," and John said, "Smell my hand." And whoever asked him took a whiff and said "Ugh," and then everybody laughed.

Cars: "What you got under the hood?" or "How's it do, zero to sixty?" or "You think you can take me? Shit, son, come on out to Thrill Hill right now, and I'll run your ass in the ground!"

Me, I wasn't in those conversations. I was just listening. Even as a teenager I was a good little boy. Didn't hang out much at the Dixie Drive-In. Sex was of interest but I didn't know enough about it to even begin talking. Besides that, I wasn't interested in making up the lies that most of the boys told. As for cars, I couldn't think of anything more boring on earth than talking about valves and cubic inches of engine under some hood. The only thing that saved me from total teenage obscurity and the scorn of my coevals was football.

Our cheerleaders never rested, not even in between quarters. Now, as we changed ends of the field, they were working on another cheer. It was one of the big ones in their repertoire. They screamed up at the fans: "Now, we're going to do 'He's Our Man,' and y'all *yell!*

"Frankie Peck, he's our man. If he can't do it—Vanzant can! Billy Vanzant, he's our man. If he can't do it—Lavin can! John Lavin, he's our man. If he can't do it—etc., etc." This would go on until nearly the whole team was named. But it always ended up with, "Billy Moon, he's our man. If he can't do it—NOBODY CAN!" It was unfair that Billy Moon always got to be the one without whom it couldn't be done, but, after all, his girl, Janie Huett, was captain of the cheerleaders!

Are you out there in the audience tonight, Janie Huett Moon? What about Carol Simpson? Mary Lou Davidson? Shorty Johnson? Judy Sadler? Janet Scott? Patsy Spear? Greetings and glory to all the former cheerleaders at good old MDHS! Y'all deserve a lot of credit. Dan Spear didn't want you anywhere near his boys. He always thought mixing women with football made for bad medicine! He used to tell us, "During football season you don't smoke, you don't drink cokes, and you stay away from girls. You understand me? The three taboos: cokes, women and smokes. You got that, Parker? You hear me, Cane? Make damn sure you do."

Actually, Roland Cane was drinking beer, not cokes, but little Bobby Bowie always did what you told him, Dan Spear. Besides, Bobby didn't care for cokes or cigarettes, and at that point in his life he hadn't figured out what you're supposed to do with a woman. I was a prude. Even if I had been up in the stands at the Groveland game that year, sitting watching the halftime show with my parents, with Austin and Virginia Simpson, I probably would have agreed with the views of the female contingent of Mt. Dora fans:

"Well, I never..."

"Disgraceful."

"How anybody could allow those girls to parade around in outfits like that, I'll never know."

"Disgusting."

"Somebody ought to talk to somebody about this."

When my daddy heard these comments all around him in the stands, coming out of the joint mouths of Mt. Dora's mothers, including Myrt Bowie and Virginia Simpson, he probably muttered something like, "You're durn tooting," which was his way of saying he agreed. But I bet he never took his eyes off the field while he was agreeing. God knows what Austin said, but I'm sure he had some choice comments. Austin Simpson has always had a great sense of humor.

Of course, I didn't get to see the halftime show. I was back by the Groveland gym, with our demoralized team, trying to figure out how we would make it through the second half, listening to Earle Williams telling me that, after all, we were only down 20-0—all we had to do was hold Groveland and score three touchdowns, with all the extra points.

Funny how air bubbles from the past kind of burble up in your memory and burst. When I was a patient in Botkins Hospital, Moscow, USSR, fifteen years after that Groveland game, I was lying awake one night in the dark. And suddenly I got a clear image of the very scene I just described: Daddy and Austin up in the stands staring intently. And though I don't remember looking at those majorettes while we were getting creamed that evening, my subconscious must have gawked, because I had a totally vivid image in Botkins of the white cotton outfits, form-fitting, very tightly, over the crotch. Mike Tcheekar, another American and fellow patient, lay snoring away in the hospital bed beside mine, but I was awake for another hour, feasting my eyes on the Groveland majorettes of 1957.

3

Rootedy-toot, rootedy-toot/ Flush B.M./ Knickers/ Arrested in Tijuana, although not guilty/ Article 15/ San Diego, thirty years later/ The Unknown Soldier/ "Fella, would you wee in my bottle for me?"/ Sleepwalking in mine fields/ Jasmine and happiness blend in the mind of The Walking Jesus/ Blooming azaleas, lantana, Spanish moss/ Florida mountain high/ Are you still there, Tinker Durden?/ "Yeah, but God sees them"/ The thoughts of youth are short, short thoughts/ "We like short shorts"/ Aubrey Snell is drowned/ "Yeah, Smith"/ Thanks, Nana T.!/ The vicious joy of racking/ "Watch out for Number 50—L.E. Williams, Jr."/ A theological question: does God love football?/ Surprise, surprise, B.M.!/ Catholics vs. Protestants/ Wade Simpson flies away forever/ The evanescence of Jimmy Pavilliard/ Bowie Mom and Colonel Bob/ Heaven and Hell/ I owe one to the Pope/ Uncle Russ and Aunt Cille/ Daddy rolls down the Grand Canyon/ Doc Montgomery says, "I don't know what it is."/ My father cries/ Bobby Green's sister/ Head gets run over—no problem/ Have you been in Samarkand?/ I have/ The white stucco house/ Hibiscus blooming yellow/ Flame vine on the fence/ Ahead half way!

People don't change much, but the cheers change over the years. When my father played football in Seneca, South Carolina, their favorite cheer went like this: "Rootedy-toot, rootedy-toot, Seneca Technical Institute. Peaches and cream, peaches and cream, TEAM, TEAM, TEAM!" Now that's a great cheer! But I doubt if Seneca still uses it. Nowadays opposing grandstands shout obscenities at each other. The cheerleaders on the teams Bishop Moore plays in 1994 are probably chanting "Flush B.M.! Flush B.M.!"

Most likely they've got male cheerleaders at MDHS these days too, big bruisers who hold up the girls by their bottoms or heels, and the girls, hair teased high and wild, balanced on those paws, making chopping motions with their hands and yelling, "Yaaaay! We're No. 1!" Then somebody counts one-two-three HEP! and the male bruisers let go of the bottoms or heels and down, down, straight down they come, those fresh-faced girls full of trust and daring, in their pleated white skirts, which flare out to show the orange of their knickers as they fall. Youth knows it will be caught when it falls. Youth believes, fervently, in its own immortality.

"Knickers" is the British word for underpants. Did I tell you I lived in England for two years? In the army. After my summer in the wheat field overlooking East Germany (1964), they sent me to the only American army post in the U.K., near Harrogate, Yorkshire. When I arrived the top sergeant called me into his office, put a nasty squint on, and said, "Now I want you to get one thing straight from the start—we don't tolerate any bullshit trouble-makers here."

Me, little Bobby? A trouble-maker? Well, of course I wasn't, but they still had the "Article Fifteen" in my file, and the story of how they caught me in Tijuana, Mexico. Let me tell you how this whole crazy business developed.

I was taking Russian classes at the Presidio of Monterey, six hours a day, five days a week. It's the best language school in the country and I loved it. Of course, they couldn't do without the usual army crap: weekly inspections and Saturday details, policing up the ice plant. Once we had a Friday off coming up, for some holiday, and three of us, Tim Gormann, Jack Kemel and I, decided we'd take a trip to Tijuana. We put in all the proper papers, requesting permission to exceed the distance limitations. Gormann had the use of his father's Chevy, so we would have plenty of time to drive down to Mexico and be back for classes on Monday. But our request came back "DENIED," in the big illiterate scrawl of the first sergeant.

Well, naturally, we were angry. We sat around that Friday, wearing the blue jeans of free civilian life, fuming, contemplating our lost long weekend. After a few choice expressions directed at the army, I said, "Is America still a free country, or not?" Kemel and Gormann, all hangdog, just looked over at me and then looked back down at the fresh shellac on our barracks floor. Then I said, "Well, I know we're in the military, but are we still Americans, or not?" They perked up a little bit, and this time they said "Yeah" and smiled a wan smile. I started screaming, "Yeah is right! You're damn right yeah!" I danced around the barracks, inciting my friends to riot: "Are we free, or not? Huh? Huh? Let me hear it! Are we free Americans?" And with that they jumped up, started yelling "We're free, we're free!" So, in a word, we all three upped and made a mad dash for the car, whooping all the way. We hopped in and took off, giggling hysterically. We drove 450 miles, to Mexico.

We stopped to buy beer. We drank that beer as we rode, joking and singing. God, what a riot the army was! In the army, when you got away from the making of beds and shining of shoes and the "Son, get your hands out of your pockets!" your soul could run rampant. We slept in the car that night, in an empty lot at Disneyland. The next day we tooled into San Diego and parked walking distance from the border. We strolled across to Tijuana. Nobody checked any papers.

We spent all day wandering the streets, drinking Mexican beer and eating tamales. Hustlers approached, selling drugs, trinkets, sex ("Hey, man, you wanna get you rocks off?"). We partied half the night in the "Hotel de Paris," where we rented luxurious rooms. We spoke Russian among ourselves and I used my Spanish, from Eudell Sutley's class, on the locals. I told them we were tourists from Russia, '*rusos*'. Early the next morning we arose, with a sense of time well spent, and we set off to walk back to the U.S.A. Gormann and I went right through the border checkpoint, but Kemel was held up. Only later did we learn that the imported Austrian jacket he was wearing attracted attention, and when they searched its pockets, they found illegal amphetamines that he had had the stupidity to buy on the streets.

So Gormann and I waited a few minutes on the U.S. side, by the crossing. No Kemel. We went back to the parking lot and sat in the grey Chevy. Still no Kemel. I said, "We better get moving. They've got him, and we're here against orders. Pretty soon they'll have us too." But Gormann said, "No, we'll wait. He didn't do anything wrong. They'll let him go in a minute."

I said, "They got him, and by now they know he's in the army, and they're going to ask him who he's with, and he's going to tell them where we are." Gormann said, "No, he won't tell. We'll just wait a while longer."

We waited maybe forty-five minutes in that parking lot. Still no Kemel. "Listen," I told Gormann, "I'm waiting five more minutes, and if he's not here, I'm going to be out on the highway hitch-hiking back to Monterey. If they don't get you, you can pick me up later, by the roadside."

Gormann laughed. "Get me? Nobody's going to get me. What are you so paranoid about?" Speaking of paranoid, Gormann was out of the army on a general discharge (loony tunes) two months later. After they busted us down he just totally lost it. The last time I saw him he was a hippy, shambling around downtown Monterey in a beard and ragged jeans, walking the walk of The Walking Jesus.

Three minutes after I said I'd wait five minutes we saw the San Diego white police cruiser come circling around the parking lot, and I said, "Oh, shit, you know who he's looking for, don't you?" Gormann said, "Not us."

The cruiser stopped, and the policeman got out, walked over to our car and said, "You boys in the army, by any chance, stationed up at Presidio of Monterey?"

So that's how I landed in a San Diego jail, and then in a military drunk tank. When they threw us in that drunk tank, there was one sailor passed out and drooling on the floor, into a drain, and there was one bewildered soldier, namely Jack Kemel (still in his Austrian jacket), huddled over in the corner. By this time Gormann and I had decided we would speak only Russian, as a way of protesting our arrest. After all, we were free Americans, and we hadn't done anything wrong. Besides that, we weren't drinking, and they had the gall to stick us in a drunk tank. We also gave Kemel hell, in Russian, for turning us in.

After that, we laughed and sang Russian songs in that drunk tank, Gormann and I, while Kemel remained disconsolate in his corner. Finally, some noncom came up to the bars and told us the only language to be spoken in the drunk tank was English, was that clear? and after that we shut up. In fact, the lingua franca of the drunk tank wasn't English either. It was the retching noise the sailor on the floor made, when he came to for a minute.

On the whole, though, they treated us well there, at the drunk tank. They were even respectful. Their primary clients were intoxicated sailors from the naval base in San Diego, and they could see that we were of a higher class, what with us speaking Russian and not being sloshed. They held us all afternoon, and then they let us go. Our only offense was "out of bounds," which means we had exceeded the distance limitations from our military station by some 450 miles.

So we got in Gormannn's Chevy and drove back to Monterey, knowing that those considerate people at the drunk tank would make a phone call to The Defense Language Institute. Sure enough, right in the middle of classes the next day, we got notice to report to the orderly room. There sat "the old man," i.e., Lt. Zilch, the young officer who was company commander and didn't know diddley about anything. He had an angry look on the white sidewalls of his narrow head, knowing that was the look he was supposed to put there. He took all his cues from the redneck mannerisms of first sergeant Emory Skagson, who stood puffing and blowing beside "the old man's" desk.

Of course, the first sergeant handled the proceedings. He was the real company commander, just like first sergeants are everywhere. After we did our "Private First Class So-and-So, reporting as ordered" bit, he just glared for a full thirty seconds with that nasty sneer, and then he jumped on us, all four feet. After he got through reaming us out, he informed us of our rights. We could either go through a court martial, or we could simplify matters by accepting what they called an "Article Fifteen," which is just like a court martial, except you plead guilty and they stick it to you right then and there.

"So," said the first sergeant, "What will it be, the court martial or the Article 15?" I looked at Kemel, and his eyes were wandering, his mouth was open. I looked at Gormann, and he was looking at the floor. I told the first sergeant, "We'll take the Article 15." Since I had spoken for all three, they looked upon me as the ringleader. I suppose I was.

Well, they busted us down on the spot, took away our precious PFC stripe, and restricted us to our barracks, with signing in at the orderly room on the hour. This incident made big changes in my subsequent army career. In the first place, my superiors looked upon me thereafter as a quiet, dangerous type, who would never really fit in the army, and they went out of their way to leave me alone. In the second place, I knew now that I'd never make any rank for the rest of my three-year sentence, so I didn't worry about the petty chickenshit that they wanted me pecking about in. I always performed my job the best I could, but I didn't polish my shoes. When I got to Europe I took every opportunity, off duty or on leave, to have a wild time, from Germany to Spain and back to England. I laughed a lot, when I wasn't quietly doing my work. But I never was a trouble-maker; I was just "uncoachable."

A strange thing happened last year. I was on a plane for San Diego, going to a conference for Russian language teachers. I was talking to the middle-aged folks beside me, a couple who reminded me of people I grew up around. They spoke of the "It's a Small World" teacup ride at Disneyland, which was the main goal of their California trip. Then the man turned to me with his earnest, all-American face and asked, "And have you ever been to San Diego before?"

I stopped and thought for a minute, and then I put on a look of solemn wonder and I said, "You know, it's funny you ask me that, because I was in San Diego only once in my life, and that was exactly thirty years ago, and I was in *jail!*"

He looked at me and he just said, "Oh..." His wife looked away. She went back to her copy of *The Reader's Digest*. They didn't even ask me to tell the story, but if they had, they would have heard what I just told you, Dan Spear.

Getting back to the issue of cheerleading, I'd like to speak now from the viewpoint of the crotchety older generation: I, frankly, just can't see the point of this new stuff. Holding girls up, yelling out choppy cheers like robots. And, worst of all, male cheerleaders. Back in the fifties Dan Spear hounded every able-bodied boy in the school to go out for football. He wouldn't have stood for those big bruisers being cheerleaders. We had only one male cheerleader at MDHS in my memory. That was Bud Ligon, and he was the object of the whole town's derision. Why, down at the "O.K.

Barber Shop" the customers and the barbers (Mr. Landis and Mr. Hardy) mulled incessantly over the case of Bud Ligon. They aired out the issue for months on end, and they concluded, unanimously, that what Bud was doing (cheerleading) was tinged with moral turpitude.

While I'm in the crotchety mode, let me get one more thing off my chest. When I played football, if we scored a touchdown we handed the ball to the referee and then rejoiced in a sportsmanlike way. No throwing the ball up in the air, no wallowing in a huge pile on the ground with team mates, no dancing around showing your ass, no pounding one another up side the head, no ostentatious giving of thanks to the Lord God above (down on one knee, head bowed in prayer). Can you imagine what Dan Spear would have done to our linemen, had they demeaned their own dignity, and showed up the other team, by beating their breasts and howling to the skies after every tackle they made?

My father was a good football player in his high school days, a half-back just like me. He even played some semi-pro ball in New Jersey, until he took that job in the airplane factory. Then, later, as I told you before, he got so sick of New Jersey that he quit the job right in the middle of the war and we headed for Florida. Of course, they yanked his military deferment, and when we pulled up to the white stucco house at 820 E. Seventh Ave., his draft notice was waiting for him in the mailbox.

Winter was coming on, and Daddy always had bad sinus trouble. So on that army bus, all the way up to Jacksonville, he kept leaning his head out the window, letting the cold air blow on his sinuses. A couple of days later he came back to Mt. Dora, "4-F," rejected as unfit for military service. That must have been a time of great rejoicing for us, his family, although I don't have any memory of the occasion. Ask my sister June.

Robert N. Bowie never found out exactly how he earned his 4-F, but he didn't think it was the sinus trouble. He believed, in retrospect, that he owed his good fortune to a certain unknown soldier. When the recruits took their bottles into the latrine for a urine sample, Daddy, for some reason, couldn't get his stream going. Five or six different groups came and went, and there he was, still straining his kidneys and scrotum. The sergeant in charge of his bunch came in three times to get him moving, and each time he yelled a little bit louder, so finally Daddy said to a man standing next to him, "Hey, fellow, would you mind weeing in my bottle for me?" That good Samaritan, soon to be dead of some dire disease, smiled and said, "Sure, I got piss and vinegar to spare." Thanks to him, thought my father, he got his 4-F and came home to Mt. Dora.

He went back to his job, delivering chicken feed on a big truck, for the local Purina store. I used to ride with him on his rounds sometimes. I was four years old, wearing what they called a "sun suit" (shorts with suspenders sewed onto them, no shirt). People always said, "Well, I see you got your helper with you today." If it was a woman she would say, "You want to come be my little boy?" Daddy would laugh and joke around with everybody. Later on he hurt his back toting those feed bags around. That's when he found his real niche. He became a "policy man," selling insurance for Peninsular Life, a Florida company. Robert N. Bowie had a natural talent for sales, and he serviced his debit well. By the time I was in high school, he was selling life insurance great guns all over Lake County, Florida.

As for the army business, when it came my turn to be drafted in 1963, I was hoping for something similar to Daddy's experience. But it didn't work out that way. I made the same trip, to Jacksonville, for the physical. I asked to see an orthopedic specialist, hoping my old gimpy leg would serve me well. After the operation in Dec., 1957, that leg never was quite the same.

The army doctor manipulated the thing a little bit, and then he said, with subtle irony, that he had good news for me: my leg was fully fit for service!

On the forms we filled out I put a check by the question about sleep-walking, and that gave the army pause. They sent me home while they thought it over. As a child I used to sleepwalk all over the place. I'd even go outside and wander around in the orange grove. They say that's an indication of emotional disturbance, but it didn't stop me from getting a high security clearance later on. Of course, there were people all around me in the army with top clearances, and a lot of them would have been right at home in the loony bin at Chattahoochee. "Only in America," as Yogi Berra supposedly said, when they told him the mayor of Dublin was a Jew.

Riding the Greyhound back to Mt. Dora, I ran into Buddles Ledford on the bus. Hadn't seen him for years. We sat together all the way, and he told me Korean War stories. I always liked Buddles, used to play baseball with him on the town team. We got to Mt. Dora late at night, and I walked home to the pink house from the bus station down town. It was hot. In all of my memories and dreams of home, it's always hot.

I'll never forget how happy my parents were to see me when I walked through that door. They didn't say much. But their happiness wafted through the humid air of the house and then flowed out the windows, to blend with the smells of the night blooming jasmine and all the other moist thick aromas enveloping beautiful, subtropical Mt. Dora, Florida. If The Walking Jesus happened to be ambling down Seventh Ave. that night, the mixture of happiness and jasmine would have gone through his left ear and out past the white fluff on the right, leaving a splendrous ray aglow in his maundering brain.

Of course, two weeks later the army called and said they wanted me. When I joined in March of 1963 they were on the verge of drafting me for the standard two years. I took an extra year after they promised me Russian language instruction at the Defense Language Institute in Monterey,

California. I was in the army during the early Vietnam Era, but they never posted me to Asia. They needed me in Europe, to keep an eye and ear on what the Russians were doing. In place of me they sent my little sister Peggy into the jungles of Vietnam.

By the way, I did some more sleepwalking in the army. When I was in Monterey we lived in a huge common barracks. One night some fellow soldiers were horsing around and the noise roused me from a deep sleep. But it didn't wake me all the way up; I just climbed in a daze out of my cot and started staggering around. I went up to the bed of a guy in the cubicle across from me, a stupid twerp of a kid named Marty Fitzsimmons, and I tucked him in. He was lying there awake, looking at me and wondering what to do. How would you like to be tucked under your army blanket by a crazed sleepwalker? Maybe this was a foreshadowing of ten years of tucking in my three sons later on in life. Anyway, there were several witnesses to this incident, which I heard about only when I woke up the next morning. I was running scared, figuring they would pull my security clearance before I even got it, then send me off to cook school. But, apparently, nobody reported the sleepwalking and the tucking in. Later on, when I lived up on a hill, in a wheat field on the East German border, I would sometimes sleepwalk out of the huge tent we slept in and wander down by the mine fields. My friend Fred came down there and got me one night, talked my muddled self, which was bent on climbing a grapefruit tree, into returning to my bunk. Where are you now, gentle, fat-faced Fred Schoellhumper? Do I still have a friend in Pennsylvania?

Mt. Dora, Florida. What is it like, growing up in a subtropical paradise? Well, when you're a kid you don't think about it. Kids don't bother to look at the world of nature all around them. But when I go back to Mt. Dora now, as an adult, I just stand there with my mouth hanging open: you mean I'm from this? God Almighty, where on earth is there a place more lovely?

Say you live in Ohio and you want to see what I mean. Well, you can go any time of the year, but try, for example, mid March, when the spring flowers are putting on a show. Drive in from Tavares on the back road, along Lake Dora. Blooming azaleas, lantana, hibiscus, the green of the St. Augustine grass on the lawns, or the brighter green of the Bermuda, huge slash pines overhead, Spanish moss on the oaks, perpetual sunshine pouring down over the great blue herons that stand knee deep in the water, next to the cypress knees. Across the lake you'll see the town on the hill, the spot that once was the Grandview Hotel and the condo where The Castle once stood, and you'll say, "My God, my God, I'm in Paradise!"

The flora looks so familiar to me, but it must be an exotic sight for anyone who grew up farther north. Camphor trees, bougainvilleas, Florida banana trees, palmettos, gardenias, ear trees. Ask your relatives from Ohio, Dan Spear, ask them if they've ever heard of an ear tree. The fauna includes blue jays and mocking birds, cranes, herons, alligators, coral snakes and cottonmouths, rattlesnakes as thick as Buddles Ledford's arms, possums and gophers (land turtles), armadillos. Beetles of all descriptions, spiders the size of your hand, huge colonies of red and black ants, dirt daubers, horseflies, red bugs, voracious mosquitoes. Any kind of insect that bites.

Of course, they've got bugs, snakes, and subtropical foliage all over Florida. They've got armadillos in Texas, opossums in Ohio. What's so special about Mt. Dora, Florida? Well, maybe it's the total ensemble effect. This is one of the few hilly areas in the State of Florida, which lies mostly at sea level, or below. Around here we've got Howey-in-the-Hills, where Eudell Sutley used to live (maybe still does), and we've got Clermont ("Clear Mount") and Montverde ("Green Mountain"), and then, finally, we've got the jewel of them all on the hill, overlooking the lake: luxurious,

76

blooming, green, hot, humid, lethargic, marvelous Mount Dora ("Gift of the Mountain").

Now, you've lived there most of your lifetime, Dan Spear, and you may think it's changed. But to me it's still the same place. Okay, so they've put in some condominiums. They've made it more touristy and quaintsy, with all the little shops down town. They've closed the old Princess Theatre, where Billy Brown, Class of '58, helped me get my first job (ticket taker and popcorn maker), they've desegregated the schools. But there's still an East Town, isn't there? And there's still a Pistolville (Is there still a Pistolville?) and still a Sylvan Shores. In light of the enormous, egregious transformation of Orlando since they built Mouseland, just take a look at Mt. Dora. It's still standing serene in sunshine. Its population hasn't even changed that much, has it? It was maybe five or six thousand in the fifties. What is it now? Seven? And how many people are the same ones who were there when I was? Is Margaret Rigdon still around? Flavell Bagwell? Carol Spang? Bobby Partridge? Doc Walker, the chiropractor? Where's Gladys Aldrich these days? Or Roberta Aldrich (no kin)? Gwynne Godell? Ross Swartsel? June Guest? Cecil Barker? Buddy Atkins? Frederick Gosnell? Is one-armed L.C. Gimple still riding his airboat, poaching alligators? Is J.W. Shaw still writing prescriptions down at the Rexall Drug Store? Is Neal Durden working for the city? And Tinker Durden, his brother, where's he? Carolyn Cox? Charlene Edenfield? Sylvia Adams? Charlie Manson?

In the spring of 1993 a huge storm, accompanied by tornadoes, tried to blow Mt. Dora off the map. You think Mt. Dora let that bother it one whit? So a few hundred live oaks went down. So the water supply and electricity were off for a week. Mt. Dora just smiled serenely and went on about its business. What is its business? Its business is going on forever in the sunshine about its business.

Did Mt. Dora lose its cool when one of those twisters blew over a water oak and knocked a huge hole in the roof of Prof Roseborough's old

77

house on Clayton St.? No. That's not Mt. Dora's business. If Prof were still alive, and his wife, Precious, I can't see it bothering them all that much either. Remember the way he laughed? Remember the soft chuckle of D.D. Roseborough, principal of the Mt. Dora School? Remember the way he tiptoed into the back of any auditorium where anyone was speaking, and then yelled out "LOUD-UH!" disconcerting the speaker and breaking up the audience and then chuckling along with them all as they laughed?

Prof and Precious, if they still lived there, would walk outside, glance at that hole in their roof, and then take the time to go for a walk. They would set off strolling, slowly, slowly, through the heat, ever so slowly and serenely down Clayton St. toward Fifth Avenue, past Roseborough Elementary. Stopping to smell the hydrangeas, begonias, gardenias. Doing their best to be kind. Knowing deep down in their souls that God loves Mt. Dora, Florida.

When I was in Botkins Hospital, Moscow, in 1972, with dysentery, the woman head doctor on our ward was the portly aggressive type of Russian woman. She would come by and preach to me and my American room mate, Michael Tsheecar, the capitalist unconverted, from the Marxist-Leninist Bible. One day she noticed that Mike was wearing a cross around his neck, and she said, "You mean that here in the modern progressive age you still believe in all that Grandfather Frost (Santa Claus) stuff?" Meek Michael, who had the look of an apostle (skinny, blonde-haired, well disposed to any and all), smiled and said, "Sure." Then she said, with the fervor of the true-believer communist-atheist, "Well, our cosmonauts fly up in space all the time, and they never see any *God* up there!" And Michael said, still smiling, "Well, yeah, but God sees *them*."

If God has eyes to see the cosmonauts in space and the beauties of Mother Earth, how could His eyes miss Mt. Dora, Florida, and not love what He sees? Was it really any different here thirty-seven years ago, on the happiest day of my life? Only in a few particulars. When I grew up in Lake County citrus was king. You could climb the Citrus Tower in Clermont (had it then existed) and you'd see the green of the trees dotted with the orange of the oranges for miles in all directions. But then the winters got colder, too cold for the fruit; the freezes of the eighties wiped out many of the groves. I remember stealing mangoes from a mango tree down by the Lakeside Inn, I remember climbing a tree with Clarence Sims, right next to where the Aldriches lived, and coming down with two avocados. Well, I know they still have papaya trees growing in Mt. Dora, but I doubt if you could find avocados or mangoes these days. Mt. Dora is more straight subtropical now, less tropical. But they say the groves are coming back. Are there any guavas left? My mother and Virginia Simpson used to pick guavas from a tree out by the cemetery on Donnelly St. It was right next to the chinaberry tree next to the garage apartment where the Simpsons lived at the time. Virginia would make that wonderful guava butter and guava jelly. Do you still do that, Virginia Simpson?

What else was different? Well, when I grew up, in the forties and fifties, the racial tension was so pervasive you could smell it in the air. Black folks stayed in East Town, and if they wanted to go into downtown Mt. Dora they damn well better go by one street, and one only—Grandview. Now the races are more mixed, and a little more at ease with one another, and you can't help feeling good about how one little town has made some steps toward harmony. Of course, the only thing that will resolve once and for all the issue of race in America is miscegenation. That, eventually, will happen, and then we'll all be grey (a color intermediate between black and white), but not until some time in the new millenium.

When I went to segregated Mt. Dora School some students and teachers used the "n-word" on a regular basis. Now, that sounds extreme today, when "nigger" (at least in public usage) has become one of the biggest taboo words in our language. Rightly so. Why pronounce a word so wrapped up in contumely and hatred? Nowadays most Americans are trying to be tolerant, and we deserve some credit for that. But don't expect a sudden burst of magnanimity out of people, black or white. I've been working for twenty-five years in the liberal academic world, where folks who don't believe in Original Sin spend scads of creative energy to change the names of sports teams from "Redskins" to just plain "Skins." They're wasting their time—because people aren't ready to look at somebody's skin and think "neutral generic skin." Folks aren't put together that way. I'm not complaining about human nature, mind you. It's just the way we are.

At the MDHS of the fifties not many pupils questioned the dominant stance of the South—the insistence on segregation. Kids just tend to go along. And, of course, not many of us wanted the agony that goes with contemplating a complex issue like race. What were we preoccupied with? Well, we were, for one thing, in the throes of our developing hormones. Anonymous Jones brought a poem to school: "What a Soldier Dreams About." Everyone read it with relish, with laughter and lust. Once, early in our high school years, I remember a fellow student, another Anonymous, passing around a note that read, "Smile if you've got a hard on." And a friend of mine, a good-looking and basically decent anonymous girl, leered at my crotch when I read the note, and then she smiled too. Those were the things that went on in class, and I'm sure the same things are repeating themselves in the classrooms of Mt. Dora High School today, and in classrooms all over this wonderful mindless country of ours.

Most of us studied Spanish in those days. We were very close to Cuba, and Fidel Castro wasn't in power yet. He was already up in the mountains, though, preparing his revolution. A man living in Mt. Dora, Edmund Chester, was advisor to the then Cuban dictator. He even published a book, *A Sergeant Named Batista*, in which he described the humble origins of a boy who was raised in a poor cane-cutter family. When Castro's biographies came out later, he was probably described in similar terms, as a four-year-old sweating away with a machete. Our Spanish class was the first in years not to take a trip to Cuba. We had held all the fund raisers, the bake sales, etc., we even had our itinerary in hand, but then Spanish teacher Eudell Sutley announced that he refused to take responsibility for a group of adolescents in a war-torn country.

More scattered memories of 1954-1958. The Peppermint Stick Restaurant, the soda fountain at the Rexall Drug Store, the Villa Dora Hotel, the Lakeside Inn, the Club Rudo, Sally's Dress Shop. The Movie Garden Drive-In Theater in Eustis, with its back rows known as the "passion pit." Town luminaries: James Orr (police chief), Roy Christopher (attorney-at-law), Mabel Norris Reese (crusading newspaperwoman), J.G. Ray, Jr. (contractor) and his beautiful wife Bettye, Cauley Lott (principal of the Milner-Rosenwald Academy in East Town), Sam Shaw (businessman), Jimmie Jones (preacher), Howard Simpson (orange grower), Walking Jesus (eccentric), George White (banker), Eula Lee (pharmacist), Cecil Bowie (policy man), Arthur Colaianni (band director), Frank Stewart (radio and t.v. repairman), Press Atkins (laundry man), Florence Atkins (housewife), Austin Simpson (policy man), Abby Jo Land (socialite), Tiny Smith (hardware salesman), Don Conway (school teacher and pariah), Homer Morris (how would you define Homer Morris? Was Homer definable?).

In 1954 there were two drownings in two days at the Lake Gertrude beach, the one you used to drive us kids out to on the school bus, Dan Spear. The second victim was Aubrey Snell, age twelve. That same year Buster Williams was badly injured in a freak accident, hit by a car when a bee distracted the driver. It happened right about the time I was honored as a safety patrol boy—picked to take a trip to the convention in Washington, D.C.

Our best teacher from ninth grade on was Nana T. Laney, the English teacher. She would read aloud from her favorite poetry, and she would read with feeling, about how the thoughts of youth are long, long thoughts. She emoted, carried away by the power of art. Meanwhile, we would sit there and snigger at her emoting. David Brown would scrape his shoe leather across the floor to produce an unseemly sound, something like the sound that Ronnie Parker liked to make by fwapping a palm under an armpit. Everybody was highly entertained by this. The poet was wrong, of course: the thoughts of youth are idiotic, and very short thoughts.

The class character was L.C. (Larry) Smith, who, for some unknown reason, took to wearing his pajama top to school instead of a shirt. Larry was tall, blonde-haired and gangly, acne on his chin and braces on his teeth. Dan Spear held a longstanding grudge against him because he couldn't get him to go out for football. The fact was that Larry's parents, Mildred and J. Mac ("Tiny") Smith, stood firmly united against football, for fear he would get the teeth, which they had spent so much money straightening, kicked out of his mouth.

Somewhere around junior high we invented the game called, "Yeah, Smith," and we played it for years. Like many games that people play, it mixed good clean fun with cruelty. Whatever Larry would do, somebody would make a derogatory comment. Then somebody else would say, "Yeah, Smith," and after that everyone joined in with a chorus of "Yeah, Smiths." We used all different voices: old lady voices, Prof Roseborough voices, high black voices, Sylvan Shores voices, Mr. Clements voices, Spencer Beebe voices, Pistolville voices, spastic voices, little squeaky kid voices, Leebo McCree voices, all saying the same thing over and over: "Yeah, Smith."

One day, in the eleventh grade, right in the middle of an important literary point that Nana T. Laney was imparting to us, Larry took out a tissue, loudly blew his nose, then slowly arose in his pajama top, holding that used tissue gingerly between forefinger and thumb. All eyes were on him and all eyes were smiling. He loped his slow loping gait to the waste basket at the front of the room. Mrs. Laney went on with her lecture, but no one was listening. Larry stood briefly over the waste basket, holding the tissue above it, while Nana T. stopped talking and glared at him. He dropped the tissue, did a smart about face, and began his slow perambulation back to his desk. He didn't make it all the way before the explosion: "Larry, how dare you interrupt me in the middle of class! From now on you ask permission before getting out of your seat! Is that clear?"

Then Donald ("Butchie") Alexander said, "Yeah, Smith," and somebody else took up the call. C.M. tried the spastic retard voice, and I used my favorite, the little kid with the lisp, and soon the whole class was reverberating with variations on the theme of "Yeah, Smith." Well, as you can well understand, Coach Spear, since you knew Mrs. Laney, the repercussions were serious. But God, what fun it was while it lasted!

Yet, let me just tell you, Nana T. Laney, wherever your spirit may be tergiversating in the time called Now, that it wasn't all wasted. I learned the word 'lugubrious' in your class and I still think it's a great word. Despite all our mindless reactions to literature, I learned to love Shakespeare from you. At age fourteen I was thrilled by Mark Antony's oration from Julius Caesar: "But Brutus says he was ambitious, and Brutus is an honorable man." Wonderful! It must have seemed a hopeless task at the time, but you did it, Nana T. Laney! I'm a professor of Russian literature in a college now. And what's more, you taught me, and plenty of others, to write. So you've got a lot to be proud of.

I look back with gratitude upon the teachers at the Mt. Dora School in the forties and fifties. Among others: Charlotte Bennett, Helen Kurras, Buck Dandridge, Evelyn Cassady, Fred Sandwald, Jim Jackson, George Clements, Edna TeStrake, Jimmie G. Batton (from Mississippi) and her sister Alto Gary, who wrote on my report card, June 8, 1951: "Bobby is a joy to teach." But two of them stand out: Nana T. Laney and Dan Spear. Mrs. Laney taught me to love literature and to write. Mr. Spear taught me how to be like Bobby Correll, how to throw a body block with my hip, how to rack!

Take a running start, leave your feet and launch your body into the air. From a position parallel to the ground, twist a hip into the point just above the knees of the enemy, crack him on the legs and roll, knocking his feet out from under him. In my senior year I loved to use that block on some poor soul who didn't see me coming. When we shifted to the right, with our unbalanced line single wing, Neil Stoothoff played tailback and I played wingback. On Right 27 he carried the ball and my job was to block the end. Sometimes, instead of lining up in wingback position I would flank way out toward the sideline. I could hear the other team yelling, "Watch out for a pass!" The defensive halfback, who knew that the cardinal sin was letting me get behind him, would be backing up before the play even started.

Billy Moon, our center, hiked the ball to Stoothoff, giving him a running lead. Meanwhile, I took a few quick steps down field, and the half-back was in full retreat. Then, as the sweep began developing, as Stoothoff made his way toward the right, I would sneak back in, keeping my eye on my prey. He, the enemy end, was watching the ball, of course, and the blocking back running interference. He never saw me. And just when Stoothoff made his turn to head downfield, just when that left end made his move toward tackling him, I would race in and hit him hard with a hip block from his blind side.

What nasty joy I took in making that block. Bobby Green, fullback and star for Eustis in my senior, angry year, played left end on defense. He had some kind of leg injury late in the season, and we knew about that. I clearly remember how I pulled the flank-out trick, how I blindsided him on Right 27, rolled my hip into his leg and knocked him down. He had to leave the game, temporarily, after that play. Dirty football. It felt so good at the time, and when I think of it now I'm ashamed.

It's true, we hated Eustis, beating Eustis always made our season. It's certainly true that the Eustis players (Ron Stahl, Bill Barnes, Butch Somebody, Hausermann, Igou, Fred Pait, Ron Mulder, L. Dunlope) would have taken sadistic joy in delivering a solid lick to my bad leg, then watching me limp off the field, grimacing in pain. All of that is true. But Bobby Green wasn't only the best player on that team: he may have been the best person. After it was over, after we beat Eustis (in the next-to-last game of the season) on their home field, 12-7, in a game we were lucky to win, we sat on our school bus, sweating in our pads, preparing for the short ride home. That's when Bobby Green climbed up the steps of that bus to congratulate us. He told us we played a great game. Now, could I have done that if things had turned out the opposite? Could I have got on a Eustis bus in Mt. Dora and congratulated their team? Never. I didn't have the class. Harry Pearce, from Tavares, now, he had it. And Bobby Green had that kind of class.

Bishop Moore's John Ellis had class too. As we lined up on Nov. 1, 1957, to start the second quarter, I saw him standing at ease, serenely confident, the blue-eyed, blonde-haired golden boy, star of the team. The look on his face said he knew that B.M.'s wild offensive machine would soon break the game open. After all, he had the amazing total of something like twenty touchdowns already that season.

I was just reading some old clippings in the scrapbook my mother kept for me. One of them quotes an interview before the contest, with the Bishop Moore coach: "Mt. Dora will be one of the toughest ball clubs we've met this season, and I know they'll be up for us." Did he really believe that, after the Groveland debacle? I doubt it. Did he say anything to his team when Barry Keitel reported Dan Spear's threat, to forfeit the game if they ran up the score? No. He wouldn't make that mistake. His pre-game lecture may have gone something like this:

"Now, boys, we're up against one of the toughest ball clubs we've met this season, and I hope nobody's taking them lightly. I been telling you in practice all week. Forget that 40-0 score against Groveland. That'll just make them hungrier. Forget what you've heard about all the injuries. About Bowie being hurt, for instance. Remember what Bowie did to us last year? They've got a good passer, this Studuff, or however you say it. He can run too. All their backs can run. Their line is small but quick. Now remember, Stuart, watch out for Number 50—he gets through fast, you got to block him fast. This is a lean, mean-assed team we're up against tonight, boys. People say they're banged up. Well, when they get out on that playing field, when the adrenalin starts to flowing, they'll forget they hurt."

Next comes the change in tone and tempo, the appeal to visceral emotions: "I want you boys to get mad, now, you hear? I want you playing mean and hard. I want you knocking people down. I want to see some grit out there! You hear? I want sharp blocking and tackling, give me some gut passion, show me you've got tight balls!" Etc. We'll skip the build-up to the peroration, which has the whole team jumping around, pounding pads and making animal sounds.

I don't think Coach John Bryan believed what he was saying (if that's what he said; keep in mind that I wasn't there, so the speech cited above is speculation). No matter how he tried to psyche himself and his team up, he knew the Golden Hurricanes had blown out to sea. Or at least that they were downgraded to a minor tropical storm, which, after hitting the brick wall that was Groveland, would chug along erratically, puffing and wheezing its way through the rest of the season. The vibrations going out to his team in that pep talk, if not the words, were saying, "Don't worry. We beat Eustis, 44-21, we ran their ass all over the field. And Eustis has a lot better team than this bunch. No problem, boys. We're going to kick us some butt tonight."

And I just bet that if you had a film of those big Irish and Italian boys sitting there listening to Coach Bryan, and then whooping at the end of his speech, you would see on their faces that they didn't buy any of his cautionary tales. They whooped insincerely. They knew we had six starters in the stands, they knew Robbie Vanzant got his bell rung against Umatilla, they knew Moon had an arm injury, they knew Bowie would play limping if he played at all. They planned on reminding us how much we were hurting by racking all the tender spots early on. Then, after they had us softened up, they'd run all over us, same way they ran on Eustis.

Now, B.M. was a parochial school. You reckon they thought God was on their side too? I have to give you credit, Dan Spear. You never held any prayers in the pre-game huddle, asking the Lord to let the most deserving team, the most All-American Christian bunch, namely us, win the game. I think you realized that God would have only a passing interest in a football game in the trifling Mid-Lakes Conference, on a humid night, in lovely, subtropical Mt. Dora, Florida. Besides that, God can't keep up with all the games. He just watches bits and pieces of Notre Dame on a Saturday afternoon. You see, God is a busy man and he's got lots to do, especially on All Saints Day. Important things. Like manufacturing thunderbolts to throw down at folks who make Him mad with their seven deadly sins, and their saying nasty words like "God damn." That's what gets to God, not football.

But I can imagine some of those big Irish and Italian boys fingering their rosaries during Coach Bryan's pep talk, boys who'd had cod for their pre-game meal, because the Pope didn't want them eating meat on Friday. They may have even invoked the power of the true, the Roman Catholic Lord to help them kick the crap out of these redneck Protestants in this chickenshit little town, so far from the big city lights of Orlando.

Actually, Orlando was a pretty podunk town in those days too. As for the cod, well, here's a confession: I had fish for my pre-game meal. On Fridays my Catholic mommy always fried freshwater bass in corn meal. Or shell crackers, speckled perch, whatever catch Daddy brought home. I played my Friday night football with fish, the symbol of Christ, digesting in my insides. But I didn't cross myself, the way I saw some of the B.M.

players doing as they lined up on defense to start the second quarter. In 1957 I was mad at God.

Our cheerleaders, Janice Coffield, Mary Lou Davidson, Patsy Grantham, Janie Huett, Shorty Johnson, Judy Sadler, Janet Scott, Patsy Spear (your daughter) were finishing up their long litany of names: "Fred Thibault, he's our man. If he can't do it, MOON can! Billy Moon, he's our man. If he can't do it, NOBODY CAN!" With that the second quarter was ready to begin.

We had the ball. We started running it, and things started happening. It was in the second quarter, in fact, that it must have begun dawning on Coach John Bryan that the words in the private speech that ran in his mind were wrong. That maybe the words he had said *pro forma*, aloud, about our line speed, about our running backs, about how we'd forget the pain once we hit the field, that maybe those were the true words after all. Could be the key thing about that Eustis game was not the forty-four points B.M. had scored. It was the twenty-one points they had allowed. Bobby Green of Eustis was a powerful runner, but we, the Mt. Dora Golden Hurricanes, had faster backs. And most important of all: those big B.M. Hornet defensive linemen were slow. They could be beat to the snap and blocked, and in the second quarter, we (Donny Dake at blocking back, me at wingback, Billy Vanzant, John Lavin, Williams and Potter and Flavell and the others on the line) were blocking them.

Which gave us (Stoothoff, Gardner, and me) room to run. One simple fact that people who know nothing about football often neglect: when the linemen don't make any space for the backs, those backs don't go far. Take a look at my yardage against Eustis a week later. True, I scored the winning touchdown, but my aggregate rushing gains that night amounted to twenty-nine yards. Gardner had 39, Stoothoff 50. Now, compare that to our total rushing yardage on Nov. 1, 1957. The difference tells you that on the night we played Bishop Moore we were knocking people down!

So, in a word, surprise, surprise. They were a great offensive team, but their weakness was defense. They kept on running over us, but when we got the ball we started running over them, reeling off long gainers. Neither team did much passing all night. In the second period the one pass we threw, Stoothoff to Thibault, was intercepted by John Ellis in the end zone. He ran it out to the twenty. But then, on the next play, Lew Earle Williams, Jr., Number 50, broke through and tackled Musante behind the line of scrimmage. He fumbled, we recovered, and I scored on the double reverse, a ten yard run. We missed the extra point, and the game was tied, 6-6.

They got the ball and started coming at us. Ellis, Jim Ellis, Musante. Ellis, Musante, Ellis. John Ellis, John Ellis, John Ellis. Pushing on, making gains. Now the Mt. Dora fans had the spirit, our cheerleaders were revving them up. They got the loud "Push 'em back" cheer going steadily: "Push 'em back, push 'em back, WAAAAAAY BACK! Push 'em back, push 'em back, WAAAAAAY BACK!" But whenever The Hornets had the ball it was *them* pushing *us* way back!

Somehow we always managed to hold. Their long drives would, eventually, bog down. We'd go onto offense, and then it was our turn to ramble. See-saw, Margery daw, up and down the field. I was carrying the ball a lot, and the right leg felt great. It felt fast. Could it be, I thought? Even after Herschel Stone? The leg was laughing as I ran! Did my mother have her rosary in the stands? My beautiful, sad, brown-eyed Irish Catholic mother. Maybe it was her mojo medicine seeping into my bad leg that night!

My sisters and I were baptized in the Roman Catholic church. But my mother lived her whole life in the shadow of one irremediable tragedy: her children weren't raised in the Church. To know what this meant to her, you have to understand the precepts that had been pounded into her head from birth. Eating meat on Friday is a blasphemy. If you don't go to mass on

Sunday, you'll end up in Purgatory, at best. Commit the sin of contraception and you're finished for all eternity. This is contraception, mind you, not abortion. And, finally, all good children belong to the Pope—if they're not catechized, well, the catechizers tell God, who sends those kids to burn in Hell, along with the mother who didn't send them to catechism.

Before my parents were married in New Jersey, Daddy had to make an appearance before the local priest and bishop. He, a Southern Protestant heretic, had to swear, by all that was sacred to him, that any children born into this marriage would be raised under the mantle of Roman Catholicism. Why did he later renege on this promise, bringing down upon Mommy a grief beyond all measure? Because he hated the Catholic church, and he believed truly in his heart that the genuine Christian religion was the one where the Lord's Prayer had an ending: "For Thine is the Kingdom, and the Power, and the Glory, forever and ever n'ever, never, never, etc."

That dispute over where to stop the Lord's Prayer reminds me of the Russian Old Believers in the Seventeenth Century, who refused to make the sign of the cross with three fingers instead of two. There was a church reform and The New Ways said you had to do it with three, but the Old Believers would lock themselves in their wooden churches, set them aflame, and die, singing the praises of the True God, while faithfully gesticulating with those sacred two fingers. I'm sure that somewhere in the world there's a sectarian group that believes you bare your ass and show it to the skies every morning at sunrise. And if some folks don't want to do that, well the Ass Bearers sect believes those folks deserve to have their butts kicked.

When we moved to Florida, Mommy left her Irish Catholic relatives behind in New Jersey. There was nobody to enforce the promise Daddy had made. On the other hand, he had plenty of South Carolina kinfolks to support his position on religion. In addition to his brother Cecil, who was the first to move to Mt. Dora, there was his sister, my Aunt Cille, and later on his parents also immigrated from Seneca, settling into their "mobile home" (they called it a trailer back then) at Riley's Trailer Park.

I guess Riley's is still out there, just on the other side of what was once the Dixie Drive-In. In those days the Simpson family ran it: Grady Simpson, Austin's brother, a good-natured joker type. His wife Thelma. Their children, L.G., Martha and Wade. Really fine folks. After college Wade became a Navy pilot, and one fine day, somewhere in the Pacific Ocean, he climbed in his jet, put up a thumb in the air, roared off his carrier on a training flight, and flew away into sheer nullity. They couldn't find a trace of him or the plane, and Thelma and Grady never did get over that. Martha later married George Johnson, a jovial man with a quick laugh, who worked with my father at Peninsular Life. Are you still around, George? Still got that orange grove on the road to Sorrento?

The thing that happened with Wade, it's not as infrequent as you might think. Just in Mt. Dora I know of two more examples. Jimmy Pavilliard was in the C.I.A., so they say, and he just disappeared. Is he back yet? Same thing happened to John Keller, who used to work as an aide when he was a senior at MDHS, teaching mechanical drawing to us eighth graders. Are you trapped in some twilight zone dimension now, kindhearted benign John Keller? Or do these disappearance stories amount to myths? Even more interesting is the tale still told about the evaporation of The Walking Jesus. They say one day he just traipsed down a clay road lined with chinaberry trees, muttering the Twenty-third Psalm in a soft voice, getting smaller and smaller, a tiny white and chartreuse spot that faded, eventually, like a wisp of mist, into eternity. But nobody knows when this was or where he went.

My friend Donald ("Butch," "Jack," "Dutch") Alexander lived in one of those rented cottages out at Riley's, while my grandparents, whom we kids called Bowie Mom and Colonel Bob, occupied their tiny trailer. I'm sure it would be against federal law today for anybody to live in space that small, but they seemed to manage. As for the Catholic issue, Mommy always said Bowie Mom was to blame—she was the one who harped at Daddy until he finally reneged on his promise. Who knows? His mother always had a lot of influence on him.

Anyway, after he decided he wasn't letting his kids be Catholics, the perpetual battle began. The predominant image I have of my mother depicts her sitting by a window, at 820 E. Seventh Ave., looking sadly out that window. I know she could sometimes laugh. She had a loud cackling laugh that my Daddy made fun of. But the way I best remember her is in that scene beside the window. Sad brown eyes. If she wasn't sad she was angry. Because the dominant emotion in that marriage was anger. He was mad at her and she was mad at him.

He sold insurance three days a week and went fishing Thursday through Saturday. To get away from her, though he never admitted that. She didn't want him doing nothing but fishing. She wanted some kind of social life, but he didn't need one. They lived together apart, the way a lot of marriages live. If they ever experienced conjugal harmony it was before my time. They sniped at one another over trifles. He brought home his fish, the freshwater catch that we ate every Friday. He told her to clean them, and she told him he could clean them himself. He did. But he was mad. She was mad.

On Sundays she went to church in Eustis, by herself. There was no Catholic church in Mt. Dora back then; there weren't many Catholics even in Eustis. My classmates, Louis Bedell and John Lavin, were the only two I knew at MDHS. Lake County, Florida, was basically Southern Baptist territory. Catholics were aliens, most of them Yankees, always suspect. So were Jews. But there wasn't much prejudice against Jews in Lake County because most of the locals had never seen a Jew. I hadn't. Our bigotry was reserved for blacks, with some left over for Catholics.

So she went over there to that church in Eustis, taking me or June with her once in a while, when she could wrench us away. I still remember how impressed I was by the incense, the statues of Virgin and Child, the candles, the officiants all in black, the muttering in a foreign language, the getting up and down off your knees. I never knew exactly what was going on, so I watched my mother. She worked from bead to bead on her rosary. The favorite repetitive lines were, "Holy Mary, Mother of God, pray for us sinners now, and at the hour of our death."

When I was a little kid I watched and listened a lot, and I did a lot of wondering. I thought, So what about *after* our death? Mary will be interceding with God at the hour of our death, but who's going to pray for us when we're gone? Even now it seems to me that we might still need some prayers, after we pass over to the Other Side. Or is everything "hunky-dory" (one of Mommy's favorite expressions) Over There? Maybe we just rest a lot, sit on clouds playing harps. I'll tell you, though, one thing I'm looking forward to about death: I'll sleep a lot better at night.

But then, finally, Daddy put his foot down. His kids weren't going to any God damn Catholic church. Not once a week, not once a month, not ever anymore. After that, she'd show up for the Sunday service, and the Catholics would start harassing her. The meddling dolt of a priest couldn't let her, the best, most devoted Catholic he had, worship in peace. He'd grab her after mass and demand to know why her children weren't coming to church and catechism. "It's your duty as a Catholic to bring those children up Catholic," he would tell her, with the implication that anyone who didn't would roast in Gehenna.

If there is a Hell, which I doubt, my vindictive side hopes he's there now, in his black robe, roasting away. Together with all the nuns who helped him torment my mother. She would come home devastated, then go on trying to live her intolerable life. What a shame she believed that business about Reward or Punishment, which some devious somebody invented long before the Year One, as a way of trying to make folks behave.

Looking back on it all, I would have happily become Catholic to save my mother from the agony she went through. Even an altar boy. The catechizers never would have got my mind anyway, even if they had me from age two. Because I'm uncoachable. What the strife in our family did was make an angry person of me. Wouldn't you be angry, Dan Spear, if you saw that happen to your mother? Wouldn't you be angry if you grew up with anger in the air all around you? Maybe you did. After all, your temperament was always choleric. I understand angry people, because most of my life I've been one. But you never knew that. Bobby was a nice, shy boy. Bobby Bowie was very very quiet.

For all that, as I said before, I'm grateful to the Pope for instigating the conception of my sisters, Jacquelyn Teresa Bowie and Mary Margaret Bowie. After they came along, of course, a new battle began. My mother knew the first two children were lost creatures, but she was determined to save the last two. So on and on they went, the Great Protestant-Catholic Wars. I didn't want to take sides, so I opted to do without organized religion altogether.

Mad at my parents for perpetuating the battle. Mad at the Catholic priests, fingering their St. Christopher amulets. St. Christopher, by the way, was later declared bogus, and they said that God had also changed His mind about eating meat on Fridays—now it was okay. Can you imagine my mother's reaction to these New Truths? Mad at the Protestant pastors, mouthing banalities in their Holy Joe voices. Mad at my mother for believing the Catholic propaganda, mad at my daddy for soaking up the Holy Joe proclamations. Mad at my mother for sniping at my father, mad at my beloved father for mocking my beloved mother.

One day she mentioned how she had always hated her real name, Myrtle. People called her, affectionately, 'Myrt,' and that was okay. But one day Daddy said, "Well, okay, if you don't like 'Myrtle' I think I'll just start calling you 'Merle.' And he did, for years. With sarcasm. Anger, rancor, rage. But I didn't know true rage until after Oct. 22, 1956.

Why, how, could they live together for forty years? Daddy told me before he died, with tears in his eyes, he said, "Once she said to me, 'You know, I'd leave you today if I could, but I don't have anywhere to go. If I did I'd leave you today.' That's what she said to me," said my daddy, with tears in his eyes. He was seventy-five years old when he told me that, and she had been dead for twelve years.

In April of 1956 I saw him with tears in his eyes for the first time in my life. He came out of the master bedroom, in the pink house on Seventh Avenue, and he was crying. I had always thought my father was the toughest man on earth. My great dream as a boy was to be strong like him. He used to box in high school and he could throw a mean punch.

I remember how he beat up Uncle Russell occasionally, when Russ got drunk and started strong-arming his wife, my Aunt Cille. Of course Cille, Daddy's older sister, was drunk too; she was an alcoholic by her early twenties. Russ and Cille lived in a big two-storied rotting wooden house over on Fifth Ave. Right up the street from Sellers Lovelady, but on the other side. Cille would phone us crying in the night, saying Russ was hitting her, and Daddy would go over there and make mincemeat out of that poor, drunk, bald-headed man. Russell was a nice person when he wasn't drinking. So was Aunt Cille. She had a kind heart.

As a little boy I spent a lot of time with my father, riding around with him on his chicken feed truck, and later on his collections. I saw how he behaved in public, and that always impressed me. He had a lot of self-confidence and a friendly way about him that folks liked. At one point in the fifties he probably knew three-fourths of the people in Eustis and Tavares, where he sold life insurance. He serviced his debit, got their claims paid quickly. They appreciated that and recommended him to their friends. I remember you once remarking in class, Dan Spear, apropos of nothing, that those Bowies must be filthy rich, because every time you turn around they've got a new car. It was true. Daddy had to drive a lot on his job, and every two years he bought Chevies (later Plymouths and Chryslers) and wrote them off his taxes.

He was cordial, but he never took any crap. Anybody who riled him was soon backing off. I witnessed this more than once. People could see that "Don't push me" in his grey eyes, when the light of good will went out and something else shone forth. But what I didn't realize about my father was this: he still had a lot left in him of the soft-hearted boy who rolled down the Grand Canyon in 1931.

"After taking a good look at the 'Big Hole' from the rim, we ventured down Bright Angel Trail but at first did not expect to go to the bottom. The scenes became more beautiful the deeper we got, so naturally we wished to see what it was like at the bottom.

The soft rocks, which had been cut into all kinds of forms imaginable and showed every color of the rainbow, glistened and gleamed in the early morning sun-light. The trail wound around with one lap about four or five feet above the other, sometimes further on a good grade. We did not walk down the trail, sliding from one to the other on the loose rocks. . .

When we reached the bottom about eight thirty o'clock we

were pretty dry, tired and hot. We satisfied our thirst at a spring
and washed our hair and bodies too in a small clear
stream on the banks of the Colorado River... This scene
from the bottom of the Canyon looking up at the billions of
tons of rocks, each one a picture by itself, is undoubtedly
the most beautiful scene that can be witnessed by any human
on the earth..."

from *"Seven Months of Boyhood Adventures"*
by Robert N. Bowie

In April, 1956, when he came out of that bedroom, where he and
Mommy had been consulting with Dr. Andrews, I was shocked. My daddy
was crying. After that my mother came out. She had a strained sober look,
but her eyes were dry. Later on she told me, with a sense of pride, that Dr.
Andrews had said to her, "I thought your husband would be the strong one,
but it looks like the strong one is you."

First they had taken Jacqi to Dr. Montgomery, but he said he couldn't
figure out why the lymph glands were swollen on both sides of her neck. My
parents later surmised that good old Robert Montgomery, one of the
kindest men in Mt. Dora, just hadn't had the heart to tell them. They called
Dr. Andrews, and he came to our house to examine my nine-year-old
blonde blue-eyed sister. What he told them in that master bedroom was
that Jacqi had acute lymphatic leukemia.

I remember the sunny day, when was it? Must have been about 1959,
when Bobby Green drove over from Eustis to that same pink house to pick
up an insurance check. I was home on vacation from the University of
Florida. After he talked to Daddy I came out to say hello. We spoke for a
few minutes, but I couldn't find the important words, if there were any. His
thirteen-year-old sister had had a freak accident at a local carnival. Imagine

a scene like this. You're eating cotton candy, you're trying to knock down wooden milk bottles with a light rubber ball to win a teddy bear, you're stopping off at a freak show or going in to peer at "the boy in the iron lung." You're just a kid. You're giggling nonstop, having a wonderful time. Then you get on a loop-de-loop ride with two other girls, and you're packed into that caged compartment, shrieking joyously, laughing at the wild centrifugal force, and then, suddenly, the car you're whirling around in comes loose from its moorings and you're sailing off into space. You've got just a few seconds of sailing through the sunlit humid blue silence. You're not screaming any more. But your mouth is still open, you're awestruck—riding out the splendor of your final moments of life. Then the ride comes to an end.

Bobby Green and I engaged in some small talk, mostly about football. I walked him out to his car, past the palm trees in our front yard, he climbed in the car and left. People never know what to say to each other, so they end up saying nothing. But I felt for him that day.

The second quarter was nearing a close. Score still 6-6. Gardner carried the ball off tackle, I made a block for him, and as I started to get up off the ground somebody ran right over my head. I went back to the huddle with blood flowing out my nose, smeared all over my face. I must have been wild-eyed, but I was smiling. Everybody looked at me and laughed. "You okay?" said Lavin. "Sure, I'm okay," and I laughed back. But that blood and the look on my face kind of worried them, so they called time out and waved Dan Spear onto the field. He came running with his smelling salts, stuck it up under my bloody nose, and asked the ritual questions: "What day is it? Where are you now? Etc." Well, I was in the mood to answer, "Today is the fourth of July, and I'm in Samarkand, at the tomb of Timur the Lame." But I knew he'd take me out of the game, so I gave him the right answers, wiped the blood off on my jersey, and went back to the huddle. Years later, by the way, in 1992, I really was in Samarkand, and I visited the mausoleum of the great Mongol warrior Tamerlane.

Stoothoff called the next play in the huddle, we broke to take up our positions, and through the haze in my head I heard the cheerleaders going into another extended chant: "We want a touchdown, we want a touchdown..." As I ran out to line up at wingback, I realized I didn't know what the play was. The chant was pounding away in my mind: "We want a touchdown, we want a touchdown, we want a touchdown." Was I carrying the ball? What a laugh, I thought. Here we are running a play, and I don't know what it is. I started chuckling out loud. They want a touchdown. Maybe I'll just accidentally score one on this play!

I got into my three point stance, listened to Neil yelling out the count, and waited to see what would happen. I didn't run, I didn't block. As it turned out I didn't have to do anything. Richard Gardner went down field, took a pass from Stoothoff, and scored a twenty-five yard touchdown. We kicked the extra point this time and took the lead, 13-6.

The lead, I say! We took the lead! Time ran out in the second quarter. We ran off the field for the halftime break, leading in the game! We ran beneath the crossbar with the orange and white crepe streamers, we ran, single file, through the gate by the scoreboard, past the white stucco house where I used to live, with the hibiscus blooming yellow out front. We clattered our cleats across Seventh Avenue, kicking hunks of pumpkin, we ran back down the alleyway, past the flame vine on the fence, into our locker room in the gym. We were winning. Nobody could believe it. B.M. couldn't. Barry Keitel couldn't. Our cheerleaders, the Mt. Dora fans couldn't. I'm sure you couldn't either, Coach Spear. Only Earle Williams could.

4

H a l f T I M E

A mix of immiscibles/ Something like love/ Alligator sicced on Larry Smith/ Sheriff Willis McCall/ Groveland rape case/ Mabel Norris Reese/ Her dog Cubby poisoned?/ The Platts come to town/ "These people are not Niggras"/ The shape of Laura Belle's nose/ Carpetbaggers and scalawags/ "Students Sign Platt Petition"/ The Walking Jesus/ "Cauley ain't no uppity son of a bitch"/ Old Lady Drives into Post Office/ Billy Pat Harding/ My neighbor, Mr. Forsythe, killed by shotgun blast/ "Lord God Almighty, it's hot"/ "Ain't that the truth"/ To the rescue: Doc Montgomery and George Hall/ Doc and George shotgunned/ Buddles Ledford—hero/ Doc Montgomery decides the only disease is the human condition itself/ Are we all miscegenated?/ Leebo McCree floods the playground/ Coffee and doughnuts in Vietnam/ Recalcitrant libidos/ Robert Jeffrey Roepke Reed/ The most aggravating gnats on earth/ David Coffield talks philosophy with Elvis/ Black asphalt, melting in the heat/ Mewling mourning doves/ Clayton Squibb/ Driblets and droplets on Daytona Beach/ Prof Roseborough picks up a branch/ St. Augustine Bishop outraged by Groveland majorettes/ But drools/ Barry Keitel feeling queasy/ Who thought we could win?/ Lew Earle Williams, Jr.

What a strange, dreary, beautiful and excruciating, lyrical little town. They once had some kind of call-in contest on an Orlando radio station, and the prize was a copy of the Mt. Dora phone book. "It's a book without much of a plot," said the wise-assed D.J., "but it sure does have a lot of characters." Take just the people I went to school with: Alma Jean Jones, Lawrence Cheatham, Larry Bill Elliot, Linda Lee Lane, Patti Jean Wilds, Alice Faye Johnson, Betty Lou Sills, Mary Lou Davidson, David Coffield (who once met Elvis), Sylvia Lister, Bobby Joe Cook, Richard Stout, Lynn Rector, Sylvia Adams (my secret love—ninth grade), Pinckney Turner, Henry Land, Shirley Wiley, Frank Laugherty (I recently heard he shot himself; I don't believe it; wild, friendly, beer-drinking, happy-go-lucky Frank? I don't believe it), Anna Pearl Haskins, Lowell Frisbee, Levy Grantham, Ducker McHaffie. The plot of the phone book goes on and on, culminating in Jan Ziegengeist, and every one of them a character. (904) 383-3087. That was our number at the pink house, but now it's probably somebody else's, and whoever that somebody is, you can count on it: he/she's a character. But who on earth isn't?

Most who attended the Mt. Dora School lived in town, but since Zellwood, Tangerine and Sorrento had no high schools, we got students from those hamlets too. The population of Mt. Dora, about five thousand back then, was a strange amalgamation. The blacks lived out in East Town, and what the insensitive called "po white trash" lived in a ghetto on the Orange County end of town—known as Pistolville. Then there was Mt. Dora proper, containing upper middle and lower middle class, and, finally, Sylvan Shores, out on Lake Gertrude, where the rich luxuriated.

My friend Larry Smith lived there too, but his modest home was on the poor folks end of Sylvan Shores. His father, "Tiny," a large bald man who worked down at Rehbaum's Hardware and read books on history in his spare time, had scraped up enough money to buy a small house over by the no-name lake, where they later built the shopping center. Not far up Old

441 from there, across from the Dixie Drive-In, was Homer Morris' shanty: a combination Texaco station and beer joint. Larry had the misfortune to grow up with his front teeth sticking out, which provoked a lot of commentary from well-wishers. He claims, and I don't believe this, that one day as he was riding his bicycle past Homer Morris' establishment, some of the ole boys drinking beer out back shouted unkind remarks. Then they commenced to sic a three foot alligator on him. "Yeah, Smith" (squeaky little kid voice, with lisp). No, I don't believe the gator part.

The white people in Mt. Dora could be divided, roughly, into two groups: Rebels or Yankees. The Rebels, who had drifted in from various Southern states, were represented in all the residential subsections above, except East Town. The Yankees were primarily elderly retirees, living in Mt. Dora proper or Sylvan Shores. Many of them were "sunbirds," migratory avians who flew back North every spring.

Of course, the Rebels loathed the Yankees, and the Yankees held the Rebels in contempt. Besides that, the Rebels who lived in Pistolville hated the blacks in East Town on principle, and they also hated the rich folks in Sylvan Shores and most of the middle class in Mt. Dora proper, for occupying a superior social and economic position. The middle class hated the blacks on principle too, looked down on the "white trash" of Pistolville, and despised the Sylvan Shores elite for being rich and snooty. The Sylvan Shores folks hated the blacks on principle, sneered at the nocount hicks out in Pistolville, and looked down on the middle class in Mt. Dora proper. God knows how the blacks in East Town felt about all this. Oh yeah, one more thing: in some strange twisted way everybody loved everybody.

Not too long ago a black woman who grew up in backwoods Mississippi was over at my Ohio home, cooking me a mess of collards, ribs with hot sauce, black-eyed peas, real corn bread and over-salted okra. This is what's called "soul food," and I love it because it's what I grew up eating.

While she was cooking I was explaining what it was like between the races in my home town.

"Despite all the ill will," I lectured (I'm a professor), "despite the rancor and the inveterate racial antagonism, there was a special feeling between black folks and white folks in the rural South."

"Something like love?" she asked, and she smiled.

"Yeah, that's it. Something like love."

Of course, the author Raymond Carver was right when he said you got to be nuts to talk like you know what you're talking about when you talk about love. The way I look at it, though, is that nearly all the love on earth is a lot more like something like love than it is like love. Or something like that.

Lake County, Florida, in the forties and fifties, was notorious for its racial tensions. The prevalent attitude of white Southerners back then was "Give a nigger an inch and he'll take a mile." That attitude prevailed in most of Mt. Dora (everywhere but East Town): in the schools, the churches, the O.K. Barber Shop and the Rexall Drug Store down town. Except among the Yankees, who adopted one of two policies: (1) they tried to outdo the Southerners by taking outrageous racist positions, or (2) they went around spreading "Yankee propaganda" about equal rights.

While I was growing up the subsections of our town lived in a state of uneasy truce. The Ku Klux Klan would ride through Mt. Dora in long cavalcades of cars, wearing their white robes, their hoods with the eye holes. I can remember watching one of these processions pass slowly through the darkness, as I sat on the front porch of our stucco house, across from the football field. People stayed inside until all the cars went by. You couldn't make out much of the passengers except the whiteness of the conical hoods.

They ended their parade out at East Town, where they would put up a huge cross wrapped in rags, on the corner of Grandview and Grant Streets. They would douse the rags with kerosene and set the cross aflame. This was called "keeping the niggers in line." The Ku Kluxers also made it their business to enforce moral standards among the poor white population. For example, they once took my aunt's second husband for a long long ride down a country road. He was too intoxicated to remember exactly what happened. The next morning he was found beaten, naked, lying out in a clay pit. All because he was a drunk.

Does this sound like ancient history to you, Dan Spear? Nowadays the schools are integrated, and black folks can walk the streets. They don't have any more Ku Kluxer cavalcades or cross burnings. Lake County Sheriff Willis McCall, who developed a national reputation, is dead by now, and for all I know Lake County has a black sheriff. I'm aware that they've had black football coaches at Mount Dora High, and I'd imagine many of the players now are big bulked-up boys from East Town. What chance would our little team of 1957 have against them? We didn't have a weight room. Why, I, the great Bobby Booby, weighing 150, probably couldn't even make today's teams. I said that recently in a phone conversation with an old friend, Berl Oiuyam, who lives these days in a town where the local high school produces world-class black football players in droves. Berl said, "No, Bobby. You'd make it. You know why? Because even back in the fifties you didn't just have speed; you had *black* speed."

What do you remember about when you were a young man in Lake County, Coach Spear? Do you remember, for example, the Groveland rape case of 1949? It involved four black men and one white woman. The youngest perpetrator, Charles Greenlee, sixteen years old at the time of the rape, was sentenced to life in prison. Another, Ernest Thomas, was killed trying to escape from jail in North Florida. Samuel Sheppard and Walter Lee Irvin were the other two. Irvin was, eventually, sentenced to die in the electric chair, in Sept., 1949. You can read about all this in old issues of *The Topic*.

Do you recall the day Irvin and Sheppard were shot? Willis McCall's Lake County Sheriff's Department was transporting the prisoners back from Raiford, where they had been taken for a pre-trial hearing. Emotions among the white populace were volatile, so Willis and his deputies were driving in the middle of the night, trying to be inconspicuous. Way out in the countryside, somewhere around Bushnell, they took a urination break in an orange grove. From that point the story told by the surviving Negro diverges from that of the deputies. Willis' men said the prisoners tried to escape and they were forced to fire upon them. Samuel Sheppard was shot dead, but, much to the chagrin of white Lake County, Walter Lee Irvin recovered from his wounds. He testified later that they had taken off his handcuffs and leg shackles and then said, "All right, nigger. Now run."

This case was notorious enough to make *Time* magazine, and after that the name of Willis McCall reverberated all over the U.S.A. His biggest enemy in the whole of Lake County was Mabel Norris Reese, editor of our weekly newspaper, *The Mt. Dora Topic*. She was a Yankee interloper in a small Southern town, working for black civil rights before the term "civil rights" was even used. In sum, she was what at least three-quarters of white folks in Lake County abominated: a "nigger lover." Her daughter, Punky Reese, went to our high school. What a difficult thing that must have been for her; you had to be tough to be the daughter of Mabel Norris Reese in Mt. Dora, Florida.

Do you remember, Coach Spear, when they burned a cross in front of Mabel Norris Reese's house in 1954? When they poisoned her dog, "Cubby," with strychnine? Later on it was, apparently, established that the dog died of natural causes, and Sheriff McCall was quoted in *The Topic* as follows: "I am glad to learn that the dog was not poisoned, as I despise dog poisoners almost as much as I do a communist" (Dec. 30, 1954). These events developed, of course, consequent upon the infamous Platt case. You certainly remember the day Willis McCall evicted the Platt children from our school. That set off a controversy that went on for years.

The Platts were a dirt-poor family that had migrated into Lake County from Holly Hill, South Carolina. Allan Platt, the father, found a job as an orange picker, and they enrolled their five children (Raymond, Laura Belle, Esther, Linda, and Violet) in the Mt. Dora School. Shortly after that the trouble began. The Platts had dark skin and claimed to be of "Croatan Indian" descent, but people in Mt. Dora soon decided there was a lot more of Africa in these folks than there was American Indian.

Parents showed up at the office of Principal D.D. Roseborough, complaining that the school had been surreptitiously integrated. Prof called in the Platt parents, who affirmed their Indian and Irish background. They showed him their marriage license, which read, "Allan Platt, white American" and "Laura Dangerfield, white American." Mr. Platt claimed that his father had served as a Confederate soldier in the Civil War. The white denizens of Lake County said, "Yeah, tell me another one," and the parents of schoolchildren started getting obstreperous.

Prof put in a phone call to the South Carolina school that the children had previously attended. "No sir, it's no problem," they told him. "The Platts always went to white schools here." Later came a letter from one G.E. Brant, Superintendent of Schools for the district of Orangeburg Co., S.C., attesting that the Platt children had gone to the Crane Pond School in Holly Hill. "These people," wrote Mr. Brant, "have no social dealings with Negroes and I am of the opinion that there is no Negro blood involved."

Lake County continued to rumble disgruntledly. Occasional strident voices rang out amidst the rumblings. "Ain't no way I'm going to school with no niggers. That's what I say, that's what my momma says, that's what my daddy says: you're not going to school with no niggers!" Then one fine sunny day Sheriff Willis McCall drove over from Tavares in his big white Lake County cruiser, loaded up the Platt children, and off they drove, out of our day-to-day lives. The Mt. Dora School was officially resegregated, but that was when Mabel Norris Reese really got into the act. She began an extensive campaign in *The Topic*, defending the Platts and fighting for their reinstatement. Willis McCall, with the backing of most Caucasians in Lake County, stood firm in his resolve. He said he did not like the shape of Laura Belle Platt's nose. Mabel Norris Reese published pictures of Laura Belle with the rest of the family, along with a human interest article about what this turmoil meant, in personal terms, to a little girl.

Soon the children were admitted to the Christian Home and Bible School, a private denominational school, but then the Christian Home parents got up in arms, and the principal buckled under the pressure. On and on raged the controversy. Sheriff McCall was quoted as saying that the Platt children were mulattoes, and that "carpetbaggers and scalawags" were responsible for Lake County's bad publicity.

Amidst all the fanfaronade, *The Topic* continued publishing the wonderful articles of East Town reporter T.M. Thomas, dedicated to the church and social life of his community: "Our souls shouted for joy while Brother Michaels preached and everybody did enjoy the message fine. The collection was very good, too" (Jan. 26, 1956). The style makes him sound naive, but maybe T.M. Thomas had a better perspective than the feuders and fighters on what was really important in life.

Were your souls shouting for joy on Jan. 26, 1956, Gay Heist, Spider Bennett, Bud Ligon, Wheeler MacDonald, Vernon Swartzel, Arlene Hejna, Bill Baker, Alan Burhenne, Patsy Penn (from Tavares), Barbara Brown, Dickie Jean Reich, Ima Burns, Michael Ray, Weymon Moore, Mary Anne Brotherson, Joe Graf, Cora Ann Sadler, Donald Alexander, Latrelle Funderburk? Well, you (my fellow students) probably don't remember what your souls were doing on that particular day, but you certainly remember the Platt case. The family eventually got the kids back into the Christian Home and Bible School. There were a few more incidents. For example, someone fired shotgun rounds into the Platt residence near Sorrento in May of 1956, and Waiford Bedford or somebody (I'm not accusing you, Waiford; this is just an old rumor) got ahold of a hand grenade at the National Guard Armory, and a group of beer-drinking night riders tossed that thing out somewhere, then roared off whooping with glee.

Early in the fray a small minority of Mt. Dora students had aligned themselves with Mr. Conway, practically the only staunch ally of Mabel Norris Reese among the teachers at our school. He was eventually hounded out of town. Another brouhaha developed when *The Topic* printed a petition supporting the Platt children, signed by large numbers of Mt. Dora high school students. Now, I recently reread those signatures, and it's a fact that some of the signers were among the most vociferous anti-Plattists I knew. Mabel Norris Reese, apparently, had pulled another fast one. Of course, there were immediate retractions. Students claimed they did not know what they were signing. My sister June was among the purported signatories. As for me, I didn't sign, and the first I heard of that petition was when it was run in *The Topic*. All my life I've been standing apart, looking at how people act, listening to what they say. Nobody bothers to tell me any gossip, nobody confides. I'm a lifelong non-signer of petitions too. But then, nobody ever asks me to sign.

Anyway, the Platt Case went nationwide, and once again notorious Lake County, Florida, was in the news. Lucky for us, there was not much t.v. back then, no CBS muckrakers, like Mike Wallace. If Wallace had been skulking around in the shadows of the citrus trees, he would have heard certain locals voice the same frank opinion over and over: "One thing you can say for Willis: Willis keeps the niggers in line. Whatever else he may be up to, that's not my bidness—cause Willis keeps the niggers in line."

A lot of us who lived through those days are still alive. I wonder how
T.M. Thomas is doing? What about Cauley Lott? Everybody liked Cauley,
principal of the East Town school. "Cauley's a good nigger," the white folks
used to say. "Cauley ain't no uppity son of a bitch; Cauley knows his place."
People don't talk that way any more, at least not so openly, and Mt. Dora's
a better place for having "got shed" of the controversies. Of course, when
you grow up in that environment, you never overcome it totally. Am I
accusing my fellow students of being, and remaining, racists? No. I have no
right to accuse anybody. But what I'm saying is that even when that stuff is
in the air all around you, you can still find ways to treat people with kindness. Earle Williams, for example, ended up a high school teacher, working
in predominantly black schools. He likes his job and he knows how to be
human. There's not a mean bone in the body of Lew Earle Williams, Jr.
Ask his students.

What ever happened to the Platts? Are they still living out there in
Sorrento? Or did the whole family pile, one fine sunny day, into their truck
and drive out of Lake County, and out of history? Let's imagine, say, the
Joad family, from Steinbeck's novel *The Grapes of Wrath*, on the day of their
departure. Chugging along in a rusted-out Ford with a hole in the muffler,
tail pipe dragging along the cracks in the asphalt, belching black smoke.
Wash tubs and wicker chairs with broken legs lashed to the roof, ladders,
kids hanging out the windows. Taking one last tour through the city center,
Mt. Dora, circling the roundabout down at Evans Park, then up the hill past
the lawn bowling club, over the railroad tracks and right through the heart
of the business district, Donnelly Street: Larson's Texaco station, Moon's
and Rehbaum's hardware stores, the O.K. Barber Shop, the Rexall Drug
Store and Horsley's Jewelry. Stopping at the red light with George White's
bank to their left and Sally's Dress Shop cater-cornered, the Roy
Christopher law office on the right.

While the Joads wait for the traffic light to change, Doc Walker, chiropractor, crosses the street, heading uphill to his office, talking to Roy Landis, Jr., shoemaker, who limps alongside him. Obie Alexander peers from behind the show window of Sally's, just as Tom Joad leans out the driver-side window and spits. Then, making a left turn onto Fifth Avenue, they rattle and smoke past the Princess Theatre and Reggie Parker's market, shying away from the flashing police lights down by the old post office (that was the day a senile Yankee lady forgot where the brake pedal was and drove her Cadillac right up the steps into the small lobby, and Billy Pat standing there sorting mail, looking up at her with his mouth open, and her looking back at him from behind the wheel of that car, maybe wondering if she should buy stamps, being she was there in the post office anyway). Next, past Millard Reid's Standard station on the right, and just then the '54 Ford backfires loudly and blows out a mass of smoke, as if passing gas one last time in the face of Mt. Dora, Florida, and then the car surges forward picking up speed and the Joads are out free and clear, swinging onto the beautiful drive overlooking Lake Dora, and who should they see just then but The Walking Jesus (Rose-of-Sharon, the prettiest daughter, leans out the back window, smiles and waves at him), loping, as usual, barefooted, in his white mane, down the highway beneath The Castle, silk chartreuse shirt and white satin pants, muttering prophecies. Of course, he doesn't wave back. The Walking Jesus never waves.

Maybe the Platts went back to Holly Hill, where folks didn't worry about how much of their blood was African and how much was Irish, or "Croatan" Indian. I don't know. I never heard the final chapter in the story known as *The Notorious Saga of the Platts*. Wherever they are, I hope life turned out well for them.

As for our personal family drama, the Platt case went just like the religious issue, with combatants taking diametrically opposed positions. You see, my mother was a "nigger lover" herself. She was from New Jersey, and believed in equal rights. My father was, basically, a fair-minded individual too. But Daddy was from a red-clay-digging sharecropper family in South Carolina, so there couldn't be much doubt about his views on the Platts. Outside Yankee agitators, promoting the cause of miscegenation, had paid them to move into Mt. Dora and stir up trouble. There was Daddy's position, and that of many others in Lake County.

What highlights do you remember, Dan Spear, from the annals of Mt. Dora, Florida, forty-fifty years ago? Do you remember, for example, the big shooting out in East Town? That must have been about 1958. It started with a very calm phone call one hot afternoon, to the Mt. Dora police station. The retired folks who lived across the street from our pink house were the Forsythes. He was a tall man with grey hair and a perpetual smile, a Yankee immigrant who earned a little money to supplement his pension by working as auxiliary policeman. He was on duty when that phone call came in.

There wasn't much crime in Mt. Dora, and the police force was small. I'm not sure the auxiliary policemen even carried weapons. That particular phone call sounded like small-potatoes police work, a domestic dispute, so they sent Mr. Forsythe. He drove out to East Town, down the main drag, the only road that was paved. He turned off onto a side, dirt road. The wheels of the police car spun in the soft, off-white dirt, but, unfortunately, the car did not get stuck. Corpulent black ladies sat around on the front porches of the unpainted shacks, wearing skirts and white brassieres, sweating, shooing away the voracious gnats with the kind of hand-operated fans that folks used in church. One of them would sigh and say something like, "Lord God Almighty, it's hot." And then another would sigh back and say, "Ain't that the truth." But when they saw the police car they just shut up and watched.

Very little breeze to stir the thick air. Insects humming in the silent humidity; mocking birds agitating, but softly. Grasshoppers over in the tall weeds, long as your two thumbs put together, twitching their feelers and chomping on sandspur stems. Gruesome monstrous hoppers, slime green. Dragonflies flickering through the sunlight and dappled shade.

The neighbor who phoned in the complaint pointed out the shack, where the trouble supposedly was. "They been carrying on two hours straight," she said. "Her screeching, him kicking her around. Be like to drive me crazy." But there was no evidence of any domestic problem. That shack, too, was quiet, innocuous. Its front porch was empty, except for a decrepit white wicker rocking chair, lame of one leg, and a geranium plant dying of thirst. Then Mr. Forsythe walked calmly up onto the front porch of that shack and took a shotgun blast in the chest. The force of the blast knocked him back off the porch, and he fell in the dirt and pine needles of the front yard.

After that sudden boom the humid silence set back in. The gigantic slimy grasshoppers in the weeds all around took a look to the right, to the left, then went back to chewing their cuds. The ladies in brassieres didn't say a word. They stopped fanning themselves, opened their mouths, and just sat. Mr. Forsythe, my next-door neighbor, lay there with mosquitoes buzzing the white fluff on his ears and big red ants crawling over the grey stripes of his police pants. He was dead.

Then came another calm phone call to the police station. Still no word about a crazed man with a gun. The voice on the phone said there'd been a little trouble, and maybe they better send a doctor. So they called good old Doc Montgomery. They weren't sure what was going on, so, just to be on the safe side, George Hall, fireman and assistant police chief, rode out to East Town with Doc.

They drove up to that shack, saw Mr. Forsythe in the dirt near the front porch, and ran to help him. But before they even got close they both were shot. After that George Hall and Doc Montgomery lay huddled together on the ground, wounded, afraid to move. On the dirty white sand in the middle of the yard, next to a stunted palmetto.

The third phone call was not so calm. Word soon spread through Mt. Dora that a "crazy Niggra" had shot three men and was still holed up in a shack. Police from all over Lake County converged on East Town and cordoned off the area. Volunteers appeared with deer rifles, shotguns and pistols. Doc Montgomery and George were still lying there, bleeding into the white sand. Nobody dared get close enough to help them. Deputies from Willis McCall's Lake County Sheriff's Department in Tavares crouched with drawn pistols by the tires of their cruisers. Others took cover behind the huge live oak trees all around the shack. They could almost make out their adversary in the murk, periodically cracking the screen door and pointing out the barrel of the shotgun.

There was a long stalemate. They got on police megaphones and called for him to throw down his weapon and come out. No response. A few volunteers, who had watched too many Johnny Mack Brown Western movies, were shouting, "Cover me!" then dashing from one tree to another. The deputies got out their field glasses. First they directed them at the shack. "Look to me like that fucker is just inside the door, but he's so god damn black I can't tell for sure." Then they peered through the binoculars at George and Doc. Both still breathing. But after an hour of waiting people started getting worried they would bleed to death. By the look of Mr. Forsythe, the twisted way he lay on the ground, they realized he was beyond worrying about.

So they stood there, and crouched there, behind police cars, fire trucks and huge oak trees, holding their pistols and shotguns, wondering what to do next. Then Tom ("Buddles") Ledford settled the issue. What big, brawny Buddles was even doing there only God knows. I don't recall him being part of the police force or even the auxiliary police. He was a veteran who had seen action in the Korean War. My guess is that he was one of the volunteers who heard about the shooting, hauled out his weapon, and headed for East Town to do what he could.

Anyway, Buddles was standing behind the cover of a live oak tree, full of mistletoe and Spanish moss. That tree was about as close as anybody could get to the house. Why wasn't some regular policeman behind it, why not one of Willis McCall's deputies? I can't remember. All I know is that, for some reason, Buddles Ledford was behind that tree, and Buddles suddenly took it upon himself to step out with his shotgun into the open, and when the "crazy Niggra" saw him standing there, he cracked the screen door of his shack to point out the barrel of *his* gun, and when he did that Buddles shot him in the head and killed him.

At least that's the way I remember it. You, Dan Spear, and some of you out in the audience tonight might have different recollections of the incident. What about it, George Keen, Carol Rector, Charles Wareing? Was that the way it was, Clark Vanderoef, Junior Bell, Helen Davidson, Dedrick Dollar (of Eustis), Lavonia Bowie (my cousin), Charles Kinsey?

Bobby Lofroos, Josephine Brown, George Johnson, Hazel Ann Avery, Herman Kicklighter (of Umatilla), Lee Dettra, Cecil Barks, Lennie Vincenti, Jan Ziegengeist, Patsy Grantham, Al Rehbaum III, Sonny Hughes, Johnny Groves, Charles Norton, Nancy Werder, Joe Swift, Walter TeStrake, Ruby Aldrich? What about you, Mr. Hardy and Mr. Landis, down at the O.K. Barbershop on Donnelly St.? You must have heard the details inside out, back to front and front to back. That's what a barber shop is for.

Mr. Hardy and Mr. Landis can't tell us anything; they've been dead for twenty-thirty years now. I wonder if Buddles is still alive. What about my old family practitioner, the team physician for MDHS football, Doc Montgomery? A fine man, a human being. He recovered from his wounds and went back to practicing medicine. But then I heard that one day, years later, he decided there was nothing that the medical profession could do in light of the human condition. Retired from his practice and moved to North Carolina. That's what I heard, anyway. Are you out there somewhere, climbing smokey mountains, good-hearted, amiable Robert Montgomery?

People come and people go. I wonder if Mt. Dora is still the town of transients that it was then: Yankees wintering here, summering there, rednecks drifting in, drifting out. Everybody from somewhere else, nothing permanent, everything as frangible and wispy as the Spanish moss in the humid air. Life is from elsewhere, and on its way elsewhere, all the time.

Most of my friends at school were migrants. Some of them, such as Bobby Joe Cook, were always on the go. His family would live in Mt. Dora for a while, then move away, then move back. It was a joy for me as a little kid, every time the fat, smirking, friendly close-cropped head of Bobby Joe Cook would reappear at the Mt. Dora School.

Earle Williams was from the land of Lake Okeechobee, Belle Glade, Florida, where his father was a harvester. L.E. Williams, Sr. came up to Zellwood to work the corn one year and stayed for the winter harvesting on the muck farms. That's how Earle ended up spending his senior year at Mt. Dora and playing football with us. His mother's side of the family was from North Florida. Earle himself, black-haired, hook-nosed, walking hunched over and slow, grinning that awkward grin, spoke with a Southern accent that blended the pines of Palatka and the South Florida saw grass. He had an American Indian look about him. But so did a lot of others, like Ronnie Gardner and Benjy Rahls. My grandfather, from South Carolina, also claimed Indian (Cherokee) ancestry. The Coffields had those high cheekbones and gaunt faces. Although everyone was het up about miscegenation in the fifties, we ourselves were pretty damn miscegenated.

I once was back for a visit in the seventies, talking to some people down in Gilbert Park, and they said, "You mean you grew up here? You came from Mt. Dora? You're the first person I ever met who really came from here!" But they were wrong. I came from somewhere else too (Metuchen, N.J.), stayed a few formative years, then left and went somewhere else. But I never got Mt. Dora out of my soul.

C.M. Jones, III was known as 'Bub' to his family, which immigrated from Alabama (Fayette), to Zellwood, Florida, in 1947. His grandfather, known as 'Claude' (and that was his real name—all three generations were "Claude Marion Jones"), became a haberdasher. When he opened Sun State Stores, a combination gas station and clothing shop, in Zellwood, he asked his son, C.M. Jones, Jr., known, for some reason, as 'Bill,' to join him in the business. Bub Jones also worked there, pumping gas and serving a primarily black clientele from the part of Zellwood called "The Quarters." In his spare time Bub hung out around Locklin Lake, especially at the old deserted house, where he and the Gardner boys played war—using oranges as hand grenades and booming each other up side the head.

Where was Judy Sadler, "The Queen of Tangerine," originally from? I think she was born in the Orange Memorial Hospital in Orlando, where Gary Potter died eighteen years later. The Sadlers (Buck, Gail, etc.) lived out toward Zellwood, in the metropolis named after a mandarin-style orange. In my recollection she was at the Mt. Dora Public Schools almost from the start. I still have a photograph of Mrs. Bennett's second grade rhythm band, and skinny, blonde Judy Sadler is smiling on the front row, waving a tambourine around. I think that was the same year that Leebo McCree got the water fountain jammed out on the playground. Then he told Judy, "Run for your life! This whole place is fixing to flood!" Well, Judy, as they used to say, "lack to died" when she heard that. She ran. Much later she became the belle of the class, making all the boys' loins tingle, but that wasn't until the ninth or tenth grade, and by that time Gary had claimed her for his own.

The Potter family had migrated from the desolation of Brady, Texas, where Gary's body was shipped back for burial in 1958. Long, thin Neil Stoothoff, with his quick laugh and loping stride, moved over from Sanford at age fifteen, so he was from somewhere else too. Maybe Billy Moon, Mary Kay Rehbaum, and Larry Smith were the only true natives of Mt. Dora in our Class of '58.

People like me, who had the temerity to be born above the Mason-Dixon line, were not readily accepted. We were labeled "Yankees," taunted, ostracized. Ronald Aldrich, Jr., who came from Bath, N.Y., was one who took a lot of flak, especially since his father was Assistant Principal of Mt. Dora High School. My sister June, an MDHS cheerleader, overcame her Northern origins to become what they called "popular." Me, I was quiet and weird from Day One, and I didn't redeem myself with athletic prowess until late in my high school years. I had problems, in the early times, with wrestling and clay fights. In fact, every clay fight I took part in ended the same way: with little Bobby Bowie hit in the eye by a big hunk of clay and going bawling home to his mommy.

Sorry, Mr. Spear. I seem to have digressed far afield from the original story. About that one football game. Somehow everything gets connected: what I did in 1957 to what was going on in 1947 to where I was in 1987, etc. And, you know, the stuff that happened to me earlier seems to have *pre-determined* what was to come along thirty-forty years later! One reason I'm writing about Nov. 1, 1957, is that a certain spirit fully manifested itself for the first time on that day, and ever since then that spirit revisits me periodically, and rejuvenates me when it comes.

Another thing that happens—one memory of Mt. Dora gets all kinds of other memories flooding through my brain:

My sister Jacqi getting her picture taken with cowboy sidekick star,

Smiley Burnett, down at the Princess Theatre. She had two years to live, and old Smiley lasted for another twenty. My sister Peggy practicing her cheerleading from age six on. Plump little Peggy in her pedal pushers, out under the palm trees in our front yard, singing the "Hurrah for Hurricanes" song. She was the final honoree in Mabel Norris Reese's "Citizens of Tomorrow" series, featuring selected Mt. Dora children (see her smiling eight-year-old face in *The Mount Dora Topic*, Aug. 22, 1957, p. 3). Sure enough, she did become a good citizen of tomorrow, when it turned into today.

Who would have thought that after four safe years in a sorority at F.S.U., she would end up in the Vietnam War? She volunteered as a Red Cross doughnut girl, flying on choppers to the fire bases, transporting coffee and pastries for the grunts. Go out and shoot and be shot at. Bring back your point man in a body bag. Then relax with smiling, fresh-faced girls, over coffee and doughnuts. There is something quintessentially American about that.

Peggy returned from Vietnam with a new outlook on life; Vietnam tended to do that to people. She became a hippie and went around in bib overalls, and a lot of folks in Mt. Dora, like Billy Pat down at the new post office on Donnelly, didn't appreciate that. Later on, after she got a Master's in counseling, she had a job in Gainesville, rehabilitating sex offenders. Trouble was, at the center where she worked they weren't finding a lot of cures. In fact, they eventually gave up on the idea that human libidos could be repaired and sent their clients back to prison. That experience dealt one more blow to my little sister's belief in all-embracing God-given human decency. But to this very day Peggy still thinks most folks are okay. In fact, so do I.

More memories. My sister June, after an argument, spitefully ripping up my comic books. Why'd you do that to your baby brother? June later worked for the Red Cross too. In fact, all three of us have had a Red Cross connection, since I was a volunteer in Central Asia (1992) and gave seminars on fund raising to Red Cross officials in Kiev (Ukraine) and Minsk

(Belorus) a year later. June also can be found in the pages of *The Topic:* her wedding announcement appears on Aug. 15, 1957, and the picture of the beautiful bride on Aug. 22. That marriage was brief, but it produced Jeff, blonde blue-eyed R. J. R. Reed, who grew up to become an army airborne special forces ranger, sitting out with his unit in the Egyptian desert, on the way to Iran, when Jimmy Carter called off the operation to rescue the American hostages there.

Vivid memories. My parents, sitting out on a torrid day with our next door neighbors, the Frenches, in those slatted white aluminum chairs, under the Spanish moss of the live oak tree in front of the pink house, sweating, fanning away the insects, drinking ice water, or Welch's grape juice, Hawaiian punch, making endless fatuous conversation. Self-important old Gulliver French, retired engineer from Tennessee, and his officious wife. The descendants of those nasty little gnats are probably still hovering around there, near the offspring of the Spanish moss, still looking for sweaty bodies to buzz, struggling to crawl into the eyes and ears of new people sitting under that same huge oak tree (it's still there, though our palm trees froze out and died thirty years ago). I don't know who irritated me more, the gnats or the Frenches. No, that's not true; I do know: the Frenches.

What else? Mommy going to her Brownie groups (she was a scout leader) or to her women's gatherings (she was a member of the Azalea Circle of the Lakes and Hills Garden Club). Daddy going off to Reggie Parker's Market, to buy a week's worth of meat, or to his Lions Club (until he quit the Lions, so he could have more time for fishing). David Coffield going to Orlando to see Elvis. In 1956.

Why did I miss that? I, the greatest of Elvis fans, an Elvis impersonator, who could sing "Heartbreak Hotel" in the voice of the King Himself, how did I make that decision *not* to go to the concert that day? C.M. and I had planned to go, that's all I remember. But we didn't go. David Coffield did. He came to school on the following Monday and repeated over and over, to a bevy of fascinated listeners, the tale of his conversation with Elvis:

"So we're outside there, sitting in the park, waiting for them to open the doors, and we see some folks hanging around a little trailer. You know, they've got this trailer set up over on the grass, so we go over there to see what's up, and I swear to God, it's Elvis in that trailer! We can see his head in there, behind the slats of the jalousies. His greased-back hair and that d.a., and some fellows are talking to him. We walk up there, and I said, 'Hey, Elvis. How you doing?' And he looked at us and he said, 'Just fine. How y'all?' So then we hung around there a few minutes, just shooting the bull. With Elvis! Until some girls ran up and screamed 'ELVIS' real loud, and a whole horde of other girls started hustling across that field in our direction, and right quick Elvis rolled the jalousies shut. Later on we could see him, once in a while, cracking the blinds and peeking out, but he wouldn't talk any more, not after those shrieking girls came running up there, showing their butts. He must have figured they'd tear down the trailer to get to him."

Good old David Coffield. He had that same gaunt Coffield look as his sisters did—the friendly face and sunken cheeks. Janice, Joyce and David. Wasn't there a baby John too? Wonder what they're doing now? David's probably a Baptist preacher, like his father was. As for his Elvis story, he's probably still telling it today, with him and his memory working out some brand-new variants. Like maybe about how Elvis opened those jalousie slats once too often and herds of overstimulated girls ripped out every wall of that trailer, got in there and stripped Elvis down, and he's running, guitar in one hand, buck-naked across the park, hoping he can make it to his pink Cadillac before they pounce on him and have their way with him, right there on the green Bermuda grass. Well, that's my imagination getting carried away, not David's.

There's the great thing about Elvis, though: he's giving people a reason for living years after he's dead. Not just listening to his songs, but imitating his voice, telling Elvis stories, writing Elvis books, making pilgrimages to

Graceland. Or take all the women who slept with Elvis. There must be lots of them still alive in America today. They're aging a little bit now, and you can bet they're not all living the good life. But on the worst days, when it seems like there's just no reason to go on, they can smile to themselves and say: "Yeah, but anyway, I once screwed Elvis."

Although I've been living in Ohio for twenty-five years, teaching the Russian language in college, I still dream about home. I don't dream about the violence, though, or about the racism. Not about Ephraim punching out David, or the KKK burning their crosses, or even about Sheriff McCall in the George Washington's Birthday Parade, riding his palomino down the streets of Tavares (Eustis?), tipping his white cowboy hat to the adoring crowd. No. My dreams are calm and peaceful, dripping with sweat and steeped in humidity. In most of the dreams I'm still very young and still living in the white stucco house at 820 E. 7th.

The barefoot years. We never wore shoes in the summer, and that left our feet at the mercy of the hot pavement and sandspurs. In my dreams I'm running down the torrid sidewalks, dashing from one shady spot to the next, on my way to Mr. Kuechler's filling station on the corner, where Old Highway 441 makes that big right turn. I've got a nickel in my hand. I'm off to buy a big twelve-ounce bottle of Barq's Root Beer from the cooler there. Or a Dr. Pepper. The "cold drink box," bottles bathed in ice water, with a rag hanging there, to dry them off when you pull them out. Sometimes my sister June is running with me. Our feet are getting blistered, and that makes us run all the faster. In my dreams it's always unbearably hot, the kind of Florida heat that people today can't imagine. Because today they've got air conditioning. In my dreams the black asphalt is melting on the road, leaving huge cracks when it cools in the night. When I get back home from Mr. Kuechler's, my mother is sitting by the window, staring out at the heat, which rises off the asphalt in quavering sheets.

Or I'm riding my twenty-four-inch bike with Clarence Sims. Down the big hill near Lake Franklin, where the new stadium is now—the one that you built with your own hands and the sweat of your brow, Dan Spear. Or I'm playing tackle football (in 1948) with Bobby Partridge, Sonny Hughes, Robert Morehead, Billy Simpson. Or I'm sitting high up in a grapefruit tree behind the pink house, watching the Dakes' boxer dog, Rex, making his rounds of the neighborhood property. In my dreams somebody, or some dog, or lizard is in motion, walking, bike riding, running, and the sun is always bright, it's hot, hot, hot, and the mourning doves are mewling through the viscous air.

In some of my dreams I'm watching those old home movies that Uncle Johnny made, over at New Smyrna Beach, about 1949. Uncle John was the husband of my Aunt Doris, my mother's sister. He was a great photographer and a fine army officer. Dreaming and watching in the movie all the dead people still walking around: Uncle Cecil, Aunt Wren, smiling and waving, splashing through the shallow water, Aunt Cille, Uncle Elliot, building sand castles with turrets formed from muddy driblets of yellow-grey sand.

You sit in the heat, just clear of where the tide washes in, your mother, your sisters, you make a little pool for your driblets, you pick up a fistful of muddy seashore and you let it ooze through your fingers, drip, drip, dribble drip, slowly raising your fist all the while till the water-mud quits running, then grabbing another fistful, building higher and higher with your castle tower made of mud drops, construction booming great guns until you go too high and the tower collapses, but then you start over. Why not? You've got all the time in the world, you and the dead people in those movies, who are helping you build that driblet castle, so on and on you all build together, Daddy's other sister Aunt Peg, her son Walt, Nettie Kubista (from New

Jersey), her husband Ted, who once drove a taxi in New York City and took me to my first major league baseball game (Ebbets Field in Brooklyn, 1953, Cubs vs. Dodgers: Kiner, Sauer, Eddie Miksis, Frankie Baumholtz, Jackie Robinson, Duke Snider, Peewee Reese), making idle summer conversation as the sun burns your back crisp, but never mind the sunburn, you've got Noxema for the night, when you lie in the hot bed with the scorched skin soothed by white cream, listening to the most comforting sound on earth—waves breaking on beaches in darkness—so on and on you build it with droolings and driblets, your daddy seated beside you, construction foreman, grabbing mud and letting fall the droplets, his belly sagging over faded blue trunks, tongue tip between his front teeth, the way it always is, protruding, when he concentrates, his grey-black waves of hair shining wet with salt spray, he mixes in a periwinkle with his beach mud so your castle wall has one spot like mother of pearl, and on and on we all dribble in concert until finally it's done, a veritable work of art, thousands of tiny grey dried driblets coalesced, gleaming in the sun, and just then the tide sploshes forth and gently washes our castle back into sand and sea water.

Everybody moans—-OOOOOOOOOH! But then we back up and regroup a short distance closer to the dunes and start playing the driblet game all over again. Like pissants commencing with reconstruction plans, after a red-haired kid (with green eyes the color of my son Nathan's) lays waste to their anthill, or like people on the day following a monstrous hurricane near Miami, which blew a swath of destruction through their lives. Building driblet sand castles is a metaphor for the relentless never-say-die of insect and human life, throughout the history of the world.

Land crabs on spindly legs were the main residents of the sand dunes in those days, where the condos live today. In my dreams I sometimes see myself running through the hillocks of fine white sand, trying to avoid those weird creatures with the eyes up on top of their heads, and they avoid me too, rushing to the shelter of the perfectly round holes they've dug. But most of my dreams are still set in Mt. Dora, I'm mostly in the white house, with the satsuma trees behind it, but sometimes in the green house, with the grove, or the pink house with the grove. The dreams are full of citrus, orange or grapefruit leaves with that extra miniature leaflet at the stem, the orange-yellow fruit with brownish traceries on the peel, looking like maps of exotic places.

The other night I dreamed of Prof Roseborough, walking down the sidewalk past the pink house. I was sitting in the living room, watching him through the picture window. He was old already, retired, rambling along at a leisurely pace, stopping, bending on creaky knees, ever so slowly, to retrieve a branch from a water oak tree, Spanish moss and dull-green leaves hanging to that branch, picking it up ever so slowly, white shock of hair glistening in the sun, lenses of his frameless spectacles flashing as the light caught them, slowly straightening his back with that twig in his hand, creeping over to lay it by the curbside, then strolling on down the hill, dragging behind him the arm that was crippled by the stroke, trudging along Seventh Avenue, fading into transparency, then nullity, the way the Walking Jesus did.

Those are the kind of dreams I still dream about Florida—soothing visions full of moist lassitude and the cooing of doves. I never dream about the manic exhilaration, about the happiest day of my life: Nov. 1, 1957.

During the halftime break it began to dawn on us, and maybe on Dan Spear, that we had a chance to win this game. But he and we preferred not to think about that. There was no halftime pep talk. Dan Spear went back to his office. We sat around in the gym and talked quietly. Somebody was telling jokes. We laughed but we didn't laugh as loudly as we had before the game. The hysteria was tempered, but we were still in a light frame of mind.

Was Father Lawler, principal of Bishop Moore, out in the stands of the enemy camp that night? Did he and Sister Maria, head sister, walk over at halftime, to pay their respects to Prof Roseborough on the other side? I don't know. Who else was there, in the Bishop Moore stands? Among the students, say? Peggy Bazzell? Ken Shattuck? Jeanne Balog? Enrico E. Caruso? Johnny Klein? Janet Fanvele? Barbara L. Pfetsch? Phil Ragozzino? I don't know. I'm just guessing. Did Howard Earle Stivers, B.M. band director, have his bunch out on the field for a halftime marching show? "Eight steps to five yards." I don't think so. It was a fresh band and they didn't put on many travelling shows in those days. B.M. was a new school, built only about 1954. I can't remember why it replaced the old St. James School.

The girls in that band weren't allowed to wear long boys' pants; they had to be in dresses. Later on Howard Stivers found a way to get around that. He put the girls in bloomer-style pants, gold, with a black stripe down the side, had them looking like the Swiss Guards at the Vatican. But he was always running scared, afraid the Bishop from St. Augustine might make an unexpected appearance, then consign those girls' outfits to perdition. I'd like to have given the Bishop a free ticket to our Groveland game that year, then watched his eyes pop out during the halftime show, when the majorettes marched by.

You run into some strange coincidences sometimes. The reason I know about the B.M. band is that I was in a taxi in San Diego recently, and the driver of that taxi turned out to be Howard Earle Stivers' son. I'd love to talk to a B.M. player who recalls the halftime pep talk of Bishop Moore Hornets coach John Bryan. Or even better, go back in a time machine and eavesdrop on it. Maybe athletic director Barry Keitel added a few words to the tongue lashing. I doubt it, though. By this time Barry must have felt a certain queasiness revving up in his insides. But he wasn't about to transmit these vibrations to the team. He just walked around smiling, patting shoulders and slapping butts: "We're okay, guys. No sweat. Plenty of time to get 'em in the second half!" But it's a fascinating thing about athletics, you know. Once you start out playing in a certain frame of mind, it's hard to change in the middle of the game. Even after the opponent has proven to you that the original frame of mind was far from appropriate. Bishop Moore had started out overconfident. Now, at halftime, they weren't overconfident any more, but what were they? They didn't know exactly, and that was part of their problem.

Of course, in his halftime remarks John Bryan would try to build up the anger. These puny hicks are playing over their heads, but we ought to be ashamed for letting them run on us the way they're running. How about some defense? Have you boys got balls or not? The second half is going to show me if you've got balls, etc, etc. Coach Bryan must have known that working on the anger was no total solution. But it was the best he could do. He was sure they were still going to win this game. He just wasn't sure how.

As for us, nobody dared to do much thinking or hoping. We didn't want to jinx ourselves. There's where we had the psychological advantage. B.M. was in desperate need of a new frame of mind to play the second half, but all we had to do was to stay in the one we were in. Win or lose, we were happy. We were having fun. What about you, Coach Spear, sitting down in your office, breathing in the fumes of the analgesic balm? Were you talking second-half strategy with Assistant Coach Shanks Hansel? If you were you never let us in on it. You knew we had a chance now, just like we knew. But you didn't dare hope too hard. You didn't dare change anything for fear of losing the just right tunings of minds and psyches. And you still didn't believe we could win the game, did you? Nobody believed that except Earle Williams.

Stories, stories, and more stories. Everybody's got a story to tell. I'd like to hear all the interesting stories from all the lives of all the MDHS students of the decade of the fifties. I'd like to hear what became of them. We used to have "Career Day" every year at the high school. People made presentations for the students, talked about their professions. The most popular speaker was always Highway Patrolman Bryant Speers. But I bet some of those listening to his spiel about chasing down speeders "clocked at 110 m.p.h." ended up working even more interesting jobs than his.

A lot of people I went to school with became very successful. Take just your and Bert's three kids, Dan Spear—two PhDs and one medical doctor! Now, that's not bad for a son of humble South Slavic immigrants. Others have had exciting adventures in exotic places. Walter TeStrake ended up in Moscow. Is he still there? Bill Brown became a corrections officer in California, Janice Reid a professional ballet dancer. John Wilson did spook work all over the world. C.M. Jones, last I heard, was doing big bidness in Boston. Even those who never left the lassitude of Lake County, Florida, must have some crazy tales to tell. Life can be exotic at home. Who knows, maybe Anna Pearl Strump, e.g., relocated a short piece down the road, say to Okahumpka, where she was abducted by aliens in 1965 and returned to tell about it. They did experiments on her, Anna Pearl said, and they implanted alien two-headed babies in her uterus, and that's how come she got pregnant.

Or one day Waiford Bedford, say, was sitting in an armchair, in a trailer park near Lake Minnehaha, or Astatula, Altoona, Cassia (this was 1988), watching a Florida Gators football game on t.v., drinking a Genesee beer and eating salted peanuts, and he up and underwent spontaneous combustion. Nothing left of Waiford or his trailer but a heap of smoking grey-blue ashes.

Well, those are just possibilities, and I certainly hope nothing like that happened to Anna Pearl or Waiford. But I'm saying that it could have. Anything can happen in life. What I'd give to hear all the enthralling things everybody's been through since they strolled down the aisles of the Mt. Dora Community Building, to the strains of "Pomp and Circumstance."

But since I haven't heard all the future stories, I'll give you one representative sample. It's about what happened to me on June 6-7, 1992, thirty-four years after I walked that aisle.

We're still in halftime, the band's still marching, or the mosquito trucks are fogging, or they're chasing that mongrel around, trying to get him off the playing field, and he's still smiling, tail at half mast, trying to cooperate, but every time they almost get him he scoots off a little further and the crowd laughs again, so while they're doing that I thought I'd have time to sneak this story in. But if you're not interested, Dan Spear, we can skip Chapter Five and get right back to the game.

5

HaLf TIME TIMEOUT

The Friendly Skies of Air Azerbaijan

Kiev—St. Petersburg

June, 1992

I knew we were in trouble when I saw the passengers. They were all men, swarthy men, wearing black leather jackets. But not the kind the new mafioso of the ex-Soviet Union wear. These were chintzy cheap leather jackets. Their eyes bugged out when our blondes appeared on the tarmac. Then I saw what was written on the fuselage of the plane we were about to board. Big trouble.

We were getting into a mess that had been prepared, by accident, much earlier—in New York, before we even left for Absurdistan. Aeroflot wrote the tickets with the numbers upside down and Clark, our travel agent, didn't notice the nine where there was supposed to be a six. On May 12 they brought the tickets, along with the visas, out to Kennedy Airport, where my students and I were waiting to take a Czech Air flight to Prague, en route to Moscow, then Kiev, Ukraine. We, the group of twelve from Miami University (the one in Ohio), were doing a Russian language study-tour: three weeks of classes in Kiev, plus a week of touring in Moscow and St. Petersburg. As group leader and professor of Russian language and literature, I was responsible for straightening out the glitches. I'd been running student groups into the Soviet Union since the eighties. Now that the country was dead, I was running them into the un-Soviet Union. Absurdistan. That's the term they use, with characteristic Russian black humor, to designate the countries left over after the Union collapsed.

I knew we were in trouble when Tolya came back from the Aeroflot office in Kiev, where he had taken the tickets to confirm our flight to St. Petersburg. He said, "Weren't you leaving for 'Peter' on June 6? These tickets are written for June 9. And you're supposed to be on a plane back to New York on the tenth. I looked at the tickets and moaned. When Clark's people brought the stuff out to JFK it was only an hour before departure for Prague, and the first thing I noticed was that my own return ticket to the States was dated wrong. Czech Air had fouled that one up, and we scurried around trying to straighten it out. That's why I didn't notice the bigger problem: the sixes on our Kiev—Petersburg tickets were upside down.

The upshot was that we arrived in Kiev with that flight still scheduled three days late. Of course, changing an airline ticket should be a minor problem. But here's the cardinal rule in the rule book of Absurdistan: minor problems are major. Whatever you do will take you ten times more time and effort than in the West. That covers everything from buying a book of matches to walking across the street. If there's a book of matches to be bought or a street to walk across.

Well, at least the flight in was uneventful. A year later, with a different group, I flew Czech Air into Kiev, this time with a stopover in Lvov (Lviv), New Ukraine. We sat on the ground for an hour, taking on passengers, while (as we learned upon landing in Kiev) the Lvivian baggage handlers were cutting the locks off our luggage. Here's some advice for the tourist: when flying in the ex-Soviet Union, don't use suitcases. Especially the Samsonite matching stuff, which might as well have a sign in big cyrillic letters: I'M RICH. ROB ME. If you have to check anything, put it in cardboard boxes, with handles improvised from cord. That's the way the Soviets travel; it won't attract attention.

In a word, here we are back in May, 1992, in Kiev, and Tolya says the dates are wrong for our flight to St. Petersburg, and I know this won't be easy. Tolya, whose title was assistant dean for something, worked as chief facilitator for the Kiev Foreign Language Institute, where we did our study program. Soviets come in several varieties. Tolya fell into the good-hearted simple-souled category. But keep in mind that beneath the mask any Soviet citizen wears, even such a cordial type as Tolya, lurks what Russians call *khitrozhopost'* (an untranslatable term that combines skillful cunning with an obscene word for the backside).

Tolya was maybe thirty-five, tall, gregarious, with a permanent five o'clock shadow on his jaws. His bow-legged walk and simple manner were endearing. But he was always in a sweat about something. For our whole three weeks in Kiev he wore the same strained grin and the same pair of faded Levis every day. He was eager to please, almost to a fault. For example, when the hot water was turned off at our hotel, Tolya apologized for the inconvenience and arranged daily trips to a Kiev bathhouse. We went once. The steam room platform was made up of boards so rotten they could have collapsed any minute, and the woman attendant was drunk and abusive. Until she realized she was dealing with foreigners—after that she became drunkenly fawning.

Tolya sat naked on the slime of the topmost rotted boards, steaming his body and showing my students (Chuck and David) how to thrash themselves with the birch *veniki*, the bundles of leaves and twigs used to stimulate circulation. He kept apologizing for the filthiness of the bath house and the drunken state of the attendant. We didn't complain. When in Russia (Ukraine—same thing) don't expect the convenience and cleanliness of a Finnish sauna. While we sat and steamed, Tolya went on beating himself with his *venik*. He found more things to be apologetic about. The frazzled old bus we used for excursions had broken down again, but they'd have it fixed by tomorrow. The hotel people were promising hot water some time next week. The day trip to Uman had not materialized, but they'd find a way to make it up to us. Meanwhile, there was a special treat in store for me, the group leader. My students were learning Ukrainian songs and poems to recite at the farewell party, in addition to the usual Russian songs and poems.

"What about the flight to Petersburg?" I asked. Tolya whipped himself still harder on the shoulders. Then he stood up and worked the *venik* across his buttocks and the backs of his legs. Whoosh, whoosh, whoosh, bits of wet birch leaves coming loose and wafting in lovely twists and turns through the steam. Chuck and David sat on the less rotted boards of the first level and looked at Tolya in wonder, admiring his steaming and thrashing techniques. They each held a soggy *venik*, but were none too eager to begin lashing their bodies.

Tolya explained that he was working things out with the Soviet airline, Aeroflot; he expected to have it done in a matter of days. When he heard me moan back in mid May about that June 9 date on the tickets, he blanched, but immediately recovered. He put the strained smile back on his face and gave me the response that Russians have given foreign travellers since time out of mind: "No problem. We'll get it straight." Now, from my experience in the Soviet Union, I knew that when a Soviet tells you, "No problem," you can assume you've got big problems.

They had put us up at the Sport Hotel, right next to the big "Dynamo" soccer stadium. It had its amenities: the rooms were new and clean by Soviet standards, they hadn't shut the hot water off right away (if you're travelling in spring or early summer, expect to lose the hot water within a day of arrival), and the location was good. On weekends there was an enormous bazaar on the stadium grounds. Traders came out and stood in long lines, holding up Western cigarettes, irons, brassieres, goldfish, crockery, vodka, puppies of every breed imaginable. In the new capitalist un-Soviet Union huckstering has taken over the country. One day I saw a small forlorn man in the line, dressed in the colorless beiges and browns of Sovietdom. He was holding up one Adidas running shoe, the left, size 9. He was desperate to sell, since he didn't have the shoe for the other foot and knew his bargaining position was weak. Therefore, he was asking for payment in the new Ukrainian currency, the so-called "coupon." In May, 1992, the coupon had just come into existence; it was artificially rated as equivalent to the Russian ruble (which was still legal currency in New Independent Ukraine). But if you talked to the black market money dealers in the bazaar, you realized that the decline had already begun. You could get 130 coupons for a dollar but only 125 rubles. A year later the dollar-coupon exchange was one to three thousand and the ruble-coupon was one to four. Now, at the moment I write (Apr., 1994), the ruble is at 4000 to the dollar, and you need a wheelbarrow full of "coupons" to buy anything.

That bazaar featured Ukrainian, Roumanian, Moldovian, Armenian black marketeers, and even a small contingent of Vietnamese. How did these people from Vietnam end up in Ukraine and how could they compete, in the black market trade, with the locals? One of them tried to hustle me into trading dollars, which might have worked, had he been able to communicate in English, Russian, or even Ukrainian. He apparently spoke only Vietnamese. Yet there he was, making a living in the big Stadium Bazaar. How? It's like being a deaf and dumb used car salesman in Talladega, Alabama. One thing about Russia or the Soviet Union or the F.S.U. or the N.I.S. (whatever you want to call it, it's still the same place), one rule that always holds: Absurdistan is full of unanswerable questions.

Our program was into the third week and going fine. We had good classes at the Institute and interesting excursions around lovely Kiev, the Mother of All Russian Cities. Our personal sightseeing bus, half the size of the usual red Intourist bus, was emblazoned with colorful patterns of white and yellow daises. It reminded me of something California hippies would live in back in the sixties. The food was tolerable, no one was sick, and the chambermaids at the Hotel Sport were not pilfering anything valuable from the Americans' rooms. In a word, all was well, but we still didn't know how or when we would get to St. Petersburg.

Finally, only three days before our scheduled departure, Tolya came knocking at my door, bearing broad smiles and good news. "It wasn't as hard as we thought. We got the tickets changed. True, you'll have to take a night flight instead of early afternoon, but you'll get to Peter on time. No problem." I thanked him profusely, aware that it had taken him two and a half weeks of standing in lines, then wheedling and begging, to win over the Aeroflot people.

Airline personnel are just like anyone in any service capacity anywhere in the Soviet Union. You walk up to their counter, and they'll treat you the way any shop girl treats any Soviet citizen in shops from Minsk to Khabarovsk. Let's say you're in a grocery and you're hoping she's maybe got a hunk of beef stashed under the empty shelves, so you put a fawning smile on your face. You have to fawn if you expect to get anywhere with her, because she knows she has the power to sell you that fatback or not sell it to you. Power is the only thing anybody in the Soviet Union, or the un-Union, understands. She's sitting on a stool, in her long white smock, looking out the window, taking a cigarette break. She's young but jaded. She has on her face the same look of bored disgust that you see on every shop girl's face in every shop from Tbilisi to Yakutia (Sakha). Out of the corner of her eye she watches you sidling uneasily up, but she pretends you're not there. You stand by the counter and smile sheepishly. She's busy smoking her cigarette and looking out the window. You clear your throat, meekly, make a low baaing sound. She slowly, ever so slowly, turns her head, glares at you with that disgusted expression, blows out some cigarette smoke, and finally says, "Yeah? What do *you* want?"

After this whether you get your fatback depends on one of two things: (1) How well you can kiss her behind (2) How much hard cash you can offer. Unless you're American. If they know you're an American the shop girls will almost smile. But poor Tolya was a Soviet, and he must have sweated and kissed butt at Aeroflot on a daily basis, so I thanked him for the new tickets and tried to put the prospect of that flight, only a few days away, out of my mind. You see, I had flown Aeroflot before, and I had learned that some things are best not dwelled upon. Of course, my student group, reveling in blitheful ignorance, went on about its business, enjoying the courses, excursions and night life of Kiev.

They went out on the town every night. We were in luck to be at Hotel Sport, right beside a subway station and walking distance from central Kiev. My 1993 group stayed at a mafia hotel, the *Mir*, in a dangerous part of town. On their first evening in Kiev, Brent and a few other intrepid souls, out for an evening stroll, came across a drunken fight in an underground crossway. They saw three young men grab another and repeatedly smash his head against the concrete wall. They didn't go out again for a while after that.

I first flew Aeroflot in the summer of 1972, back when Brezhnev "stagnancy" ruled the country, when, to hear a lot of Russians talk today, everything was peaches and cream. I was on my first trip to the Soviet Union, a young scholar with a group of American teachers of Russian, studying at Moscow State University. We took a break from our program and made two flights on Aeroflot: first to Kiev, then to Leningrad. Even back then the airline had a wild reputation. As for its safety record, there could only be rumors, since the government never announced disasters. You could have a nuclear accident in Chelyabinsk, killing maybe ten thousand people, and the next day the headline story in the Soviet newspapers would feature a new brick factory they were proudly building in Omsk.

The Russians running our exchange program in 1972 were busy telling us "No problem," but we came across other Russians, unconnected with our program, who were happy to provide the rumors about Aeroflot. People such as the pensioners sitting at doorways to check passes, the ones who always had advice for you: "Don't go out without a hat. You'll get sunstroke." Or, "Close your window. There's a draft. You'll get pneumonia." Or, "Never eat in a student dining hall. You'll get cancer." Folks everywhere love spreading bad news, but Russians are world champions at this.

What first astounded me, twenty years ago, were the dimensions of the airports. In those days big cities like Kiev or Leningrad had airports the size of the one in Daytona Beach, Florida, from which I had flown to New York before departure to Moscow. The stewardesses on Aeroflot wore the standard look of the shop girl on their faces. You need not bother asking them for anything. Before takeoff they distributed small pieces of hard candy, which would help you cope with the changing air pressure in your ears. Other than that nothing was served. Not even a cup of mineral water. The seasoned Aeroflot traveller brought his own lunch.

The impressive thing about those flights in 1972 was the way the pilots took off. Straight up and fast. It's like you're in a rocket heading for the moon. Grit your teeth and hang on. Why these straight-up takeoffs? I never did get a logical answer, but some said it was because all the pilots were World War II veterans. They were used to short airstrips and didn't know how to take off on a long runway.

During the vertical departure from Moscow, I remember wondering whether we would be landing in Kiev the same way, without benefit of a glide path. Well, in a word, we did. Straight down. Just fasten seat belts, suck on your piece of candy, and hang on. Trust your pilot. He knows what he's doing. We didn't crash, so let's assume he did know. At least there was some order and discipline back then. Recently a French-built Aeroflot airbus crashed on a flight from Moscow to Hong Kong. There were rumored to be children's voices on the black box recording, and later the truth came out. The pilot had let his fifteen-year-old son fly the airplane.

While messing around with the instruments, the boy had knocked off the auto-pilot and sent the plane into a dive. They never pulled out of that dive.

After my 1972 flights I didn't use Aeroflot again until the eighties, when I began running student groups into the country. Expecting the straight up straight down pattern, I was relieved to find they were using a normal glide path. Apparently the military aviators were reaching retirement age.

So here we are, back in June of 1992, the twentieth anniversary of my first Aeroflot flight, and the day of our departure for Petersburg has arrived. At nine p.m. we stow our baggage in our bus at the Sport Hotel. The flight is scheduled for shortly after midnight, but I've asked Tolya to send the flower child bus early. It has broken down three times in three weeks, and I'm none too confident it can make it all the way out to Borispol Airport.

It seems the whole bunch is ready on time, which doesn't always happen with student groups. One year two of my students got into one of these Russian drinking things with a Moscow friend and missed the bus to the Sheremetevo Airport. The Russian kept waving away their worries about the shortness of time, while drinking to eternal friendship between the Russian and American peoples. He ended up, of course, in the sentimental stage of inebriation, hugging and kissing them, weeping over their departure. Then, finally, he looked at his watch.

They borrowed a car from some neighbor and made a mad dash for the airport. As they raced along, they saw a man step off a bus and right into the path of a car that was driving on the wrong side of the road. The car that hit him, going fifty miles per hour, screeched to a stop, then backed up at tremendous speed to where he lay in the road. Two men got out, tossed the victim into the back of the hit car, and squealed off, apparently bound for a hospital, or a morgue. Then the police arrived and tied up traffic.

My anxious students sat there stalled and sick to their stomachs. After all, they had just observed how a man looks when run over by a car moving at a high rate of speed. They arrived at Sheremetevo shaken, completely sober despite hours of farewell toasts, in time to fly home with our group.

Anyway, this year I've got them together, under control, and the bus is chugging along for Borispol. All is well. I've bought myself a bottle of black market Ukrainian vodka to fortify me for the trip. Westerners in Russia tend to drink three times as much as they drink at home. There's something (actually, a lot of things) about the country that drive you to drink. Bound to be some kind of glitch, I'm thinking. Am I a pessimist? No, I'm an American who has travelled extensively in the Soviet Union, who knows Russian culture and literature, speaks the language. Who knows, therefore, that the one thing you can expect is the unexpected.

Tolya is riding along with us to the airport. He's in that teary mood, the way Russians get when saying good-bye. Even to people they've known only a few weeks. And some of my students are a little bit maudlin over Tolya too. If you spend much time around Russians, you find yourself, one fine day, with the emotions they wear on their sleeves having rubbed off onto yours. At the farewell party-performance my students had slouched through their skits and dutifully sang Russian and Ukrainian songs. David, a good sport, played, though reluctantly, the role of a turnip, in the students' enactment of the Russian folk tale. About how the grandma pulled and pulled, but she couldn't pull the turnip up, and then grandpa joined her, and they pulled and pulled, but they couldn't pull the turnip up, and then came mother, father, daughter, son, cat, etc., etc., and they all hung on to one another and they pulled and they pulled, but they couldn't pull the turnip up, until finally a little mouse came up and joined the end of the line, and that gave them just enough strength, so that they all pulled and they pulled, and they finally pulled the dour turnip (David) up out of the ground! What is the moral of that tale? The eternal Russian message: collective effort wins out in the end; the individual is nil.

Then the American students gave their teachers gifts and bid them an emotional farewell. They also loaded Tolya down with presents (calendars of Ohio wildlife, miniature American flags, guidebooks to the Grand Canyon). They appreciated all his efforts as facilitator on their behalf. Now, during the final bus ride, one student, Charles, presents him with a belated gift: a soccer ball, for Tolya's four-year-old son. This gift moves Tolya to full-blown streaming tears, and he hugs the donor for a full two minutes, while the rest of the students snigger and Chuck struggles feebly to detach himself.

Caught up in the valedictory spirit, Tolya can't admit, even to himself, that he is immensely relieved to be getting rid of us. Americans present special problems for a facilitator in the Soviet Union, since they must be given the best of everything. Not because they necessarily demand more. It's just that on the unwritten prestige list that every Soviet knows by heart Americans rank Number One. Right beneath them come the Germans, British and French. After all the Western capitalist peoples you have the South African whites and the Japanese, who, being highly organized, successful and prosperous, get special dispensation for their slanted eyes and yellow skin. Most Russians are inveterate racists, so other Orientals rank way down on the list, not far above the Africans, who are absolute bottom line. In the view of a Soviet in a service position it's fine to abuse an Oriental or black customer. But when nationalities on the top of the list come under your purview, you, the Soviet service personnel, must smile and kowtow. Get them the best that can be got. Which is still far below what they've come to expect at home.

A Soviet facilitator is aware of this, and that's why he's so perpetually embarrassed and apologetic. As for Tolya, he is glad we're going for at least one more reason: he'll be relieved of the tremendous burden of safeguarding American valuables. I could see the joy shining palpably on his brow that afternoon, when we went to his office, opened his small excuse for a safe, and took out our tickets, passports and spare dollars. Whenever I arrive with my students for a study program, I collect all airline tickets and pass-ports. Then I recommend that students give me most of their extra money and traveller's checks too, for safekeeping. Leaving these things in hotel rooms or carrying them around with you can cause problems.

Of course, after I take up the passports and tickets, after I inventory the student money, my big problem is finding a place to put it all. Russians running the study programs or hotel managers will tell you, invariably, that they have no safe available. Of course, they do, but nobody wants to take responsibility for the belongings of the Americans. What if the money should go missing? Historically, one reason nothing gets done in Russia is because responsibility terrifies everyone. So it sometimes amounts to several days of insistence before I get my safe. If we're at a hotel for a short stay (three-four nights) I don't get one at all. Oddly enough, the Sevastopol Hotel in Moscow, which ranks close to the bottom in sleazy Russian hotels, was the one place where they provided a wonderful safe deposit box for our group (in 1990). This year, 1992, no one but no one at the Sport Hotel or the Kiev Pedagogical Institute for Foreign Languages would agree to safe-keeping our valuables. When I insisted the fourth or fifth time somebody higher up forced this task on poor Tolya. He was visibly sweating and his hands were shaking on the day he opened up that small excuse for a safe in his office. It didn't even have a combination—he used a huge old-fashioned key. I was thinking, well, anybody who got into the office could (1) use something like a credit card to break into this thing or (2) pick it up bodily and carry it off. But I decided to take the risk. Who could imagine American dollars in such an unlikely spot as Tolya's office?

I was consoled by the thought that there were no credit cards in the ex-Soviet Union, so they couldn't be used for safe cracking. But poor Tolya. I imagined him lying awake worrying about those dollars, stashed precarious-ly in his office at the Institute for Foreign Languages. Maybe he even spent nights in there, sleeping on the floor, with a makeshift club by his side. After today, D-Day, June 6, 1992, his empty little safe would rest securely.

Our hippie bus holds out to the end, and we arrive at Borispol very early, then check in for our flight. I tell Tolya that I can handle it now, and he should go on back with the bus, but he insists on hanging around until boarding is announced. We kill two hours, maundering about the empty airport. Apparently we are the only passengers waiting for this flight. Odd. My students wander aimlessly through the sleepy hallways, I start working on my vodka, Tolya bounces his soccer ball. At midnight they still haven't made an announcement about boarding, so I go and check with the woman at the window. She says we're a little late since the plane has not arrived. This flight does not originate from Kiev, she tells me; it's coming in from Baku, Azerbaijan, on the Caspian Sea. First I've heard of this. No comment.

The plane shows up at 12:30 a.m. We wait around a little longer before the boarding call. We watch them wheel away our luggage on a huge push-cart. Tolya hugs everyone, gets emotional again, then strolls off, bowleggedly, with his soccer ball under one arm. He turns and waves one last time by the door. He's smiling, reveling in his awareness of a job well done. For the first time his smile looks natural, unconstrained. "Thanks a lot, Tolya!" we yell to him and wave our arms. "So long, Tolya!" Tomorrow he'll wash the jeans he's been wearing for three weeks.

Aeroflot flights don't use boarding gates. You walk out to where the plane is parked and wait around until they let you climb the ramp. Meanwhile, if the flight has come in from somewhere else, the passengers have to get off while they refuel. So, as we walked out onto the tarmac we saw the Baku contingent and they saw us. They were all men—dark-haired and swarthy. I don't think there was a single woman on that flight.

When they spied us their eyes bugged out. "Not ours," said their eyes. "These people are not ours" (meaning not Soviets). They watched the baggage carts roll out with our luggage. "Suitcases," said their bugged-out eyes. "These people have suitcases!" As we walked toward the plane, the men began circulating around us. They were young men, wearing mostly chintzy leather jackets. They had black hair and dark eyes. They were Azerbaijanians (Azeris). I had never been in Azerbaijan, and knew little about it. Only that it was a Muslim country, presently engaged in an internecine war with Armenia, another fragment of the former Soviet Union. The men began approaching the women in our group, especially the blondes. "Finlandia?" they asked in Russian. Then they tried English: "You Finland?" The women looked straight ahead and just kept walking.

When we got to the ramp of the small YAK-42, I looked up at the plane. It was an ordinary Aeroflot plane, Soviet built, capable of making the two-hour flight to Peter without refueling. Fine. But then I looked at the fuselage. Somebody had painted out the old Aeroflot logo and scrawled the words, in Russian: "Azerbaijanian Airlines." We were in trouble.

The passengers who had wandered off were now clustering about the ramp, waiting for the stewardess to give the re-boarding order. They made room for the foreigners (us), while elbowing in against one another for a good position. You might assume they could reclaim the seats they already had from Baku, but another rule of Absurdistan is "Never assume anything." Aeroflot seats are assigned, but no one pays attention to seat numbers. First come, first seated.

We climbed up the ramp and into the plane. It was filthy inside, and the interior was falling apart. We found seats. Mine was over the wing; four or five of my students were near the door at the front. Rebecca and Melissa had seats that faced backwards, so that they got a spectator's view of everything that happened in the next two hours. Lena, Chuck, Craig, Ted were in the rear. I don't know where David and Jenny were. I was lucky. My seat had a back that stood up and a seat belt that worked.

The Azeris re-boarded. Other passengers materialized, carrying huge cardboard boxes. They piled them up in the aisle, back near the toilet. Then a guy with a bicycle got on and tossed his bike up on top of the boxes. He appeared to be one of the Bakuans, so he must have carried the bicycle off the plane at Kiev, then back on. Was he worried it would be stolen? Or maybe he got some exercise during refueling, pedaling around the tarmac, circling the MIGs that were parked at the far end of the airport. He looked drunk, by the way, the guy with the bike. But then, so did a lot of others.

The plane was getting noisy, with loud talking in what I presumed to be the Azeri language. This struck me as unusual. Normal Soviet passenger etiquette (on planes, trains, buses) demands a silent decorum. You can ride an overnight train from Moscow to Kiev and exchange barely a word with your fellow passengers. Even though you sleep with these people all night, four to a compartment. But then, I haven't been in Baku. I was thinking that maybe the hot-blooded Southern type lives by different rules. Only later did it dawn on me who our fellow passengers were. They were, primarily, fruit and vegetable peddlers, transporting their produce to Petersburg for sale in the open-air markets.

The lone stewardess, a squat Russian woman in the standard dark blue Aeroflot uniform, hair pulled back in a bun, winged broach on her chest, was bustling around, preparing one thing or another. She seemed also to be mediating in a number of disputes between passengers. I couldn't hear what they were saying, but the arguments may have been over seats, because the plane was heavily over-booked. I began wondering if they had finagled the foreigners (us) onto a flight that was already full, and I was reminded of the way buses take on passengers in any Soviet city.

You're riding a bus, breathing the fumes. It is packed to the gills. A guy in dirty clothes, needing a shave, is shoved up against you, exuding a mixture of garlic and stale alcohol breath. From the other side you've got a huge fat woman pinning you against the wall, leaning on your ribs so hard that your toes ache. Your left ear is painfully glued against the window, because there's a disembodied elbow drilling into your right temple. Then the bus stops at the next stop. Two people get off and thirteen more form a flying wedge and jam their way on.

Luckily our plane had no more stops scheduled before St. Petersburg. I was seated beside a man whose body took up all of his own seat and part of mine. As soon as he settled in, he removed a greasy chicken wrapped in newspaper from his briefcase, put it on his knees, and began pulling its legs off. I got out my vodka bottle and took a few swigs.

Soon we were ready for takeoff. The buxom stewardess delivered the ritual speech, in Russian:

"Ladies and gentlemen, on behalf of Azerbaijanian Air, the captain and I would like to welcome aboard our Kiev passengers, for the two-hour flight to Leningrad. I mean St. Petersburg. We also hope that our continuing Baku passengers have had a good stretch of the legs, and are ready to proceed, well refreshed! Let me remind you to please observe the 'No Smoking' signs and keep your seat belts fastened while the seat belt lights are on. In fact, we recommend that at any moment you may be in your seat, for your comfort and safety you keep the belt loosely fastened, inasmuch as slight turbulence may intermittently be encountered. Upon take-off you will be served your choice of drinks, and, after that, a sumptuous dinner. Let me assure you that on Air Azerbaijan 'Service and safety are the bywords and flywords.' Feel free to call upon us if you have needs to be met. Our job is caring for you. Now please fasten your seat belts for takeoff and observe the 'No Smoking' signs. Lean back and relax. Welcome to Azeri Air!"

Actually, it's a joke; I made up that whole speech. Welcoming announcements on Aeroflot are brusque and to the point, but this was the briefest I ever heard. In a voice empty of all fakey and mellifluous intonations, the portly stewardess said, "Fasten seat belts for takeoff. No smoking." Everyone, except the Americans, laughed. In the first place, most of the seat belts didn't work. In the second place, a lot of passengers didn't have seats. They were standing back near the freight (the cardboard boxes, the bicycle) and the toilets. In the third place, those who weren't already smoking took the "no smoking" announcement as a reminder to light up. Everyone was having a wonderful time. That was when I first heard the shrieks, in English, from the front of the plane.

We took off. Back by the restrooms the standing Azeris broke out their vodka bottles and glasses. As we rose into the air I thought I recognized the screaming voices. It was our coeds, yelling, "Get off! Stop that!" The first thought I had was, How strange—here they've been in Kiev for three weeks studying Russian, and when they really need it, the best they can do is shriek out English words. Then came the anger. I thought, "These greasy bastards! How dare they molest real people!"

After that I tried to get into the mode of modern college professor. The vogue ideas of academe, of course, center on "cultural relativity," which means that when some grungy Azeri fruit peddlers grab your women, you think, Well, after all, this may be a traditional Azerbaijanian custom. Who am I to question their mores? You also can't call Azeris, or anybody else, 'swarthy' or 'greasy.' These terms number among the ever increasing lexicon of taboo words in the academic world, and anyone using them is automatically guilty of 'racism.'

So I adopted the tolerant approach, but I'm ashamed to say I've never been very good at standard American liberalism. I carefully conceal this from the other professors, of course, but when I see an article, for example, about how some guy got $2.5 million out of McDonald's after spilling hot coffee on himself, or some lady bilked $10 million out of Mike's Watering Hole in Chicago, because she sat in that bar drinking all night, then climbed in her Geo to drive home and squashed it up against a telephone pole, and, after all, Mike the bartender should have noticed she was too drunk to drive and it was his bottle of Ketel One vodka that had got her into that state, and, at the very least, he should have called her a taxi to drive her home, well, when I read about these things, my shameful secret is that

I'm not much in sympathy with the plaintiffs, or with their lawyers, who end up with two-thirds of the settlement in their own meretricious paws.

I took another sip on my bottle and wondered what to do next. Should I get up and plead with the molesters now, while the plane was still ascending, or should I stay in my fastened seat belt until the sign went off? What would the average professor do? Well, he certainly wouldn't get out of his seat while the "Fasten Seat Belts" sign was on. I waited. Maybe the harassers will get tired and go to sleep, I reasoned. If they don't I will calmly go forward and reason, professorially, with these men. Perhaps their parents beat them as children. Or maybe the traditional custom is to beat, but their progressive Western-style parents deprived them of their beatings. Either way, they are victims.

I will gently explain to them, I thought, in a language they understand, Russian, that American cultural mores frown upon the feeling up of women with whom one is not properly acquainted. Having reasoned all this through, I felt better. I waited for the plane to reach cruising altitude, calmly sipping at my vodka. The man next to me had already consumed nearly the whole of his chicken. He was licking his fingers now, rubbing the grease into his moustache and beard. I waited. The screams at the front of the plane continued. From the group of men clustered around the boxes and bicycle near the toilets, came clouds of smoke and loud drunken conversation. These guys are Muslims, I thought. The standard stereotype about Muslim men is that they think all Western women are infidels and whores. And may be treated as such. My anger soared once again, but I lectured to it in a professorial manner. "What you are doing is perpetuating simpleminded stereotypes, and letting irrational emotions run rampant."

Ever since June of 1991, when my friend Volodya was beaten unconscious in Moscow, I had carried a large hunting knife. That incident occurred five minutes after I left Volodya near his apartment complex. There were three of them, the muggers; they must have been hanging out around the Paveletskaya Metro Station. I was seeing Volodya home from a drunken revel in the suburbs of Moscow. Not that I was drunk. Years ago I gave up drinking with Russians. But Volodya had been chugging vodka Russian style, which means you try to get so drunk that you can't walk. He had succeeded.

It was late. My big mistake was not taking him all the way to his building and up the stairs to the apartment. His wife Tanya (well, actually, she was his un-wife, a category of wife unknown in the West, but that's a different story), was home, and after she finished giving him hell, she could have put him safely to bed. But I was in a hurry to get back to the metro before they closed it down at one a.m. My hotel, the Bega ("Horse Race") was on the other side of town, overlooking the Hippodrome. So I said, "Look, there's your building over there, across the street. Are you okay to stagger the last two hundred meters by yourself?" He said sure, he was fine. We embraced, Russian style, then parted. He shuffled off, still wearing a goofy grin on his big square Siberian face.

They followed him into the dark entryway of his own apartment building, hit him in the back of the head with some blunt object and knocked him down. He made the mistake of getting up and trying to fight, but, fortunately, they soon beat him unconscious. Otherwise they might have killed him. After that they took his wallet and back pack, stripped off his jacket, American jeans and running shoes, and left him in his underwear. They even got his socks.

Later on I gave Volodya some American briefs, telling him that the next time this happened, he wouldn't have to bear the shame of wearing skivvies too shabby to be worth stealing. Just a little joke. Well, anyway, ever since that happened I had carried a large knife, but for the Petersburg flight I left it packed in my luggage. Just as well, I thought. These market hucksters are probably armed. Besides that, I had often wondered what I would do with that knife if I ever pulled it. I wouldn't know how to use it, and I could end up with it taken away from me and stuck up my posterior. No, I will do this the rational, the professorial way. I will admonish them in a quiet voice. After all, I weigh one hundred sixty pounds; I've never been a fighter. I'm a professor. White beard. Glasses on my nose. Getting old. The seat belt sign went off. I got up, leaving my glasses on the seat, just in case. I squeezed by the man overflowing the seat beside me, careful to pass him with my backside turned away (in Soviet etiquette going down a row with your bottom facing people is considered offensive). I made my way toward the front of the plane. "We're going to be calm about this," I kept telling myself, "we're going to be calm."

Well, now I have a confession to make. My personality is somewhat split. Normally I'm mild-mannered and quiet. That's the side most people see, and they take that for the real me. But then, I've also got a wild and volatile side, combining anger with exhilaration, and once in a while that side kicks in. With each step toward the front of the plane I told myself that I would be calm and tolerant, and with each step the anger welled up more and more, and by the time I reached the seats near the door I was out of control.

I asked who was screaming. Two of my students, Kendall, from Shaker Heights, and one of the "Finland" blondes, Katie, halfway raised their hands. "Okay, where are they? The ones grabbing you. Point them out to me." I was in a total rage now. The women didn't get up or look around, but they made head motions rearward and said, "The guys right behind us."

The two Azeris in the next row were maybe in their early twenties. Each had pasted an innocent expression on his boyish face, and they were uncomfortable with the look on mine, especially after I stuck it right up in front of theirs.

What they had been doing was just having, in their view, some fun. They had been reaching around the seats in front of them and grabbing the American prey, preferably in the most intimate of spots. With each attack they made a short squealing noise, imitating a pig, and then they sat back and waited for the shrieking reaction: "Don't do that again! Get off me, you bastard!" Of course, they didn't understand the English words, but they got a good charge out of the shrieks.

Heather, another blonde, was sitting quite near the action. Later I asked her how she had avoided the attacks. Didn't she feel her femininity impugned, since nobody thought her worth grabbing? She said, "Well, they did try some stuff, but I didn't yell at them." Maybe that was the key: the Baku peasants were seeking, largely, the sexual gratification of making a woman shriek. By the way, Melissa, a beautiful Native American from Michigan, told me afterwards that nobody bothered her at all. "Must have thought I was one of them," she laughed.

So there I was then, right up in the face of one uncomfortable young man, screaming in Russian, "You son of a bitch, you keep your hands off these girls, you understand? You touch them one more time and I'll kick your ass all the way to the other end of this plane! You understand me? Huh?"

He had shrunk back as far as he could in his seat. He raised one hand to protect his face. Later I wondered if any of his buddies were reaching for the knives in their boots, but right then I was too mad to wonder anything. Then the formidable stewardess rushed up. "What's wrong? What's going on here?"

I said, "These slimy animals have been grabbing our girls, and I've told them, and I'm telling you right now, that if they do this just one more time, if they even look sideways at these women..."

"All right, all right," she said. "Let me handle it." She turned to the young men with a schoolmarmly manner and began lecturing them on good behavior: "Now, you boys have got to learn, etc., etc." I listened to this for no more then ten seconds before intervening with more angry threats. Finally, the one whose face I had spent most of my time in spoke out in a little boy kind of voice. He had a hurt, truly offended look on his swarthy mug. He said, "Well, we were just trying to make friends."

That set me off again, into another fit of raving. I raved on for a few more minutes. But one problem with raving is that eventually you run out of things to say, so you end up just sputtering out. Then you feel kind of foolish. After I shut up, an awkward moment of silence set in. We (the stewardess and I) and they (the two offenders) stood and sat, respectively, looking at one another.

I suddenly realized that I had been playing, one-sidedly, the Russian game of "Mad." All over Absurdistan people enjoy screaming at one another. It's an old Russian folk tradition, incomprehensible in the West. Say, for example, that you're waiting in the taxi line and somebody butts in ahead of you. You rush up to him and start screaming, while he defends his position in the line. But the rules of the game normally prohibit simultaneous screaming. In other words, each side gets its turn. You rant for a while, and then you shut up while he rants back at you. Then it's your turn again. Bystanders get into the act, with a variety of remarks yelled in favor of one side or the other ("He was in the line before!" "No, he wasn't!"). But mainly it's one on one.

Soviets derive a lot of pleasure from the game of Mad. Being righteously indignant, loudly, is gratifying. So that anywhere you go in Absurdistan you'll see folks taking great voluptuous pleasure in yelling and being yelled at. But not foreigners. "Not Ours" are, for some reason, ineligible to play Mad, and if a foreigner gets into it, the Russians are bewildered. "Is this guy playing the game of mutually raving Mad, or is he serious about being angry?" They conclude, "Well, he must be really and truly mad, because no foreigner could possibly understand the Soviet game of Mad."

So that's why the two Azeris didn't yell back at me when I got in their face. And during the moment of awkward silence, after I sputtered out, I had a definite sense of disappointment. I was wanting them to yell back, so that when my turn came again, I could yell still more indignantly. That's when I realized I had done it again. I was acting like a Soviet. If you spend too much time in the country you start playing their games. Unsuccessfully, because they don't play back. I once even played "Mad" with a young American diplomat who was (legally) trying to butt ahead of me in an Aeroflot ticket line in Kiev. When I told him to back off or I would kick his ass, he didn't realize that all I wanted for him to do was a little yelling back at me. He backed off, and the game was ruined.

Well, I stood there in front of those Azeris, thinking about how people peck at each other like chickens, about the satisfactions folks derive from wallowing in pain or mutual recrimination. And then I recalled the little-boy hurt on that young Azeri's face, how he "just wanted to make friends," and I started laughing inside.

Nothing was left for me to do except go back and sit down, but first I summoned up my ferocity, turned to the two victims, and said, "You see where I'm sitting? If you get any more flak from these guys, one of you come back and tell me. I mean the least little bit of flak!"

Then I gave the malefactors one last angry glare, turned and walked back down the aisle to my seat, looking mean but laughing inside. The other fruit peddlers were contemplating my enraged mug with curiosity and admiration. They must have been thinking, "Now, there's one hysterical foreigner." Two who had come up the aisle for a better view of the altercation moved aside to let me pass.

A drunk was sleeping on the floor, blocking my way to my seat, but his friends grabbed him by the ankles and pulled him over far enough for me to get by. I sat down, picked up my vodka bottle, and resigned myself. Even if these guys started up again, there wouldn't be a whole lot I could do. I thought about the way I had behaved and the looks on their faces, and I couldn't help laughing out loud.

We had another hour and a half, assuming the flight was on time. Onward, relentlessly, we flew, through the friendly skies. Half way there my vodka bottle was done, and my neighbor had gone to sleep. In fact a good many of the Baku contingent were out of it now. Some were sprawled across seat mates, a few more had passed out in the aisle. Calmness reigned. If you wanted to use the toilet (and I did after going through my vodka), you had to step over their snoring forms, then negotiate your way past the pile of boxes and the bicycle. Some of the seatless passengers were still drinking and smoking, occasionally breaking into song. But the music was not raucous— it sounded a lyrical note, soft and serene, maybe an Azerbaijanian lullaby.

The harmonizers deferentially glanced at the foreigner as he passed to the pissoir. I noticed that Ted and Craig had joined a different drinking party near the back, making friends with the good-natured Southerners. I think Chuck was in on that too. Meanwhile Rebecca, sitting up in the front with her backwards-facing seat, was watching the total panorama, as if enjoying an in-flight movie. She saw the sunrise too, and took a particular delight in the mingling of the soft songs with the pink and orange of the sky. That's what she told me anyway, the next day. I never noticed David. He must have been asleep, dreaming he was a turnip.

So on we flew, via Azeri Air, skimming the clouds of Absurdistan, and the passengers slept placidly and, Thank God, the pilot was fine, the engines in good repair, and we did, finally, land in St. Petersburg. True, twenty minutes before arrival a wild dispute broke out in the back of the plane, waking everyone. Two or three men were shouting in frenzied Azeri voices. There was some pushing and shoving. It didn't look like the game of Mad—it looked like Real. I wondered how the pilot would do at flying the plane, in the event of an all-out knock-down but no-place-to-drag-out brawl. The Aeroflot stewardess, nothing daunted, rushed in again to mediate, the bystanders gave her a few friendly pinches on her ample bottom, and eventually she got everybody calmed down.

In a word, we landed. Safely. I breathed a prayer of thanks. As we were disembarking, a few more of our coeds had their butts grabbed. Jenny, a feminist, retaliated with a series of wild hooks and uppercuts, which gave her assailants something more to whoop about. Then it was over. The ground personnel quickly separated the Not Ours (us) from the Ours, and ushered the American group over to the Intourist section (a special waiting room for foreigners). Benito and Kostya showed up with our bus (Benito was the travel agent from the Georgian Republic, in charge of our arrangements in St. Petersburg and Moscow—Kostya was his right hand man).

It was maybe three a.m. when we landed, and at four-thirty we were still waiting for our luggage. My students were zonked out, sleeping on the dirty benches and unspeakably filthy floors, dreaming disgruntled dreams. I knew something was wrong, but the irrepressible Kostya, a good-natured Georgian with a Saadam Hussein mustache, assured me that we'd be getting our bags any moment now. We waited. I presumed the Azeris had got their paws on our Samsonite, or if not that, then the Petersburg baggage crew was busily pilfering. We waited.

The bags arrived at five a.m., miraculously undamaged, untouched. Only later, on the long ride across Petersburg to the Sportivnaya Hotel, did Kostya tell me there had been something of a riot by the fiery Bakuans. I'm not sure what the dispute was. Maybe the Petersburg stevedores wanted a bigger cut of the fruit and vegetables, before releasing them to the open-air markets. At any rate, the police arrived in force and finally got the hot-blooded Southerners under control.

It was five-thirty and totally light; White Nights season in St. Petersburg. We rode our Intourist bus through the streets, and I admired the morning sun rays, lambent upon the Italian architecture of what must be the most beautiful city on earth. My students were snoozing in their seats, exhausted. Well, we made it, I said to myself. Anyway, we made it, and no great harm done.

We tooled down Nevsky Prospect, crossed the Griboedov Canal, and in the distance, jutting out over the water, was the beautiful Church of the Saviour on the Blood, recently restored to its original splendor. Its multicolored domes have much in common with St. Basil's, the fairyland cathedral on Red Square in Moscow. It's called the Church on the Blood because it was built on the spot where the Tsar Liberator, Alexander II, was assassinated in 1881.

I took a deep breath, closed my eyes, started dozing off. Half asleep, I saw, through a dreamy haze, a scene from far back in my past. We were on a Western motor trip (Mommy, Daddy, Peggy and I). It was the year after Jacqi died, the summer of 1957. We were cruising down Highway 50 in South Dakota (near Yankton), parallel to Nebraska. We were very close to Nebraska and Mommy wanted to make a short detour across the border. She liked to see how many states she could say she had been in, and she had never been in Nebraska. Daddy, who was driving, wouldn't do it. It was a damn fool idea, he said, a waste of time. Why go to Nebraska just to say you'd been in Nebraska? An argument ensued, then a period of aggrieved and sullen silence. We drove on down Highway 50 in my dream, which took on a disturbing anxious tonality, getting farther and farther from Nebraska. We drove through South Dakota and crossed over into the state of Iowa. Then, as happens in dreams, there was a sudden switch of scenery and setting. I had a totally clear image of Tolya, back in his bed in Kiev, deeply asleep, a smile on his face, the new soccer ball under one arm and his wife's head under the other. He was dreaming a blissful dream of his empty safe, the one in his office, and the safe itself seemed to share his contentment. It opened its door to reveal its blessed vacuity, and it smiled back at Tolya.

I guess Tolya never found out about the nightmare flight he arranged for the American group. I never saw him again, so I didn't tell him. Maybe some day he'll hear this story I'm writing for you, Dan Spear. If you do,

Tolya, let me just say one thing. You're a good facilitator. How were you to know that it was Azerbaijanian Airlines you were putting us on? What could you have known about the swarthy men of the Soviet South?

It's true, isn't it? You weren't aware of what you were getting us into, booking us (how big was the bribe?) on a fully booked flight from Baku? I'd like to believe that you didn't know. I prefer to retain my faith in the basic decency of human beings. No. You're okay, Tolya. You did a fine job, son. You can be proud of the job you did.

6

Mr. Forsythe is relieved/ He wasn't shot after all/ Mamie Lee Floyd/ "A killer yet lurked"/ Lunacy proceedings/ Daddy goes fishing—hooks Austin Simpson/ Austin almost drowns, twice!/ "Who'll be driving my new car?"/ President felled by assassin's bullet/ The Lee Oswald Museum (Minsk, Belorus)/ The facts, and then again, the facts/ The all-white-boys crew/ Minnie Belle/ Simple Lavin/ "Muff Potter Is Going to Make It"/ Muff Potter doesn't make it/ Blooming yellow hibiscus/ Mosquito trucks fog field/ Little kids romp in poisons/ Billy Moon and I almost beat John Ellis/ (But not quite)/ Black speed/ Be kind/ "Sorry and nocount, but he can fish"/ We're all haters and lovers/ Cauley Lott/ Swiping Ace's briefcase/ Why are we the way we are?/ Because/ "You want some, Frank?"/ What happened at the Thunderbird Motel/ The Walking Jesus on the beach/ Why I hate t.v./ Temple oranges, semi-tart/ Gizzard shad and leukemia/ Kicking surf at New Smyrna/ Sellers Lovelady clips a notch in my ear/ His son, "John the Jew"/ Floating away in sea spray/ A speck of foam on a glistening belly/ Naught but deathly silence

I just had a sudden shock. Asked my research assistant in Mt. Dora to find out exactly when the East Town shooting took place. Well, he called up retired fire chief Kenneth Cox, and Ken, right off the top of his head, said, "Dec. 5 or 6, 1959." What a memory! So then they xeroxed me the front page story from *The Topic* files (dated Thursday, Dec. 10, 1959), and when I read that, boy oh boy! Never trust your memory; your memory is a storyteller. In a word, that tale I told you about the shooting isn't exactly how it happened.

Turns out it wasn't my neighbor Mr. Forsythe who was killed after all. I'm sure that's a relief for him, or would be if he hadn't died of cancer in 1967. He *was* an auxiliary policeman, and my memory must have found it appealing to make somebody I knew the one who got shot. But the dead man's name was actually Clinton M.("Jack") Hyde, of whom I have no recollection whatsoever. To quote from *The Topic*, "He was killed by the blast from a shotgun in the hands of a drink-crazed Negro itinerant, Joe Henderson, who then tried to kill Fireman George Hall." Officer Hyde was standing at the corner of Simpson and Grant, filling out a warrant for the arrest of Henderson, who had made threats against East Town resident Mamie Lee Floyd. At that moment the accused flung open the door to his shack, and Jack Hyde made the mistake of walking toward him and ordering him to come out.

It seems I also mangled up the part about George Hall and Doc Montgomery. It was really police chief Jim Orr who responded, along with George Hall, to the second phone call, and George (but not Jim) was shot shortly after he got out of the cruiser. Meanwhile, Dr. Robert Montgomery and his six-year-old son, Louis, were setting off for a fishing trip. They had one foot out the door when the phone rang. Apparently nobody mentioned any danger, so Doc Montgomery took his son along out to East Town, and Louis, as *The Topic* has it, "experienced stark terror as is seen in television westerns of (or?) the Hitchcock variety murder shows."

Mabel Norris Reese, *Topic* editor, had a bent for high melodrama: "There was naught but deathly silence as Dr. Montgomery pulled to a stop behind the police car Officer Hyde had been driving," she writes. Doc and his son, unaware that "a killer yet lurked behind a dusty screen door a few feet away," got out of their car and went to the aid of George Hall. As he bent over George, who was lying on top of his own pistol (it was later established that he had fired six times and wounded Joe Henderson), Doc heard a neighbor call out, "There's a man in there with a gun!" He grabbed Louis and ran back behind the police car just before the next blast came.

So Robert Montgomery wasn't shot after all, and neither was Mr. Forsythe, but at least I had the part about Buddles Ledford right. Buddles was the one who killed Joe Henderson, a man described by East Town residents as rarely sober. He had served a term for manslaughter, had been arrested in Ft. Lauderdale on murder charges, and "underwent lunacy proceedings in 1947."

It was a Saturday when all this happened, and I may well have been out trolling for bass on Lake Beauclaire with my father. Just think. There were no beepers back then. If Doc Montgomery and Louis had left home five minutes earlier, they would have missed the whole adventure, we would have crossed paths out on the lake, as we often did, and just at the moment when Buddles was firing the fatal shot we could have trolled past Doc and Louis, and Daddy would have waved and called out the jokey thing he always yelled to passing fishermen: "Got the limit?" It's interesting to contemplate the "could have beens" and "would have beens" that might have been if you went, or didn't go, someplace five minutes earlier, or later.

One time they were out casting for a change, instead of trolling— Uncle Dedrick, Austin Simpson, and my father—and Daddy got his plug hung up in some weeds. He jerked hard and it came loose, but then he couldn't figure where it went. He said to Austin, sitting in the back of the rowboat, "Hey, Simp, what the hell became of my plug?" And Austin answered, in a strange retard mumble (because he couldn't get his mouth to move): "It's in my guggum lip." That was the only time Daddy ever went fishing and caught Austin Simpson.

When they saw the plug hanging there, Uncle Dedrick and Daddy didn't know what to do. They weren't inclined to give up on the day's outing and head back into town, just to get that artificial lure out of Austin's lip. Then they had a brainstorm. They knew the spot where Doc Montgomery usually fished, so they cranked up the five horse Johnson and headed over to that end of the lake. Sure enough, Doc was there, and he cut the plug out of Austin's lip with one of those knives used to disembowel fish. Then everybody went back to trolling and casting.

My father had a lot of adventures with Austin. There was the time they almost drowned at Daytona Beach. They were taking a walk down the seashore, strolling along through shallow water, when they stepped into a riptide that carried them a mile out into the ocean. Austin swallowed a lot of water and panicked. He was coughing and choking. Daddy got him calmed down, stuck his finger down his throat, and all the salt water came up. Then they floated on their backs to conserve energy and started working their way back in, toward the beach. Austin was/is a great lover of cars. While he was floating on his back he said to Daddy, "Reckon if we don't make it back, Virginia will get another husband? And that sumbug will be driving my new Chevy."

Another time they got caught in a violent thunderstorm in the middle of Lake Dora and their rowboat overturned. Uncle Dedrick was in on that one. The three of them were clinging to the gunwales in wind and high waves, and luckily somebody in the fish camp happened to be looking out at the storm and saw the capsized boat. You've swallowed a lot of water in your life, Austin Simpson, and since that prostate operation a couple of years ago, you've had to take things a little bit slower. But you're tough! What's a piddling prostate dysfunction to a man who's spent a lifetime nearly drowning!

Anyway, it turns out that Doc, thank God, was not "felled by the bullets of a crazed itinerant," after that man had just murdered Officer Jack Hyde. The word "felled" reminds me of my "What were you doing when Kennedy was killed?" story. Well, I was sitting in the Steinbeck Theatre in Monterey, California, watching a Russian language movie with fellow students from the Army Language School. It was an opera by Tchaikovsky, based on Pushkin's story "The Queen of Spades." As soon as the movie ended the projectionist stuck a handwritten note up in the lens. It read, "President Kennedy felled by assassin's bullet in Dallas." That was all. Nobody knew at that point if he was alive or dead. The Russian instructor sitting next to me asked in a puzzled voice, in Russian, "What does it mean, the word 'felled'?" Later on I heard that back when Lee Oswald was living in Minsk, after he defected to the USSR, his favorite opera was "The Queen of Spades."

I was in Minsk myself in the summer of 1993, giving lectures to the Red Cross on how non profits in the West raise money. I suggested that a good fund raising venture would be to buy the apartment that Lee Oswald used to live in with his Russian wife Marina and make it into a museum. Every foreigner coming through Minsk would visit there—it would be the biggest tourist attraction in town. The Red Cross people in Minsk were shocked. "What?" they said. "Open a museum dedicated to a *murderer?*" The Russians still haven't figured out Western marketing strategies.

Well, for all that, I like the story my memory made up, about Doc,

George, and Mr. Forsythe, so I'll leave it the way it is in Chapter Four. Anybody looking for the facts can go out to the *Topic* office, which is over toward Eustis now, on Highway 19. Ask to see the old bound files and read the "stark tragedy" in the words of Mabel Norris Reese. But, truth be told, I bet she was wrong about that "naught but deathly silence" as Doc pulled up. Certainly there were whirring dragonflies in the air and the aggravating whines of mosquitoes, and the heart-rending coos of lugubrious mourning doves. In Mt. Dora, Florida, the air is permeated incessantly with those sounds.

Then again, I'm not sure *The Topic* is the definitive source for that incident either. Who has the facts, anyway? They say if you get five eyewitnesses to a murder, well, one of them will say a paunchy blond man did it, and another will say it was a slender African American, the third will swear she saw a one-legged dwarf running from the scene, and the other two will declare, "Murder? We wasn't there and we don't know nothing about no murder!"

So if you want the facts on the death of Jack Hyde, you'll have to compile a book of interviews. Give one chapter to Doc's recollections, another to George Hall's. Talk to Mamie Lee Floyd, Buddles Ledford, T.M. Thomas, Ralph Forsythe, Dwight Mosteller, Herman Kicklighter (from Umatilla). Ask Kenneth Cox and Beanie Creamons what they were doing that day. Find the East Town women in brassieres, who were out fanning themselves on their front porches. Of course, the book wouldn't be complete without the testimony of the two central figures: Joe Henderson and Jack Hyde. But getting the facts from them (and from others in the list above) would require a long journey down the road called The Way of All Flesh.

In the summer of 1957 (or was it 1956?) I got a job harvesting corn at Zellwin Farms, in Zellwood, Florida, five miles from Mt. Dora. A blip in the road (Highway 441) on the way to Orlando, Zellwood was the home of C. M. Jones, the Gardner brothers (Ronnie and Richard), and the Potter boys (Gary, Jan, and Del Gene). Zellwood's economy was dependent on the "muck farms," which provide rich soil for growing vegetables on what was once the bottom of Lake Apopka. Gary and Jan Potter ended up with me that summer, on the "all-white-boys" crew, along with Herbert Flavell, John Lavin, whose nickname was 'Simple,' and a lot of others from MDHS. We were hired by Neil Stoothoff's father, Herbert, who worked for Zellwin as chief harvesting foreman. Our salary was sixty-five cents an hour.

June in Florida is already hot beyond all measure. Our co-workers on the other crews, local blacks and migrant laborers from the Caribbean, didn't seem to mind the heat. But we, pampered children of the middle class, found out quickly what twelve hours in the sun could do to you. The work day began at 7:00 a.m. and ended at 7:00 p.m.; we had a thirty minute lunch break at noon. By 8:00 a.m. the sun had devoured what little coolness was left in the air from the previous night, and we were praying for some shade to stand in. But a corn field has no shade. By 8:30 John Lavin began bleating out his favorite refrain: "What time is it?" He didn't really want to hear the answer, though, because the answer meant we had three and a half hours to go before lunch.

They ran a big truck down the corn rows ahead of us. We followed behind, ripping the ears from the stalks and tossing them up into the back of the truck. Someone was always falling off the pace. The truck would be slowly pulling out of range, and John Lavin would be frantically grabbing at his corn stalks, making long-distance heaves toward the target, yelling, "Hold the truck!" A good many of those tosses missed altogether and fell on the ground. The foreman of our all-white-boys crew was a wizened little black woman, Minnie Bell Jones. She didn't make any direct criticism of the white boys' efforts, but you could tell from the squint in her eye that she was wondering how she got herself into this mess.

We worked at a dragging pace, stopping all the time, to let the laggards catch up. Periodically Mr. Stoothoff, a burly man with a perpetual scowl, would drive by in his pickup, and he and Minnie Bell would confer. After that he wouldn't say anything, but he'd glare over at our sorry bunch before driving off. We'd go back to work, the truck would chug along ahead of us. John would start cursing, yelling, "OOOWW! Sticker bushes! Watch out for the damn sticker bushes in here!" Soon he and me and several others were behind again, screaming, "Hold the truck!" and desperately heaving ears of corn. Then Minnie Bell would call out, in a high voice dripping lassitude, "Hold de truck, driver."

Our white boys crew was working side by side with a black girls crew. It took only about twenty minutes at the beginning of the day for those black girls to leave us far behind, wallowing ignominiously in our own ineptitude. Within an hour they were rows ahead of us, and by lunch break they were out of sight. I'd like to see the statistics. How many more truckloads of corn did those girls pick than us in the course of one day? I'm sure Herbert Stoothoff knew.

There was one exceptionally nubile black girl in that bunch. Maybe fifteen years old. Very well built. Before we started in the morning some of the white boys would be looking over there and talking big about what they'd like to do with her. They were even making plans, figuring they could lead her astray amidst distant corn stalks, during lunch break. But soon their plans were forgotten. By nine o'clock the black girls crew was no longer visible and the white boys were passing out with heat stroke.

We'd be dragging along, falling behind, hollering, "Hold the truck, hold that damn truck!" Minnie Bell never removed the inscrutable look she wore on her squinched-up face. She would call out in that slow voice, "Hold de truck, driver." We'd catch up, then we'd wait for John, who was fuming and blaspheming, frantically ripping at the corn stalks. "C'mon, Lavin, move your ass," somebody would yell. "Simple Lavin," said somebody else.

Then we laughed, all but Minnie Bell, as John cursed even louder, picking and tossing, still missing the truck with half of what he threw.

When he finally caught up, Minnie Bell called out wearily, "Move on down de line, driver," and off we'd go again. But then somebody would collapse into the corn stalks. One time, I remember, it was Ben Haas (I think he was Henry's brother). Minnie Bell called, "Hold de truck, driver," while the rest of us gathered around the victim. Somebody went to find Mr. Stoothoff, and a few minutes later he drove up with a barrel of water. He stood around looking disgusted while we poured water over Ben's head and got him back on his feet. After that Mr. Stoothoff drove the casualty away in his pickup, Minnie Bell gave her tired clarion call ("Move on down de line"), and the redoubtable white boys crew plodded on.

Why didn't I quit that job? Too dumb, I guess, or too stubborn. The torment of the heat sure wasn't worth the money we made. Looking back on that cornfield, I can honestly say that I never knew any heat worse than that. Not even at your two-a-day summer football practices, Dan Spear, though I was more thirsty then. Those were the days when you weren't allowed to drink water during football practice. Apparently there was a reason for that. To make us tough? I don't remember. After practice we took salt pills, and I hear they've reversed their opinion on that one too. Nowadays water is good for football players and salt is bad.

Anyway, I would go home after practice and eat oranges, gulp water all evening, Hawaiian punch, grape juice, anything to counter the dehydration. I'm surprised there weren't more boys dying of heat exhaustion on Florida football fields back in the fifties. As for those Cornfields of Hades at Zellwin Farms, none of the all-white-boys crew died that year, but a lot didn't make it through the three weeks of the corn picking season. Among the survivors were me, John Lavin and Gary Potter.

I remember once riding away from the fields at the end of the day, in the back of the truck with all the other workers (black girls, white boys,

Puerto Ricans, black women, black kids), a truck bed reeking in enervation and sweat. We, the mighty white boys crew, were so happy to be done with it one more time that we broke into song. We serenaded John Lavin with his favorite, the Ricky Nelson hit, "Poor Little Fool." John was in unrequited love back then, and he used to wallow in the misery of that song.

John Lavin. A decent person. When I look back upon the whole of my past in Mt. Dora, Florida, that's what strikes me most of all: how many basically good human beings, like John Lavin, there were all around me. People really are okay, you know that, Dan Spear? There's hope for the human race.

As we sang in the truck bed I noticed a horny Caribbean migrant worker making heavy advances on a local black woman. She just sat there wearily, bouncing along with the truck, too tired to care, while he was feeling her up in a variety of spots. I was astounded. Blatant and open sexuality. As an adolescent I had an incredibly naive view of life.

Thinking of those searing corn fields now, I'm amazed by something else: that Gary Potter made it through the picking season. Although no one could have known, he had very little time to live. We would get a good laugh out of his getup when he first arrived in the morning. He was all in white: white shirt, white pants, even white socks. He had learned somewhere that white reflects sunlight and heat. Everything fit him very loosely and seemed to be made of sheets. He was also wearing a straw hat of enormous breadth. He'd come ambling up in his whites and sombrero, mimicking the loping gait of The Walking Jesus, smiling that Potter smile, with his bugged-out blue Potter eyes, and we'd all fall down on the ground laughing.

Gary had Bright's disease, and his kidneys were degenerating. *The Mt. Dora Topic* story (Dec. 19, 1957) has the following headline: "Gary Is Going to Make It—It's a Happy Refrain at MDHS." At that time he was in Piedmont Hospital in Atlanta, recovering from a near fatal relapse. I don't have vivid recollections of that. Maybe because in December of 1957 I myself was in the Orlando hospital, Orange Memorial, where they operated on my bad right leg.

By the spring of 1958 he was missing classes, feeling worse all the time. He had to check into Orange Memorial for a short stay, and I still have a letter he wrote me from there. His girl friend was blonde blue-eyed Judy Sadler, "The Queen of Tangerine." One night, when she and he were sitting in Gary's neat little M.G., at the favorite dating spot of Lake County—the Movie Garden Drive-In Theater—he had an attack of nausea. Judy, who didn't know how to shift the gears on the M.G., had to do her best at driving him home. We heard about this at school, but we weren't sure exactly what to make of it.

In the spring before we graduated, Gary, C.M. and I were hired to clean up a vacant lot in Zellwood, for C.M.'s grandfather, Claude Marion Jones. We took a break in the middle of the day, C.M. went down the street to pick up something at his house, and Gary Potter started talking to me about death. He said, "I wonder what it's like to die. I guess it's not so bad for old people, is it? After all, they've lived out their lives, they've got kids and grandchildren and everything. I suppose they're ready to go."

I was taken aback. Never had he, or any of my friends, brought this subject up. I knew something about dying already, but I didn't like talking about it. When it comes down to things that really matter, people can't find the right words. So I just said, "Well, I really doubt that, you know. I doubt that even old people are ready to die. Nobody wants to die. You know?"

He thought about it for a minute, and then he said, "Yeah, I guess you're right. Nobody wants to die." After that we went back to clearing brush on that lot, and we never talked about death again.

Gary Potter died a few months later, in July, 1958. C.M. went over to visit him in the last days, at the Orange Memorial Hospital. There was no conversation; Gary was beyond talking. C.M. told me he was sorry he had gone, wished he hadn't seen him like that. I didn't want to go. I knew what a person looked like toward the end. The funeral was another wild wailing business, like the funeral for Ronnie Gardner. Joan McDonald, a classmate and soprano, sang at the service, weeping as she sang. I was there, with C.M. and Butch Alexander, but none of us cried. Males weren't supposed to cry, but my insides were dripping misery.

The main thing I remember from that funeral was the way Judy Sadler looked at me. The three of us, C.M., Butch and I, were just entering the foyer of the chapel when she walked past. Understandably, she was in bad shape. Her blonde hair was not all in place, the way it usually was. Her eyes were washed out, faded with tears. She didn't acknowledge our presence. She walked by without speaking, but as she passed us she raised those blue eyes and glanced at me with a look of pure hatred. As if to say, "Why is it? Why do you deserve life and he doesn't?" I'm sure she wouldn't remember, but I can recall that look to this very day.

When I think back on Gary ("Muff") Potter, I recall, first of all, the old "Potter gang," of which I was a member. We used to do some friendly terrorizing of the younger classes, and I think they enjoyed it as much as we did. Whenever we descended upon Spencer Beebe he would scream with simulated fear, "Aaaaiieee, it's the Potter gang!" Even though I was a member in good standing, I was not immune to attack. I lived so near the school that throughout my twelve years in the Mt. Dora public education system I always went home for lunch. In my high school days I would cross Clayton St., enter the orange grove just past Pap Schott's place, walk through the trees and end up at the back door of our pink house.

My mother would have lunch ready when I arrived. We would eat together, silently, and then I would take the same route back. In the tenth grade the notorious Potter gang began hiding out in the orange grove, ambushing me on my return journey. They (Gary Potter, C.M. Jones, Larry Smith, Jack Alexander) would attack, and I would take off running. After a long pursuit we would end up on the blind alley where Frank Stewart used to live, by the fence with the flame vine, behind the gym. Whether they caught me or not depended on whether I had time to climb over that flame vine and back onto the school grounds. But even if they caught me nothing happened. The fun was in the pursuit of the quarry, not in the capture. When we caught Spencer Beebe we never knew what to do with him either. So we just let him go.

Muff Potter with his easy grin, Muff Potter playing cornet in the Manuel J. Sedano Memorial Band, marching along in one of those hot woolen orange band uniforms, obviously manufactured by a company in Ohio, where September has some coolness in the air, Muff Potter tooting his horn with his bug-eyed Potter look. He was still with us on that glorious night of Nov. 1, 1957, wearing his white Riddell helmet with the face-protector bar, in his orange home football jersey, Number 41, with that Muff Potter grin on his face, trotting back out to the field after the halftime break, past the flame vine on the fence, past the white stucco house where I used to live, with the yellow blooming hibiscus out front.

The band (which so many of us were a part of, when we weren't playing football—Jack, Gary, C.M., me, Spencer Beebe) had concluded its halftime performance. The marchers in their orange woolen coats were putting aside their instruments, and the majorettes were cooling their well-twirled batons. The mosquito truck was making its final run around the field, blowing smoke, trailing whooping little kids in its wake. The four or five small boys who had left off romping behind the truck to start a game of tackle football cleared off the field. The mongrel dog loped after them. When he got off the field somebody finally caught him, and he rolled over on his back into a submissive position (Okay, I give up; just don't beat me). They grabbed him by the scruff of the neck, where a collar should have been, escorted him to the big gate by the playground on the home side, and booted him out onto Seventh Avenue. After that he raised his tail back up, trotted off uphill, sniffing and cocking a leg at every camphor tree, every palmetto bush, every oleander. Take a last look at him; you won't meet him again in our story. He's black, with a white strip on his chest and a patch of white on one ear. The other ear, bitten once too often, kind of droops down. He's not the least concerned that he's an "integrated" dog with one defective ear. He takes life as he's got it and feels grateful to God that he can do what he really loves: piss on trees and telephone poles. What has become of him now, you might ask, thirty-seven years later? Well, he's up in dog heaven, cocking a leg beside wisps of clouds, sniffing at hems of the dog angels' gowns, still smiling.

Bishop Moore was sitting around in small clusters of gold and black, down by the far goal posts again, in front of Kenny Atkins' house. As we jogged out and got into formation for the group calisthenics, our cheerleaders ran toward us with welcoming cries, waving their arms about. Some of them stopped and beckoned to the stands, inciting the crowd. The denizens of Mt. Dora greeted the mighty Golden Hurricanes with whistles, Rebel yells, cheers. I don't think they were laughing any more. They were hoping now, but, like ours, their hope was cautious. They didn't dare hope too hard.

B.M. kicked off (or we did), and the third quarter began. There were a lot of kickoffs in the second half, and I still don't know why, but Bishop Moore kept kicking the ball to me. On account of my injury, Coach Spear had me lined up at left halfback. Stoothoff was in the center, receiving position, and ordinarily the ball would be booted straight down field, to him. Maybe Coach Bryan had told his kicker to aim for the crippled halfback. So they kicked it to me and I started running wild, bringing back every kickoff for huge yardage.

Am I bragging? No. I'm praising my blockers! God, the space they gave me to run in that night! What does a running back love more than space? It was like driving across Nevada. On those kickoffs somebody was doing some racking! Thanks, Fred Thibault, thanks Owen McCallister! You too, John Lavin, Donny Dake, Billy Vanzant. I'm also praising my bad leg. By the third quarter I knew with certitude what the first half had already suggested. That a wondrous something had occurred. My right leg was harkening back to the pure speed of the year before. My toes, in my magic low-top Kangaroos, were laughing, saying, "Don't worry, Bobby Booby. We've got it back. Deep down beneath all the tape, in the muscles, the pure speed is there. Just dig it out and turn it on."

So I listened to the laughing toes and the leg, I grabbed those kickoffs, and I turned on the afterburners. Ah, the joys of fast running! Herschel Stone just got lucky over at Tavares that night. After all, he had the angle on me all the way. And I never saw him coming, not until a split second before he hit me. If I'd seen him I'd have picked it up to a higher gear. Herschel Stone doesn't exist. Tonight you can put me up against John Ellis and we'll see who's fast! Bring back Billy Odom, the greatest halfback in the history of MDHS. He's up at FSU now, playing football with Burt Reynolds. Bring him back! I'll run him in the ground!

The third quarter was a crazy seesawing business. They ran on us, then we ran on them, then they ran on us. Lots of yards were gained. No passing to speak of, though. Everything on the ground. Mt. Dora on offense, moving with the ball. Blocking, racking people, knocking them down. On defense backing up and holding, chasing down Ellis when he went wide, digging in, giving ground, gang tackling Musante up the middle. God, it was fun, Dan Spear! It's just a shame you couldn't have been in it yourself.

Near the beginning of the quarter I remember one play, when I took a handoff deep in our own territory, and headed around left end. I ran into heavy traffic, cut sharply back against the grain, and found a lot of space.

Moving laterally, down what had just been the line of scrimmage, I saw Billy Moon standing in the middle of the field. It was weird. There wasn't a soul standing except Billy Moon, and he was yelling, "Follow me!" We headed down the right sideline, him running interference, right past the Bishop Moore bench. How did Barry Keitel look as we ran by him? What I'd give for a video chronicle of all of Mr. Keitel's facial expressions that night, beginning with what I actually saw before the game, when I was up on the ping-pong table.

Billy Moon and I got out in front of the whole Bishop Moore team, most of whom had over-pursued to their right and now had to get back in a hurry to the other side of the field. Finally, there was only the safety man left to beat, the star, John Ellis. He was giving ground, knowing he was the last man, giving ground, buying time. Billy Moon would steer him off to the left and I'd try to break free to the right. Then Billy Moon would take him to the right and I'd head back left. But Ellis kept giving ground, forearm shiver, backing up, holding him off, and Billy Moon couldn't knock him down and I couldn't get around him.

We weren't making very good time, and I was afraid somebody would catch me from behind, so I feinted right, then put on a burst of speed and broke to the inside. Ellis liked to tackle high; I knew that because I'd watched him play against Eustis. So my stiff arm was ready to use on his face when it came at me. I almost made it past Ellis, but he climbed over Moon through my stiff arm and up on my back, and he rode me ten more yards down the field before slipping off. Trouble was he hit my left foot on the way down. Trying to recover my balance, I stumbled another few yards, but finally fell. No touchdown, but a sixty-seven yard gain from scrimmage, the longest run I ever made without crossing the goal line. Stoothoff ended up scoring after that, on a twenty-six yard run.

What a night Neil Stoothoff had! Later in the same quarter John Lavin recovered a fumble on the Bishop Moore forty yard line, and Neil took it in for a touchdown again, this time on a run of thirty-two yards. We scored thirteen points in the third quarter. We were ahead, 26-6! That's when somebody dared to think, on our side of the field, or in the stands, or on the bench, somebody from Mt. Dora dared think, "We're going to win this game!" That jinxed us, when somebody thought that. Who was it, who was the culprit? L. Earle Williams doesn't count; he was thinking that way all along. Was it team physician Doc Montgomery? Was it you, Dan Spear?

We were just supposed to keep on laughing our way through this one; we shouldn't have made any assumptions. But then someone dropped the cautious hoping and hoped hard and loud, and Fate unleashed the Ellis boys. John Ellis had a forty yard touchdown run, and Jim Ellis scored on a plunge, after a fifty-five yard drive. Thirteen more points for their side: 26-19. Hold that line!

It was a wild, wild football game. I was totally in the spirit of it. Wild. Why was I so happy? Because I was laughing at the world, with the world. I didn't have to think about religious conflicts, racial tensions, death. But, above all, because the pure speed was back. The "black speed."

People I grew up with used to say, "Spades are such good athletes because they just crawled out of the jungles of Africa. They still got a lot of wild animal in them, so it's no surprise they can run." Let me speak one last time on the subject of race. I doubt if I can explain this to people who write books saying that all Germans are guilty for slaughtering Jews or that Germans did something that civilized folks, like us, could never do. Well, these people have one big problem: they don't want to admit that we human beings are the way we are.

Easy answers are so much easier. If I say there are all different degrees of bigotry, your everyday average American (even a professor in a university) doesn't want to hear that. He knows right from wrong (so he thinks), he knows what a bigot is, and a bigot is always bad. Wrong. I grew up with bigots all around me, I was a semi-bigot too, and I can tell you that bigotry, like life, is an intricate business.

People embrace consensus opinions because that's so much easier than thinking for yourself, and because if you go with the mores of the society, you don't get much flak. The most common stance at MDHS was just not to say much about the race issue. Take, for example, the assistant principal of the school, Ronald E. Aldrich. He was from the North, a Yankee, and naturally a lot of people hated him, on principle, just for that. He was not a racist either, but I never heard him beating the drums for integration. As for Nana T. Laney, she was too intelligent not to see all sides of the issue. I'm sure of that. But she, too, kept her opinions to herself and concentrated on her beloved literature. The great majority, mainly, keeps quiet. Is that so surprising? Most folks don't want to make big waves and then have to swim in them. Most prefer floating on their backs in the sunshine.

Standing in what is the camp of consensus today, looking back and calling people names is easy too. The modern, closed-minded, "politically correct" thinkers of the world might call Prof Roseborough a bigot. He originally came from Tennessee, and he was imbued with the attitudes of a white Southerner. He didn't use the word 'nigger' though, as did some of our teachers. He preferred the more genteel terms of the fifties. When he got off on the race issue in his civics class, he would talk about the 'Niggras' or the 'colored folks.' Once, when one of my most viciously black-hating classmates made a highly flavored remark in that civics class, Prof Roseborough didn't try to contradict him. Prof just said, in that slow calm drawl of his, "Now, Boone... Be kind, Boone, be kind."

As for me, if I had been the standard generic bigot that many citizens of Lake County were, it would have been a lot simpler. But being in a household where opposite opinions are perpetually voiced tends to make you think. When the arguments at our dinner table weren't about religion they were about race. Mommy was a Yankee, on the wrong side in the Civil War, from Daddy's point of view. Besides that, she was out of tune with the "niggerism" of the South. By that term I mean the tendency of the white Southerner to be obsessed with the blacks who lived apart from him, but all around him. Maybe the only thing comparable is the complicated thing that Slavs have for Jews in Eastern Europe. Back when I was a kid, a lot of white Southerners thought about "niggers" all day long, and when they went to sleep at night they dreamed "niggers." My mother was from New Jersey, and she couldn't understand that. Of course, I grew up in the South, but can't say I really understand it either.

I remember the soliloquies of the man we called Uncle Dedrick (not really an uncle, but a family friend), who lived only a couple of blocks away and often went fishing with us. Whatever topic you began with, Uncle Dedrick would bring it around to the issue of "niggers." In other words, we could be watching the speedboat regattas on Lake Dora, talking about the powerboats, and Dedrick would notice a boat painted black and white and call it an "integrated boat." You could say, "Hey, look at that blimp up there!" and Uncle Dedrick would say, "One thing you can bet on, it's a white man running that blimp. Take a nigger, he ain't got the brains to drive a blimp. Too damn dumb. He can chunk him a spear, but you put him up on a machine, tell him to run it, and he'll set up there with his mouth open and his thumb up his ass, right to the elbow. A nigger can fish, though, I'll give him that. A nigger can smell the shell crackers a mile off. So if you want to catch you some shell crackers, why, you just watch where the spear chunkers congregate, and sho nuff, that's where the best fishing's going to be. I don't see how they do it. You know, a nigger's sorry and nocount, but a nigger's got a nose that can sniff out fish."

Now, Uncle Dedrick wasn't sitting at our dinner table, but my father might sometimes repeat what he said, and that's when the fireworks began. Of course, Mommy was living in a town where that talk was on every street

corner, in the beauticians' shops, in the schools, churches, in the Rexall
Drug Store and Princess Theatre downtown, but she wouldn't put up with
it at her own dinner table. So, in a word, there we sat, for the years of our
childhood and adolescence, we kids, eating fried fish, conk peas, slimy okra,
collards and cornbread, in one of three different houses on Seventh Avenue
(the white, the green, the pink), listening to opposite sides of every story.

Some of my schoolmates complicated things even further, because
they knew I was born in New Jersey. "You ain't even from the South," they
would say. "You're a damn Yankee, and a nigger lover too." Well, to some
extent they were right—the side of me that was influenced by my mother
was Northern and non-racist. But then you put that together with the side
of me that I got from my father. And what do you end up with? Well, I can't
speak for my sisters, but me, aged seventeen on the day this story is set, Nov.
1, 1957, I could have been characterized as a Catholic-hating, Protestant-
hating semi-Catholic semi-Protestant, and a nigger-loving Negro-hating
basically fair-minded unbigoted bigoted semi-racist. Something like that.

Let me just emphasize one central fact though. My mother was a good
woman and my father was a good man. You might think I'm taking my
mother's side, because she was not racially prejudiced. Well, everybody's
prejudiced in one way or another—it's human nature. Biologically we're
haters and lovers both. People who get up on their sanctimonious high
horses and start condemning human behavior ought to dismount and take
a good deep look into their own insides.

Mommy grew up in the great melting pot of the Northeast. She used
to look at Dan Spear's Eastern European face and wonder out loud what his
real name was (Sperlovich? Spirlunsky?). Years later I asked him about that,
and he said his family came, originally, from Serbia, and the name, as long
as he had known it, was 'Spear.' Could have been spelled different at one

time. My mother's Irish parents had taught her disparaging terms that we didn't hear much in the South. All we knew was "nigger, nigger, nigger," with an occasional "po white trash" thrown in. She knew "hunkie spic polack kike wop, etc." Not that she used those terms with vicious spite, but they passed her lips. Nowadays they would put her on "diversity training." Well, she wasn't perfect. Nobody's perfect.

Daddy was a good man. You, who have lived in Mt. Dora, Florida, for so many years, Dan Spear, you knew him and you know he was a good man. You also understand what I'm saying about how complicated the human race can be. You're not like the modern thought police, who take people and box them up in simpleminded little boxes with clear labels on the lids. Nope, sorry, thought police. It won't work. People are just too damn complicated for that. My daddy may have been indoctrinated in childhood, like so many of us are. But no matter how much family, genes, and society mess you up, you can still retain some human decency. Nana T. Laney, Ronald E. Aldrich, Dan Spear, Eudell Sutley, and a whole lot of other Mt. Dora teachers did. Florence Atkins did. Bud Huett. Margaret Morton. Doc Walker. Sam Shaw. Jimmie Jones. Right here I could give you a long, long list of names from people of the once older, and now frequently dead generation, from the Mt. Dora, Florida, of the fifties. But I won't go on for fear of leaving somebody out. There are so many worth mentioning.

Now, I didn't know too many people from East Town. But I bet you that a lot of folks out there, with all the intermingled good and bad in their souls, with all they had to suffer from the abuse of their own loved ones, from their spiteful neighbors, and from the white world that looked upon them as scum, I bet a lot of them turned out to be decent human beings too. Take Cauley Lott, principal of the black school, I didn't know him very well, but I would see him around town. He didn't come on loud and proud, "acting black" like some urban Negroes do today. Cauley Lott was proud in a quiet dignified way that showed he believed in himself. That's the kind of "black pride" that holds hope for the future. If only it can overcome the exaltation of macho violence and the irresponsibility.

So there is cause for optimism. Folks, black and white, can transcend it all: the rancor and hatred that roils inside us, the nastiness instilled by genes, parents, society. Everything. That doesn't mean they end up perfect angels. No. But they end up human beings. Me, I'd settle for turning out as decent as Prof D.D. Roseborough. Not likely I can achieve that, though.

Things got even more complicated in our little family drama when the New Jersey relatives were around. They backed my mother in her struggle to reclaim the kids for Catholicism. But Daddy never wavered from his original decision, and the battle went on. I don't remember any direct confrontations with the relatives. Mainly there was just that constraint in the air when they came to visit. Trouble was, my daddy was an angry man, and some of those Jersey relatives were angry men too (why are there so many of us choleric types on earth, Coach Spear?). When Uncle Horace came to visit everything was okay until they had a few drinks, and then matters could get delicate. Of course, the volatile issue of religion underlay most of the animosity, but they kept that box of smoldering cinders clamped shut, afraid that if they opened it, the whole house would go up in flames.

I spent a lot of my childhood listening to grownups and watching them. One time it was maybe ten p.m., and Horace had passed through several stages in the drinking process: happy, euphoric, altruistic. Now he had entered a new mode, the aggressive. The antagonistic. He was sitting, looking at my father. Not saying much, just sipping occasionally from his glass, glaring. Mommy and Aunt Dolores were off on some jolly conversation of their own, paying little attention to the men, breaking, periodically, into that characteristic Handerhan cackle they both used. I was watching.

Uncle Horace finished off the whiskey in his glass, clinked around the ice in the bottom, stared over at my father, and said, very slowly, slurring his words: "You know what you are, Bob? Huh?"

"What did you say?"

"I *said*," said Uncle Horace, in a loud and nasty voice. "I *said*, 'Do you know what you are?'"

"No, I don't know what I am. You tell me. What am I?"

Horace just glared for a minute, eyes glazed, then he repeated his question:

"You know whatchew are, Bob? Huh? You know whatcheware?"

At this point Dolores intervened. Horace was getting loud and she tried to shush him up, but he wasn't about to be shushed. He spent another five minutes asking that question, staring blear-eyed at Daddy. Then, finally, he answered it himself, running the words together:

"You're a sumuvabitch, that's what you are, Bob. You're a sumuvabitch."

After that he went off to the kitchen to get another drink.

Horace is dead now, and I wouldn't want to leave the impression from this one scene that I didn't like him. Uncle Horace was a gentle man. But, like all of us, he could get emotional.

1956. It was such a big year in my life. I'm sitting here trying to conjure up memories from that year, and what I get is a jumble of isolated incidents. Some of them involve the crassness of adolescence. School life is replete with casual cruelties, perpetuated by students upon fellow students. The weak suffer indignities and impose more indignities upon the weaker. I took my share of the abuse (until I became a football hero), and gave my share too. For example, in the eleventh grade I did my best to make life miserable for band director George Moore. I also took delight in the mob spirit of "Yeah, Smith," and helped torment Ronnie Aldrich by swiping his briefcase in Mrs. Cassady's social studies class.

When I look back on my youth, it's amazing how many things I'm ashamed of. During our time on earth we should strive for compassion toward our fellow man. But as long as the human spirit takes joy in cruelty (and it does, oh yes) goodness cannot totally prevail. Why are we the way we are? Why, Mr. Spear? They say modern scientists are getting close to the solution. A recent theory is that we are all kidnapped by space creatures in our infancy. Those little green humanoids do experiments on us, implanting ten billion contradictory smaragds of personality in our souls. Then they bring us back to earth and gleefully float around in their saucers above, watching the fireworks.

In 1956 I can imagine them as spectators at the beer-drinking games of four on one with the Pistolville girls. There were numerous incidents I knew of, and you, Coach Spear, were aware of at least one of them too. I overheard the talk you had with a player on our team, one of the most likeable boys you could hope to meet. It surprised me, the fatherly, solicitous way you spoke. Not your usual angry tone. I heard you telling him that this was not the kind of thing he should be doing. It was demeaning to his dignity, you said, and it was "uncouth." It always struck me as odd that you loved such a hundred dollar word.

What he, and some of his friends, had done was this. They had taken to driving out to Pistolville after dark. They had taken to stopping off at a certain shack and picking up a certain high school girl, quite a nice person, but fat. In a word, they would place her in the back seat of their car, in a prone position, while driving around, drinking beer, and taking turns.

Another classmate of mine, L. J. Jacobs, once described to me that identical high school sport. He, Ronnie Starkus, and Frank Laughtery had a friend named Carol, a "full-figured" blonde girl. L. J. told me, laughing, how they had taken her for a drive the previous evening, out by Trimble Park. How Ronnie was zipping up his pants in the back seat, and how Carol, on her back, called out cheerfully to Frank, who was riding shotgun up front. She said, "What about you, Frank? You want some?" And Frank, who was busy shooting the shit to L. J. and working on his bottle of Pabst Blue Ribbon, said politely, "No, thanks. Not right now, Carol. Maybe a little bit later."

Ronnie Starkus was a skinny fellow with whitish hair and a dumb expression on his face. There was something of the albino about him. His main claim to fame was the incident with the giant homosexual over at Daytona Beach. It seems Ronnie was at Daytona on a beer drinking weekend. Somehow he got separated from his buddies and ended up sitting beside this big friendly guy in a bar. They drank for a while, talked, and then the big guy said, "Let's go out and see if we can't find some pussy." He and Ronnie circulated around a few more bars, and then the guy said he needed to go back to his room, at the Thunderbird Motel, to pick up some money. Well, once he got the innocent, and now quite drunken Ronnie into his room, this huge fellow overpowered him and did unspeakable things to him on the bed. So that for weeks after that Frank Laughtery, Ronnie's closest friend, kept telling everybody that Ronnie was busily composing, for publication, a true confession. Its title, said jokey Frank, was: "I Was Cornholed by a Two-Hundred-Eighty-Pound Queer at the Thunderbird Motel in Daytona Beach, Florida."

Speaking of Daytona, Waiford Bedford told me that once, in the late fifties, he saw The Walking Jesus there, strolling down the beach and kicking salt water with his big bare feet, white satin pants rolled up to the knees. He walked far and wide, apparently, The Walking Jesus did, but he confined most of his rambles to the streets of Mt. Dora and Sorrento. People waved at him all the time, but he wouldn't wave back. What I'd give to know what was running incessantly, relentlessly through the whacko mind of The Walking Jesus!

I grew up without t.v. In the early fifties t.v. was something like air conditioning—only the rich folks out in Sylvan Shores had it. Then, gradually it spread to the middle class. With voices steeped in awe people used to talk about the nights when the weather was right, and "Both Jacksonville channels were coming in perfectly clear!" In the beginning those with sets would invite their friends over, but if you got invited on a bad reception night, all you watched was the snowy screen. Then came 1956 and the new Orlando stations! Wonderful! Clear pictures! After that everybody bought sets and started watching and watching the wonderful stuff (Milton Berle, Kukla, Fran and Ollie, Jackie Gleason, Palladin).

Having lived through a childhood without t.v., I never did get addicted. Not to this very day. What a blessing it would be for the children of modern America. Growing up without t.v.! Think of all the free time to do interesting things! Like the things that MDHS teens were doing in my time: eating burgers at the Dixie Drive-In, cruising around in their cars, drag racing, stopping by for take-out beer at Fatso's, in Tangerine (with its unwritten sign: "Fatso's Place: Where the Under-Aged Are Valued Customers"), then cruising around some more while drinking that beer, listening to Little Richard on the car radio, sneaking into melon patches to swipe watermelons, getting up an orange fight, eating Japanese plums.

My mother loved t.v., but my daddy hated it. Mommy would sit there by herself at night, watching her programs, breaking into her loud cackling laugh at the antics of, say, Jack Benny. Daddy, who always got up at six a.m. for work, would don his striped pyjamas, put on his grits for their overnight soaking (Mommy didn't like grits), go into the bathroom and brush his teeth. He would be in bed by nine.

A few minutes after he said his good nights, there would come a doleful call from the bedroom: "Turn that damn thing down." Mommy would turn it down, but never low enough for Daddy. He would traipse out of the bedroom in his baggy pyjamas, bend down in front of the t.v., and, sticking out the tip of his tongue, the way he always did when a job required manual dexterity, he would adjust the volume. Of course, he got it down so low that it was inaudible, and after he went back to bed she would turn it up again. Then the game would start all over with another growl from the bedroom: "Turn that damn thing down."

1956. One day in May of that year I was idly fiddling with a tennis ball. I was standing in the orange grove behind our pink house, out by the little shed. There were some stumps there, left over from dead trees, and I was bouncing the ball off those stumps. Daddy had put in little temple trees in that open area, and by the mid fifties they were starting to bear. Do you like temple oranges, Coach Spear? I think that the red blood of the ruby orange is God's gift to the taste buds, but, next to rubies, semi-tart temples are the most luscious fruits on earth.

My father came out to talk to me, and while he talked I didn't say anything. I just kept bouncing that ball. He told me there was no treatment locally that could do anything for her. They had decided to take her up to Boston, to Children's Hospital, where they could get her the best care available. If there was a chance of finding a cure, that's where it could be done.

I didn't say anything. My brain was enveloped in a daze. Nodding to Daddy, I kept on bouncing the ball. Some thoughts are unthinkable, so you don't allow yourself to think them. Daddy went back to the house and I stayed out in the grove with that tennis ball.

My parents took her to Boston. Daddy was there for only a week; he had to be back at his job. She and Mommy stayed on in Boston until June 20, came home, then had to return on July 23. I know these exact dates because I recently reread back issues of *The Mt. Dora Topic*, where there is a running commentary over a period of several months. See, e.g., the big front page article of Oct. 4, 1956: "Little Jacqi Awaits a Triumph in that Silent Battle Within."

That was the year the rest of us rented a cottage on the beach at New Smyrna: my father, my older sister June, me, my little sister Peggy. Daddy was working three days and spending the rest of the week with us. We had that beach house for much of the summer. Meanwhile, back home, the "gizzard shad were infesting the larger lakes of the county" (*Topic*, July 19, 1956). Do you remember the gizzard shad of 1956, Carol Schey, Donald Reichert, Gordon Schieber, Joe Graf, Sue Bond, Henry Haas, Roger Roach, Claude Fralick, Jimmy Malone, Robert Morehead, Phyllis Ferrone? I do. I would be out fishing with my father on Lake Beauclair, near the spot where it joins Lake Carlton, and we would come across a huge churning mass of shad. They would be breaking water, thrashing around, trying to escape the bass that were feeding on them. When I think back on that now I am reminded of the author Camille Paglia, the way her writings wallow in the slime and ooze of the natural world: "See nature spuming and frothing, its mad spermatic bubbles endlessly spilling out and smashing in that inhuman round of waste, rot, and carnage" (*Sexual Personae*, p. 28).

Whenever I go back to New Smyrna these days, whenever I walk down the beach kicking water in the surf, I recall that summer of 1956. A vacation full of waiting, wondering. What's going to happen with her? What about the chemotherapy? Will she be okay?

We didn't talk much about it. She had the chemo, lost her hair. Mommy sent us pictures of her in a hat, with another little girl, from Mississippi. We walked on the beach, built sand castles, swam. I rode the waves and became an expert body surfer. Daddy floated on his back, out beyond the breakers, browning his prominent stomach in the sun. He could float an hour or more, drifting far down the beach with the current. It was his way of relaxing. He sometimes went to sleep as he floated. He'd wake up two miles closer to Daytona; then he'd swim into shore and spend a long time walking back, kicking through the shallow water.

My sister June spent most of her time sunbathing. She got so dark every summer that she could be taken for a Native American. In fact, a few years later she was, after she married Gordon Roepke and went over to live on the St. John's River, with the air boaters and "river rats." One night, following a fracas in a riverfront honky tonk, some soggy cracker was telling his story to the local police, claiming, "It was that little Indian girl that done it. She hit me over the head with a beer bottle." A few friends from Mt. Dora visited our New Smyrna cottage that summer of '56: Austin and Virginia Simpson, Sellers Lovelady and his wife Cora Lee. Along with the Loveladies came their sons, John and William, who my father, with the joy he took in nicknaming, always called "John the Jew" and "Bill the Bull." Cora Lee died years ago, and I last saw Sellers in 1975. When my mother passed away he came to the pink house on a condolence visit. He was overwrought that day, shaking with nerves, eyes brimming tears. Sellers had been a nervous man ever since the Second World War, when he was in on the invasion of Italy and saw heavy combat against the Germans. Sellers cut my hair once, when I was maybe eight, and clipped a notch in my ear. The haircut was so bad I had to go for repairs to Mr. Hardy at the O.K. Barbershop, and he said, "Lord a'mercy! Who got ahold of you?" I didn't tell him it was Sellers Lovelady. Sellers meant well, and he was always kind to me.

When I was about ten years old I went into business with "John the Jew" Lovelady, selling vegetable seeds. There was an ad in some comic book, about all the money kids could make. So I floated a $10 loan from my parents and sent off for the parcel. It contained potential cabbage, carrots, beets, okra, parsley—anything you could want to grow. I was scared to sell things house to house by myself, so I asked John to make the rounds with me. Our sales routine went as follows:

Knock, knock.

Yes?

Would you like to buy some seeds?

Not today, thank you.

Okay.

Later on Larry Smith and I used the same technique to "sell," among other things, tropical plants, mistletoe, and long-burning light bulbs. My father, a crack insurance salesman, tried to give me tips about how to stick my foot through the slot in the door and keep talking, but I never had the nerve to do that. I was a low pressure vendor. So was John the Jew. We finally got so desperate that we approached pedestrians on the street: You wouldn't happen to want to buy some rutabaga seeds, would you? No? I didn't think so.

That's why I never became a salesman, like my daddy. No natural talent for it. As for John the Jew, my ribald sense of humor is tempted to make up a story, but it wouldn't be very nice so I won't do it. The story would have gone like this: "the last I heard of John the Jew he was working in a fertility clinic in Orlando, as a sperm donor. So, in a way, he ended up selling seeds successfully, after all." At this point in the roast I'd like to take the opportunity to say that I liked your whole family, John Lovelady, and whatever path you're walking these days, I wish you well!

At twilight on New Smyrna Beach we went crabbing in the surf: The Bowies, the Simpsons (Austin and Virginia, Billy, Carol, Donna, Mike), the Loveladies (Cora Lee and Sellers, Bill the Bull and John the Jew). In those days the crabs washed in with the high tide. They would try to conceal themselves by burrowing under the wet sand, but you could make out the little humps and dig them out with a crab net. One evening we ran across Al Rehbaum III on the beach. His family, one of the oldest and most prominent in Mt. Dora, apparently had a beach house nearby. Al the Third ("Sonny"), who was two years older than me, got in the crabbing spirit and helped us dig a bucketful out from under the wet sand. There were also hordes of periwinkles, swarming about like infusoria in their pearly triangular shells. Sometimes we'd gather them up in buckets and take them back to cook up some periwinkle soup.

That's about all I can remember of that strange summer. The perpetual waiting, the body surfing, the un-festive air, as if we weren't really on vacation, the crabs, the long walks down the beach, kicking through the shallow salt water, Al the Third, the periwinkles. And, for some reason, one song that was popular that year: Gogi Grant's "The Wayward Wind." About being kin to a restless breeze.

I have a vivid memory, for some reason, of that song running through my head, as I sat on the beach and watched Daddy float on his back. He was far out beyond the breakers, and I always worried about that, thinking of sharks and huge sea tortoises. I was a worrier as a kid. His black wavy hair was under water, his eyes shut, nose and lips protruding, arms, legs spread wide, belly shining in the sun, drifting with the current that pulled him along, northward, toward Daytona. I watched him float to the tune of the wayward wind until he flotsamed out of sight. The last thing you could see was the little lump of the glistening belly.

Years later, after he got angina pectoris, his cardiologist ordered him to take that belly off, and he went from one hundred ninety pounds down to 160. Then, as he aged, he got skinnier and skinnier. So that if you could have seen him floating out of sight in, say, 1986, you wouldn't have seen anything toward the end, except a glint of sunlight in the foam.

A few weeks after we left our beach house, on Aug. 17, Mommy brought Jacqi home from Boston. They had the leukemia in remission, and she was preparing to start the new school year in the fifth grade. By the time they came home I was already back on the football field, running through the searing hot two-a-day practices in shorts, preparing for the season when Bobby Bowie, halfback, would become a star.

7

FOURTH quarter

The great Hurricane team of '59/ "We're gonna win, yeah, we're gonna win, yeah, we're gonna win, the people say, yaay, yaay, yaay"/ Black and white blended makes grey/ Mrs. Cook's squash casserole/ Does Oprah eat okra?/ Loud memories, vociferous ghosts/ Jess Wilmott married Celia Claflin/ Scouts stomp gleefully on wet cement/ The plants say, "You're ours"/ Shooting out the Christmas lights on Holler's Point/ The red bougainvillaea/ That same flame vine/ Its tiny orange flowers/ Uncle Dedrick defends his life/ "Shake it more than twice"/ Lives and variants of lives/ Too much emotion on Seventh Ave./ Bowie Mom and Colonel Bob/ The Walking Jesus/ Pinckney Turner stands tall/ Laughing flip-flops/ Is Arthur Dufour still around?/ Roasts and charivaris/ This is a tribute/ The screams in the night/ "Surely goodness and mercy"/ Charlie Reid, who died of cancer/ George Moore meant well/ Quick kicks and Kangaroo shoes/ Sailing a ship to Norway/ When I got quieter/ Nine years old, and shrieking obscenities/ "Will follow us all the days of our lives"/ What's behind the green door?/ Kumquats/ Playing Bishop Moore and laughing with a sister/ Who was stroking rosaries?/ Hold that line/ John Ellis needs twenty seconds/ The end, and the beginning

At this point in the roast I'd like to apologize for making all y'all from the '51 and '59 teams listen to this long account of one trifling game from 1957. By way of compensation, let me say that your names will glow brightly in the annals of Mt. Dora history. I've already made reference to the '51 glories, but the great 1959 team deserves some plaudits too. So, way to go, Charles Kinsey, Herbert Flavell, Henry Land, Arthur Norris, Owen McCallister, Bud Sadler, John Snowberger!

The score was 26-19, our favor. We were in the final period, and suddenly everybody dared to be like Earle Williams. The laughter we were laughing in our guts smelled like victorious laughter. Nobody thought we couldn't win this game any more. Not the Bishop Moore Hornets, not their athletic director, not the Mt. Dora fans in the stands (among others: Cecil Bowie, Eunice and Gordon Dake, Sam Shaw, Austin Simpson, Bobbie Clements, Betty Sue Wages, Wayne and Mary Moon, Mildred Williams and Lew Earle Williams, Sr., Herman Kicklighter, of Umatilla, Jan Potter, Christine and Herbert Stoothoff), not the cheerleaders, not team physician Doc Montgomery, seated on the end of the bench, by the water pail, and not Dan Spear.

From the start we had played with wild abandon, taking joy in just being alive, in sun-drenched Mt. Dora, Florida, where the navel oranges were early sweet that year, on the day after Halloween, 1957. That exhilaration carried us through the game. Bishop Moore's cockiness was long gone, and, along with the sweat, a nervous anxiety was seeping into the black and gold of their uniforms. But the original pre-game, overconfident B.M. vibes must have been still circulating in the humid air too, blending with our pre-game hysterical joy. Nothing disappears, and everything every human being, and every individual insect, breathes out into the air, amalgamates in a cloudy mass called LIFE.

The whole time I've been telling this I've been trying to figure how blackness blended with whiteness in the South, but it's too complicated. A progression: black, blank, blanc (the French word for 'white'). Go figure that one. If I can't even explain Uncle Dedrick, how can I hope to understand black folks, who lived in a world isolated from ours? You were there, Dan Spear, down in the basement of the Community Building, at the weekly luncheon meetings of the Lions Club, Kiwanis, or Rotary. At least you were there when I was, when they invited the MDHS football team once a year. The great white fathers of the town would be talking small talk, joshing around, eating Mrs. Cook's wonderful fried chicken and feasting on her turnip greens with hot pepper sauce, her Southern cornbread and luscious squash casserole. How would they react if you told them the food she prepared was "soul food?"

Blacks and whites in the South ate the same things. Been living in Ohio for a long time now, but when I hear the words "collards" and "okra" my mouth still starts watering. You're from Ohio, Mr. Spear; you realize that most people in Ohio don't know the overwhelmingly earthy, animal smell of collards; and don't know what okra is. Why, there are people up here so deprived they don't even eat Vidalia onions. But black folks in Ohio love okra. I bet even Oprah, long removed from her Mississippi roots, still loves okra.

There was so much in common between the races in the rural South. But we insisted on perpetuating that weird mixture of hatred and affection. Let me try to explain this one more time. People act like, you know, it's just kind of, and after all, folks do do the kind of things that the Devil himself can't make out, and then we have a sort of, like, a soul that's, well, it's good, but then it's evil too, and sometimes we do evil things while pretending loving motivations and, on the other hand, we can start out willing evil, and it comes out full of love, and I don't know, but then again, if you look at it, well, and like, after all is said and done, you take you a good look at the way Uncle Dedrick hated-loved black folks and then you'll...

I give up. No way me or nobody else will ever figure this black-white stuff because it's parcel and part of a much broader phenomenon: the insane grey blendings of life in general and of God's universal schemes. Take me, take the way I feel about Mt. Dora, Florida, my mixed feelings about the town.

When I go back for a visit, I walk the streets now, as a grown man getting old, and I hear memories screaming my name from every corner. How can you live, placidly, in a place where all those memories live? What about it, Pam Ray, Janie Huett, Richard Gardner, Clark Vanderoef, Neil Stoothoff, Johnny Driggers, Jimmy Beims, Larry Smith, Ronald E. Aldrich, Jr., John Heist, Billy Vanzant? You all are still living there, never left. Maybe that's the key: if you don't leave, the old memories speak in muted voices. What do you think, Mary Kay Rehbaum, Fred Kurras, Patty Johnson? You were gone for a while and then came back. How does the town work on your feelings? Does it seem different now?

The prime movers of Mt. Dora in the fifties must be pretty much dead by now. I know George White died. Roy Christopher. Al Rehbaum the first and the second are gone. But Howard Simpson is still around, isn't he? And Goober Ray. What about Abby Jo Land? Henry? Jess Wilmott? I remember, for some reason, when he married Celia Claflin in 1954. How does it feel for you of my generation to watch the older generation fade away and see yourselves becoming them? Who are the new town fathers? And mothers? Barbara Seiss, L.C. Durden, Patty Alexander, Jeff Ray, J.W. Shaw, Betty Lou Sills, Al the Third, Sue Bond, Asher Sodom, Tommy Houser, Mary Lou Brotherson, Bobby Partridge, Vester Stephens, Hank Link, Spider Bennett, Carmen Smith, Buddy White, Waiford Bedford, Gayle Snowberger, Russell Russell, Gringy Bahls, Buddles Ledford?

You park your car across from the lawn bowling club, right up the street from Evans Park, where Daddy and Dedrick once kept their fishing boat on the lake. Down in those swamps live the descendants of the cottonmouth moccasins who were crawling there when I was a boy. Start walking uphill, turn right before the railroad tracks and go by the old Ice House Theater (no longer an ice house, or a theater). You have the marina down below and a beautiful view of Lake Dora (palm trees, crape myrtles on the shore, quacking coots on the water). Take another right turn and go downhill, keep walking along the lake until you get to Gilbert Park on your left. If you go directly through the park, treading on the fallen moss, the brown live oak leaves and white sand, the pine needles, you'll end up near what was the old boy scout house. Our scoutmaster got involved in some sort of something and had to leave town. Rumor was he liked boys. But nobody talked openly about things like that back then. He always seemed like a good man to me. Another, later, better scoutmaster was Slater Cox, who has a bridge named after him over by Tavares, and whose son David was a safety patrol boy when I was.

The scouts had a terrible reputation around Mt. Dora in my day. Of course, I was never included in the hooliganism; everybody knew Bobby Bowie was a good little boy. He wouldn't stomp gleefully all over the fresh cement in the foundation laid for a new house, right across from our scout house down at Gilbert Park. No one would think to invite him along, as they set out to vandalize a farmer's truck. That happened when we were bivouacking at Camp Lanochee, out in the Ocala National Forest. I was in the background of all these scandals, but I heard about them only after the fact. I recall how folks anathematized us down at the O.K. Barber Shop, speaking hard words about juvenile delinquents who called themselves scouts.

Even more scandalous was what happened to the Christmas tree lights at Holler's Point. What year was that? 1956? Bill Holler used to decorate a huge tree with lights out on Lake Dora, on the little peninsula, Tavares side, where he lived. It was the pride of the town and the embodiment of the Christmas spirit. As you drove out Old Highway 441, high above the lake, you could see it glittering through ripples of distant water in all its splendor. It said, in effect (not in words, but in light), "Yea, The Saviour is Born." Then one dark night unknown malefactors rowed up silently to Holler's Point and shot out every bulb with bee-bee guns. The town was up in arms after that, and huge rewards were offered for the hides of the culprits. But they never were apprehended. I'll tell you a secret. I know who they were.

Let's continue our stroll. As you walk uphill from the scout house look to that swampy hollow on the right (just before the rail tracks) and you'll see where the Florida banana trees used to grow. At the crest of the hill you'll notice the old Beims residence down that side street, as you pass the new condominiums on the left. If you turned one way on Third Avenue, you'd soon come to the Brown residence, home of Bobby Brown, Barbara Brown, and my classmate Billy Brown, who made lots of mischief with Donald Reichert (later they both went into law enforcement). But we'll turn the other way, to the right, on Third and go all the way to Clayton St. Past the blooming lantana, the hibiscus, the bougainvillaeas. Even the plants in Mt. Dora are kindred: "You grew up with us," they call out to you as you pass. "You're ours." I wonder if that spectacular red Bowie bougainvillaea is still alive, growing up the back of our pink house? Walk Clayton St. to Fifth Ave., where you see Roseborough Elementary School, which was once just Mt. Dora School, and that's when memories start really playing havoc in your head. You spent twelve formative years in those buildings.

At the corner of Fifth and Highland, where the road (Fifth, Old 441—same thing) makes its big bend, you reach what was the Pure Station (where Bobby Poole and Lawrence Cheatham hung out), with Mr. Kuechler's store on the other side. The ghost of young Dedrick is yelling at you from that station (no longer Pure), where he pumped gas as a youth, before he became a hotshot real estate agent.

You ignore him, turning left onto Highland and heading for Seventh Avenue, walking the hot stretch you always ran down barefooted on the way to and from Kuechler's, where you purchased Barq's soda, Dr. Pepper, packets of salted peanuts to pour in your Coke bottle (do people still do that?). You pass the dead end street and see the flame vine, still blooming on the fence at its far end, near Cathy Stewart's house, beside the alleyway that runs past the gymnasium. Look carefully and you'll see a few fresh sandspurs in the weeds by the sidewalk. But don't worry—they're still green and haven't gone prickly yet. On the other hand, steer clear of the little plant with the white flower: that's a stinging nettle. Another half block and you come upon Uncle Dedrick again, middle-aged now, a little paunchy and hemorrhoidal, but still standing tall, wearing his fishing cap with the bill, waiting for you. This time you can't ignore him. You have to listen to his impassioned plea for understanding, to his protests about the unfair way you've portrayed him in your story. Yeah. From what I've told you Uncle Dedrick comes out looking like nothing but a virulent racist. "I was a complex individual," his ghost is shouting at me now, "with all the human loves, hates, hurts that anyone carries through life."

What did I see of Dedrick? I saw him blustering around a lot, deriding Austin Simpson. Austin, like my father, was an insurance man for the Peninsular Life Insurance Company. When we went cane pole fishing Dedrick used to boast about all the real estate he was selling. Then he'd get off on Austin, how the only thing Austin could sell was "nickel and dime" life insurance out in East Town. "Simpkins loves that nigger bidness. Week

after week collecting twenty-five cent from every shack on every corner.
Gives him a reason for living. Them pickaninnies love him too. They see
him coming, right quick they run out on the street with their nickels,
yelling, 'Here come Mr. Sibson, here come de policy man!' "

Austin never let any of that bother him. He liked his job and did it
well. He could enrage Uncle Dedrick just by not taking him seriously.
Dedrick tried to patronize my father too, but Daddy knew how to deflate
his ego. Once Dedrick was urinating over the side of the rowboat, and when
he finished he shook his wiener a few times, to get all the driblets off its tip,
and Daddy laughed and said, "Shake it more than twice and you're playing
with it."

But Dedrick's ghost is right to protest. I never saw the total side of him.
Ask those who were closer to him, who lived with him—his wife, Alatrocia,
his sons, his daughter—they'll give you the fully rounded Uncle Dedrick.
The one sure thing you can say about folks is, "People are complicated." I'll
tell you this, ghost of Dedrick, I'll forgive you your imperfections if you'll
forgive me mine. I don't go in for blanket condemnations, of the living or
the dead. So calm down now and go back to drifting through the spiral
nebulae of the afterworld. Your life was okay. You're fine, son, just fine.

Uncle Dedrick shuts up, smiles at me, grows elderly and gets
Alzheimer's, dematerializes, and I wonder if other countervailing opinions
are going to turn up. You know, a lot of people I've stuck into my story may
have a different view of themselves. After this stuff gets read at the roast, I
may be hearing from other ghosts and from persons in the flesh. Maybe
T.M. Thomas. Svelte Donna Potter. Joe Graf. Leebo. Rhoda Todd Horton.
Buddles. The girl who brought the pornographic comic book to school in
the seventh grade, saying, "No, that wasn't me brought that comic book to
school. I remember that comic book, but, uh-uh, no way was it me brought
that comic book to school." Lynn Rector. Mary Lou Davidson. Phyllis and
Charlie Kennedy, Tommy Hurlburt, John Lynch. Bobby Joe Cook, Beanie

Creamons. Or maybe David Coffield, insisting, "Now, look here, wait a minute, I never was what you made me out to be in high school." Or Judy Sadler, with her version of the life and death of Muff Potter. Flavell Bagwell. Waiford Bedford. Lewis Carroll, justifying his life, Louis Montgomery, setting me straight on the real story of the East Town shooting, or the shade of "crazed itinerant" Joe Henderson, explaining desperately how the vicissitudes of life drove him to do what he did. Larry Smith, asserting that the story of how they sicced a baby gator on him is really true. Or Dan Spear. Harry Meisel. This could go on forever. Everybody, with the aid of his or her creative memory, has her or his own creative version of what he or she was/is really like. I can't compete with that. Sorry. All I can do is tell it the way me and my memory remember it.

After Dedrick evaporates, I turn left onto the oldest end of Seventh Avenue. This is the street that I find most disturbing to walk on. I have to go by our little stucco house at 820 E. Seventh, and by the Pohlwright stucco house next to it and the Smarts' stucco house next to that. I'm afraid the dead of the stucco houses might descend upon me in hordes, each one wanting his say—all the Bowies, the Pohlwrights, the Smarts.

The Smarts were an elderly retired couple from Easton, Pennsylvania, and the Pohlwrights, also elderly, came from someplace else up North. Once, when I was a little kid, I returned from playing on the football field to find the house locked up and nobody home, and I waited and waited, and finally I sat down beside the wooden garage and started crying, and Mrs. Pohlwright brought me out some milk and cookies. A year or so later old man Pohlwright died. His wife came knocking at three a.m. in a panic, woke us up, asked my father to come next door.

When Daddy came back I heard him telling Mommy how he found him there, sitting in an armchair, in his bathrobe. I guess Mr. Pohlwright got up in the night, not feeling well, sat for a while, pondering over the meaning of his life, then died. I heard Daddy telling how he was slumped over in that chair, stiff already with rigor mortis. The folds of the robe were open at the waist and his organ of generation was in a standing position. I don't remember exactly how my father described that, which wasn't meant for me to hear (but I was always listening). I was maybe nine years old.

After my grandparents, Bowie Mom and Colonel Bob, moved out of Riley's Trailer Park, they lived in a small house on the Old Eustis Road. With an orange grove out back. We used to visit them every Sunday afternoon. This made for more Sunday unpleasantries, since my mother would have liked to do something different. But we kept to that eternal routine of the Sabbath visits. The only variety involved the rides, with my grandparents and all the rest of us packed into the car. Daddy would be smoking cigars, and I would get car sick.

We would drive all over Lake County, visit the oldest and largest Florida cypress tree ("3500 yrs.; 17/127 ft."), circle around Lake Johanna; sometimes we'd take long day trips, as far as Bok Tower or Cypress Gardens. We would ride, and they would make conversation. Incessant small talk was the substance of our lives. Then I would start retching, and they would stop the car to let me throw up. Was it the cigar smoke or the conversation? I remember once sitting on their screened-in porch, in the wooden house on the Old Eustis Road. It was Sunday afternoon, I was stultifying in the heat and the blather, and Bowie Mom, who was getting on in years, commented on a car that passed. "Now that car has gone by here at least three times today. I can't see why they keep driving back and forth. Up to no good, I reckon. All I can figure is they must be communists." When she said that I went into a fit of hysterical laughter and couldn't stop sputtering for twenty minutes.

Later on that house and orange grove were bulldozed, when they built new Highway 441. My grandparents got some eminent domain money and bought the former Pohlwright stucco residence on Seventh Ave. By then we were living farther up the street, in the pink house. I visited Colonel Bob for the last time in 1964. He was going senile. Drinking whiskey because it was the only thing that made him feel good, still gumming chewing tobacco and spitting into an empty baked beans can. I was home on leave from the army, just prior to shipping out for Europe. Colonel Bob, notwithstanding the nickname, had never served in the army. He said to me, "Bobby, don't you go over there. I don't want you to." His voice was emotional.

Young and impatient with the redundancy of the old, I tried to humor him. I said, "Well, you know, I'm in the army, and I have to go where they send me," and Colonel Bob said, "Bobby, don't you go off over there to Germany. You hear? If you go over there, I won't never see you again." He was right. I went and he died a year later, while I was serving in England. Bowie Mom was still alive when I got back from the army, but she was in the Golden Triangle Nursing Home, a madhouse of senescence and dementia, where she died in 1967.

So when you get to the Pohlwright house, across from what used to be the football field, you turn around. You decide not to walk on up the hill, past the Smarts' and the Roseborough School on your left and the former Roseborough home beyond the playground to your right. You want to get off Seventh Avenue and away from the voices of the ghosts. You go back down to Highland, turn left, walk past the new high school on the right, which wasn't built until the sixties. How was it to step bodily into the era of desegregation? My younger sister's generation had that experience; their world was different from ours: Georgeanne Greenwell, Alice Toy, Freddie Bickerstaff, Jackie Bolt, Sharon Daneski, Buddy Atkins, Maureen Stewart, Debbie Dodson, Jeannie Knorr, Martin Morgan, Cindy Shipes, Charles Alderman.

Walking Highland, you come to the Aldriches' old house, on the corner of Sixth. Then take a left on Sixth and head uphill, past the Atkins house, overlooking the parking lot where mosquito trucks once ran and football history was made. Look straight ahead and hum the "Hurrah for Hurricanes" song. Turn right onto Clayton at the top of the hill, go by Clarence Earl Sims' house, then the residence of Austin and Virginia, Billy, Carol, Mike and Donna Simpson at the end of the block.

Don't know where Clarence is riding his motorcycle these days, but the shade of Billy Austin Simpson, Jr., as he appeared at age ten, his dirty-blond hair in a crew cut, is playing outside on the street. You'd rather not face another ghost, so you turn around and head back in the other direction, walking fast by the Prof and Precious Roseborough residence, next to the playground on the left. This is the spot that Leebo Mcree threatened to flood in 1947, sending Judy Sadler off in a panic. It's still full of white sand and live oaks, and the swings are in the same spot, but the monkey bars I used to hang from are gone. And the teeter-totters.

Who was that just drove by? Looked like Charles Wareing. And right after that a Cadillac, and that could have been Pinckney Turner driving it. When I was a little kid I watched him play football with Correll and Odom on the great Mt. Dora teams. Those guys were my idols. I'm sure he'll be at the roast. He'll drive up in his pink Cadillac, wearing yellow pants and a fancy silk shirt. He'll swagger a little bit, maybe kid around with the organizers of the event, svelte Donna Potter and lovely Diane Cheek, wafting the self-confidence he acquired in the fifties. Pinckney Turner. You see, Dan Spear, that's what playing on an undefeated team at age sixteen does for you: you believe you're great for the whole rest of your life!

Take me, now, I never played on an undefeated team, and I never thought that much of myself. I went into the army as a private and had no ambitions to make officer. But there was one short period, in the spring of

1964, when people took me for an officer, and I had a good time with that. It happened right after the episode in Tijuana, and after the Article *15* I told you about. When they busted us back down to buck private, we didn't take a big fall, since we had only one stripe to lose. But we were unusual on the post where we were stationed, at the language school, Presidio of Monterey. Why? Because anybody who got to Monterey had been in the army long enough to acquire at least one stripe.

So, to make this brief, after they busted me down from PFC, I would be walking around post in my service cap and dress greens, and people started saluting me all over the place. They thought only officers had nothing on the sleeves of their arms. I didn't know what else to do, so I saluted back. It was fun, seeing how the other half lives. One day I was walking up to the infirmary to get some treatment for the corn on my right small toe. Troops were saluting me all over the place, saying, "Good morning, sir," and I was saluting back, using the nonchalant, abbreviated hand chop favored by cocky young lieutenants, returning the greetings with a grim-faced "Good morning, soldier." Unfortunately, my nemesis, the first sergeant, was out and about that morning, surveying his realm. I pretended I didn't see him and started walking faster, but he yelled out, "Hey, troop! Yeah, you, Bowie. Come here, son."

He didn't know exactly how to chew me out, though, since there was no rule against saluting. He selected a few choice words and sent me on my way. When I reached the waiting room at the infirmary, the medical orderly in there, an E-5 (sergeant rank) started fawning all over me, the "young officer." This was really getting funny. The doctor took a look at the corn that was rubbing inside my low quarters, and he gave me permission to wear a shower shoe on that one foot, in a black sock, until the corn medicine worked.

After that, I started walking around in one shoe and one flip-flop, saluting like mad. Officers didn't take me for one of them, though. They would stop me all the time and say, "Wait a minute, trooper, what are you doing in a shower shoe?" I would calmly take out my note from the infirmary, granting me permission to heal my corn.

Soon the laughter inside me got wilder, and I intensified the stakes of the game. I took off both low quarters and my black socks too and went to Russian classes in my dress greens and service cap, with two bare feet in shower shoes. Now officers and noncoms stopped me every few steps, and I would put on a disgusted look and pull out my note. This was great fun for a few days, until the eagle eye of the first sergeant looked out the window of the orderly room one morning and spied me flip-flopping along to the mess hall.

I was already in the chow line when he double-timed up, puffing and blowing indignation. Once again I took out my note. He read it very carefully, moving his lips. Then he looked up with the glint of malice on his red face. I always felt at home among the white sergeants in the army, because they all had faces straight out of Pistolville.

He said, "You *will* get a sock and low quarter on that left foot, and you *will* get a sock on that right foot while you're wearing that shower shoe! Is that clear?"

I said, "Yes, sir!" because I knew that, like all genuine retread sergeants, he hated being called "sir." Sir was for officers, and any army E.M. holds officers in infinite contempt. With good reason. He finished up by saying, "And you *will* get that corn healed on that right pinky toe ASAP, and I don't mean two weeks from now, and then you *will* get a low quarter back on that foot. And if you pull any more shit on me, son, your scrawny ass is going to be back up in front of the old man again, and I'm going to be right there beside him, sticking another Article 15 up the cornhole region. You got that?"

Sergeants in the army are among the most filthy talking people you'll ever meet. And they love to say, for some reason, "You *will*." I figured him threatening me with another Article 15 was funny, considering they had already busted me down in rank as far as I could go. By the way, my butt never was scrawny, although my daddy's was, and my son Rob's is. So then, that's the story of the laughing flip-flops. In regard to the story I'm telling you, though, Dan Spear, here's what's interesting. I used that laughing spirit to get me through three years of the army. But it first materialized on a school bus returning from Groveland in the fall of 1957, and it found its apotheosis on Nov. 1 of that year.

We're still strolling around Mt. Dora. We're on Clayton St., beside the old playground. Then Seventh Avenue beckons again, and you can't resist turning right and getting back on it. There's Berry Wells' little house, you wonder how Pat Wells, her daughter, is doing these days. Oh, I forgot. Patsy died in Dallas, Texas, years ago. Heading past our green house now, which doesn't have a lot to say to me. We lived there such a short time. On a whim Daddy listed it with a real estate firm, asking an exorbitant price, and two days later Mr. Dufour bought us out. That was in 1953. We had to find a new house quick. So Daddy purchased the lot just up the street, pulled out the orange trees that fronted on Seventh, and had the pink house built.

Later on Junior Bell lived in the green house, and after that his mother, Ma Bell. I think Junior's back living there today, and still farming the muck farms in Zellwood. Junior, Betty, Debbie, Terri. I walk by Lillian Christie's big old mansion on the right, past the Frisbies' on my side of the street. When I approach our pink house, the spectres come rushing up to embrace me, weeping, wailing out their so familiar tales from the past. Walk fast, Bobby Booby. Go on by. Turn left onto Grandview, hurry on past the Dakes' house. Skip the Methodist Church on your right, with its mortuary you don't want to look at, skip the Episcopal Church straight ahead, just across Fifth Ave., where you were married in 1967.

Get into that so-familiar loping gait, surely goodness and mercy will follow you, head back in a hurry to the Nissan with the Ohio plates, parked down there across from the lawn bowling courts. Start up the car, old Hank Williams song on the radio, moving on, soon be gone, drive around the lake, and head for Sorrento. I'm on my way to New Smyrna Beach, where more memories await me, kicking through the foam of the surf, white satin pants rolled up to the knees.

So you see, those are the kind of mixed feelings I have for my home town. Part of me wanting to be there, part wanting to be far from there. When you come right down to it, all human feelings are a complex blend. Take this so-called "roast" event, where you're being honored right now, Dan Spear. Why did somebody choose to call it a "roast" and not a "tribute"? A modern "roast" is something like the old thing they called a charivari, held after a wedding. Friends of the young couple would put toads in the conjugal bed and give it a short-sheeting. After the reception they would stand outside the newlyweds' bedroom, ringing cow bells, beating on pots and pans and shrieking out suggestive comments. This was their way of "honoring" the bride and groom.

The fun of a "roast" verges on the cruel fun we used to have swiping Ace Aldrich's briefcase. But with us old football players it's something like the kind of fun Ace may have experienced, had he been vindictive enough to seek revenge. As if some small thing in your former players' souls were saying, "Back when I was a callow youth, Dan Spear made me run laps, he kicked me in the butt when I missed a block, he called into question the quality of my testicles. Once, when he was reaming me out on the practice field, I said, 'But, but… I thought…' and he interrupted me with that mean look of his and said, in that nasty Yankee Joe Namath voice, 'It takes brains

to think!' Okay. Now it's my turn. I'll give it to him laughing, affectionately, but that doesn't mean I won't get back at him!"

You stepped on a lot of toes, Dan Spear. You were a passionate man,
an angry man. I can even imagine some people in Mt. Dora saying, "What?
You want me to come to a roast in honor of Dan Spear? Why that gol-
durned so and so, he hated me all the way through school. In his junior high
math class he made sarcastic remarks about the way my ears stuck out. My
ears *still* stick out, and what can I do about it? That's the way I was born!
Once when I got hurt and limped off the practice field, he yelled, 'All right,
then, grannie, you did enough hopping on that one leg. Now try hopping
on the other one for a change.' When I played football for him, I had one
great night, I scored three touchdowns. But we lost that game by two
points, and you know what Mr. Spear said after the game? He said, 'Cream
puffs. I'm ashamed of all of you. You didn't have the guts to win.' And I
wanted to say, 'But, but... But I scored three touchdowns!' He didn't even
mention it, the greatest glory night of my life! So let me tell you, and I hope
you get my drift: I wouldn't be caught dead at a testimonial dinner for that
dad-blamed blankety-blank, etc., etc."

Others decided to come and honor you at this roast tonight because a
"roast" is precisely in tune with their mixed feelings: one part rancor to one
part affection. And what about me? What about this letter I'm sending in
honor of you? Am I, maybe, deep down, getting back at you too, for the
insults you heaped on me? No. Because I've left the rancor behind, and I
never had good reason to be angry at anybody anyway. This is a tribute (not
a roast) to Dan Spear and to Mt. Dora, Florida, to all the people who lived
there in the forties and fifties.

Who is this story for? It's for Mr. Ed ("Shanks") Hansel, the basketball coach. He was also the line coach on our football team. He'd be up

riding those blocking sleds, bouncing a basketball in his head, long tall Shanks, with crew cut and sneer, while our linemen pushed him all over the field on that contraption, and he'd scream at them to hit harder and push farther. For lean Shanks Hansel, who had an unvoiced grudge against me because I didn't go out for basketball, and who flared up when I expressed a casual attitude toward the Babe Ruth Award, after they gave it to me in my senior year. I wonder if it was Shanks who talked Ronnie Parker into forgoing his last year of football, so he could dedicate himself to the round-ball season. Bringing the wrath of Dan Spear down on poor Parker, no relation to Tyrone. Ronnie is Jean Parker's brother.

For Ronnie Parker, Ivan's son, a likeable, outgoing type, whose block sprung me lose on an eighty-six yard punt return against Lake Weir in our junior year, the weirdest run I ever made. After I took the punt I couldn't find a smidgen of daylight. That whole side of the field was jammed up. I knew I was down, I lowered my head, shut my eyes and plunged forward. Then there was nothing, no impact, no collision. I opened my eyes and saw a clear field ahead. Ronnie Parker had thrown one block and knocked down three or four Lake Weir players. I turned on the afterburners. I was gone.

Then, for some reason, the afterburners burned out. With thirty yards left to go, my legs got tired and I decelerated. There was a huge lineman gaining on me fast. I had to take evasive action, weaving from side to side as he lurched along behind me. I finally made it to the goal line and weaved my way across it. But that was really strange. It was still 1956. Where was the pure speed that night?

Who else is this story for? For my mother, my father, my sisters, my friends. For L.C. Smith, for Jack Alexander, who came to love Corvettes above all things on earth, for C.M. Jones, with his pomaded hair, combed back in such perfect waves that even Elvis would have envied him, for Muff Potter, Earle Williams. For Judy Sadler, with her blue eyes and blonde hair.

How come it took me so many years to figure out why it was the blue-eyed blondes who appealed to me? For the screams in the night. For Charlie Reid.

Hmm. I just realized that I'm naming five or six males for every female I mention in this story. But it makes sense. Although I don't want to sleep with anybody but females, I've always been closer to males. My friend Alice Bolstridge once told me, "Men like sex with women, but they tend to love other men, and if there's any love left over, they give it to kids or dogs. Women may want a man, but they love other women, and kids, prefer their company." It's just one more way the human race is messed up. Biologically, the sexes somehow don't gibe, but there's this biological imperative to "pair bond," and we're not happy unless we've got a mate, and then, all too frequently, after we've got a mate we're not happy either. You figure it out. It makes me want to ask the Lord what he was thinking about when he came up with the rules for this bizarre business called human existence.

For Charlie Reid. What game was it? Dan Spear had anchored that taping on my leg to another taping around my abdomen, and midway through the game the tight tape messed up my bowels. There I am on defense, signaling from my halfback position to the sideline. Got to come out, stomach's upset. And you wouldn't take me out, Dan Spear. You needed me in there. After I finally got it across to you that I couldn't wait, you put Frankie Peck in for me, and I made a mad dash for the Mt. Dora gym.

I didn't even take time to remove my helmet, and there I am, running back, on the sidewalk inside the courtyard, past the white Spanish architecture of the school buildings along Clayton St., cleats clattering on concrete, and who do I see but Charlie Reid, ambling toward me, the usual big grin on his crew-cutted head. He had graduated the year before, was a freshman at the University of Florida, must have come home for the weekend. He stops me and says, "Hey, whoa. Where you going? The football game's in the other direction. And you're playing in it!"

I said, "Hey, Charlie, how you doing? Excuse me. No time to talk. I'm about to shit my pants." Then I ran off, him standing there laughing, got to the locker room, found some quick relief, pulled the hip pads on, headed back out to the field. Dan Spear saw me coming, jerked Peck out of the game, and right in I went. Meanwhile, Charlie Reid is back in the grandstands, spreading the story about what nice little Bobby Booby just said to him. I think he went around telling that tale for years.

For Mrs. Lofroos, who gave me the piano lessons my parents wanted me to take. Dan Spear's daughter Patsy was taking piano too, and I remember one of those horrible recitals at the old lady's house, with all the parents, mine were there, and Dan and Bert Spear, and lots of others, and we pupils struggling through the pieces we had been practicing, and screwing up, for weeks on end, and the parents had to sit there and pretend they were enjoying this, after hearing us pound out the same stuff at home incessantly, till it was a mad melody running in their dreams every night, and all I really wanted was to be out on a football or baseball field, and you had a plastered look of pleasure on your face, Dan Spear, but I know that quick kicks and Kangaroo shoes were on your mind.

How come nobody uses the quick kick anymore? We used it all the time on third and long. We had lots of razzle-dazzle. Remember the reverse-field hand offs that we halfbacks made on the kickoffs? Remember the T-formation "belly series" you added to our single-wing offense? And that shift count we used, moving out of 'T' to single wing and pulling the other team off sides? Smart coaching, Dan Spear!

For Arthur Colaianni and George Moore, successive band directors of the Manuel J. Sedano Memorial Band. Does anybody know who the great Manuel Sedano was? My sister June played flute, until she graduated in 1955. Mr. Colaianni, a patient man, gave me baritone lessons, trying hard to overcome my lack of interest. When George Moore took over, he despaired of my musical abilities. He finally asked me not to blow, just to move the valves and fake it, while bringing in trumpet players, first Pam Brown and, later, David Coffield, to shore up the baritone section.

I never got along with Mr. Moore. He caught me at a bad time, when I was in no mood to cooperate. I regret to say that I deliberately made life a misery for that man. We would be in the music room/cafeteria, playing our favorite march, "National Emblem," and I would get inspired at the point where the baritones and trombones take over the lead melody, and I would blast out the notes, missing half of them, and poor George Moore, up on his podium, was waving his baton and wincing in pain. In my junior year Mr. Moore made a desperate move to get rid of me altogether. He took my old baritone to the music store for repairs, but told the people there, it seems, to keep working on it indefinitely. I didn't mind going to study hall during the band period; I always liked reading books more than playing baritone. But then came time for the marching band competition in Jacksonville, and I didn't want to miss that trip, so I finally went to see Prof Roseborough. I told him how my instrument couldn't seem to get fixed. Well, that same day Prof phoned the music store, learned the true story, and he went over to the band room/cafeteria and reamed out poor George Moore. Soon I was on that bus for Jacksonville. True, Prof did call me in for a talk, and he told me that Mr. Moore was doing his best, and he asked me to go easy on George Moore. And after that I did.

Funny thing about this band business is the result of my aptitude test in the ninth grade. Designed to help us choose our future professions, the test had questions like: "What would you rather do? (a) Make a shelf in a carpentry shop? (b) Help an old lady across the street? (c) Sail a ship to Norway? (d) Read a book about spiders?" Well, the best I could come up with would be (d). I hated any kind of skilled manual work, was no altruist from my youngest days, and hadn't done much travelling. But when they passed out our professions a few weeks later, after they graded the tests, guess what mine came out—"musician"! How about that! And George Moore begging me just to move the valves! I must have had creative talents far beyond his pedestrian understanding of music. So, anyway, what profession, did I finally end up drifting into? I became a teacher of Russian language and literature!

By the way, I did sail a ship to Norway later on, in 1965, when I was in the army. Three of us, Don Diener, Dick Johnson, and I took leave and sailed across the North Sea, from Hull, England, to Oslo. We bought the cheapest passage, third class, in the prow where the sailors had their bunks. The ship kept pitching up and down, riding the high waves, and soon Dick Johnson turned green. Diener and I mocked him, laughed as he lay scrunched up in fetal position. Shortly after that Diener took to his bunk too, and I started razzing them both. I felt fine for maybe another half hour, and then that perpetual up and down movement, along with the shuddering of the engines, got to me. So finally all three of us were down there curled up in our racks, arising only occasionally to go to the head and throw up. That lasted all the way to Norway. What a relief to reach the calm waters of Oslo Bay, where the labor pains stopped.

The only other third class passengers were British merchant seamen. One of them said that he never had been to America, but he was eager to go because he had heard that the women rape the men in America. Was it true? I should have lied to him. What a look of despondency washed over his face when I told him that no, it wasn't so—American women didn't rape the men. He must have been so looking forward to going to America one day and getting raped.

More of who this story is for. For Lewis Carroll. For Gwyne Godtel. Fred Uhl. All the other dead classmates. And for the people, living or dead, whom I treated in a shabby way. You know, Dan Spear, there are memories about a specific thing you did to somebody, and although it happened forty years ago you still groan, and blush inwardly, when you think of it today. The kind of things you never forgive yourself. The gratuitous cruelties. For the people I did those things to. You know who you are.

For the look and the smell of the town, the most beautiful spot on earth. The parks on opposite sides of Lake Dora and the dock down by the old Yacht Club. Palms and pines, coots toodling along on the water, stilt-legged herons, lizards, cranes, brown thrushes, mockingbirds, cardinals, flickers, blue jays, birds of paradise (a plant, not a bird), cypress trees, up to their knees in water and surrounded by knees. In the center of town City Hall, overlooking another little park and the shuffleboard courts where my grandparents, Bowie Mom and Colonel Bob, used to shuffle. Possums, coons and armadillos, cockroaches (are the Mt. Dora cockroaches still as big as they used to be, back before the era of home spray services?), fungi and funguses, ringworms, mosses, kumquats (what a weird word, "kumquat"— a miniature oblong citrus fruit with no taste), camphor trees, tiny sweat-sucking gnats, palmettoes, hibiscus blooming red, yellow and pink, satsumas and calamondins (more citrus). Snakes (rattlesnakes, king snakes, coral snakes, black snakes, cottonmouth moccasins), the perfumery of orange blossoms in March and sweet-scented night blooming jasmine in July, when it was unbearably hot inside, we couldn't sleep, we retreated out onto the couches, on the side porch of the pink house.

You lie there, enveloped in the thick aroma of the jasmine, you look out the jalousies at the street lights, soft shadows of Spanish moss, chirring insects, thick sweaty air. The navel tree beside the carport blows gently in the breeze. Mt. Dora, Florida. August, 1956.

The insomnia started for me in late summer or early fall. During football season of my junior year, the season when I became a star. In the first game, against St. Cloud at home, I went around end and just kept running—eighty yards for a touchdown. After that the hype began, the articles with words like "speed demon," "jet-propelled." I didn't feel like I deserved the admiring glances of the junior high kids. I never had a high opinion of myself. I was just unobtrusive Bobby Bowie, rhymes with Booby, the shy and studious one, a listener and a watcher. Then, suddenly, I was a football hero too. But that didn't mean I could sleep.

Since I always had been quiet, I don't suppose anyone noticed when I got quieter, in the fall of 1956. You read these newspaper articles: "Teenager Snaps. Goes on Berserk Rampage." Inevitable comments from neighbors accentuate the calm and silent nature of the perpetrator. "Hard-working student. Kind of kept to himself. Never said much. Who would have thought it?" Well, you'd think someone would have thought it, but somehow nobody ever does.

I remember the first air conditioned building in Mt. Dora, Florida. It was George White's First National Bank, on the corner of Donnelly and Fifth down town. You walked in there out of the steamy humidity, and you felt like you were in a refrigerator. The tellers (my sister June was one, after her graduation) took sweaters to work with them. People complained about having to do their banking in the cold.

Nobody I knew of had air conditioning at home. How in the world did we manage? Well, there were fans whirling all over the place. Some of them on the ceilings, like in most businesses (Moon's Hardware, Link's Stationery, Rehbaum's Mortuary). You may have even had an attic fan, like we did in our house on Seventh Avenue. But all it did was circulate hot air. In mid-summer there was little relief, even at night. It was hot, hot, hot. That's when we ended up sleeping on the porch.

But there seemed to be an unwritten rule against porch sleeping in September, sort of like the Floridian's rule about beaches: nobody but Yankees goes to the beach after Labor Day. I guess we were thinking, "Well, the new school year has started, summer's over. September is fall." But

Florida pours out monstrous heat and humidity from its September furnace. So in September, 1956, I would be lying in my bedroom in the torrid pink house. Sweating. And thinking.

She came back from Boston, she started the new school year. But that didn't last long. Now she's home sick, and back on chemotherapy. It makes her itch. She goes to sleep in the bedroom next to mine, my parents' bedroom. They keep her in with them now, in case she wakes up. Which she does. She goes to sleep early. I lie there in the humidity, thinking, sweating, rolling side to side, and finally I drift off to sleep.

Then come the screams in the night. The itch, the pain. My parents trying to console her. As hot September ekes its way along, this starts happening every night. Things are getting louder: "Stop it! Do something! Stop the itching. I can't stand the itching!" It either hurts or it itches; one way or the other, it won't give her any rest. So then, when all appeals to my parents have failed, she invokes the names of anyone she can think of. My name is one. She yells, "I want Bobby!"

My distraught mother comes into my room and says, "Go and talk to her. She's calling for you." I try to talk to her, but I can't do her any good. She's yelling, "Help me! It hurts! Stop the itch!" But I can't stop the itch.

The heat of September finally eased off. October arrived, bringing relief with the cooler weather. But the screams in the night got worse. I was playing football, I needed rest. I couldn't do her any good, but she still called for me. My parents stopped coming in to get me in the night. They told me not to worry. They told me to sleep. I put pillows over my head. One night I heard her yell, "Why don't you just kill me? Why can't I die and get this over with?" As things got close to the end she started screaming out horrible obscenities, things you wouldn't think a nine-year-old girl would know. As if the utterance of taboo words could defeat the pain and the itch.

Sometime in early October they put her in the Eustis Hospital. No point in going back to Boston; nothing more could be done there. I remember visiting her a few days before she died. She was unconscious in the hospital bed, her naked body attached to various tubes and wires. I.v.'s and other hookups, in her nose, mouth, crotch. So I didn't get to talk to her. What would I have said anyway?

On Monday, Oct. 22, 1956, I was sitting in Mrs. Nana T. Laney's English class when somebody came down with a message that Prof Roseborough wanted to see me in the principal's office. This was not unexpected.

Prof didn't tell me anything. He just looked at me soberly and he said, "Your parents called, and they want you to come home." I said, "Fine. Thank you." I went back to Mrs. Laney's class to get my books from beneath the desk. I interrupted the class. They all looked at me. I told Mrs. Laney, "Excuse me. I need some books to take with me. I may not be back to school for a few days." She looked at me, and they all looked at me, my friends and classmates, but nobody said anything.

I was always the diligent student. Didn't want to get behind on the schoolwork. I walked with my books across Clayton St., past Mr. Schott's house (he was our physics teacher). I walked through the orange groves, the same way I always walked home for lunch, and after school. In those days there were citrus trees behind every house in the block that was bounded by Clayton St., Fifth Avenue, Grandview, and Seventh.

When I got to the back door of the pink house my mother was waiting for me. All she said was, "She's gone." I nodded and didn't say anything. That was my big mistake. I should have started cursing right then and there, smashing up dishes in the kitchen. But I just went off to my room and lay down on the bed. For some reason Daddy wasn't home then, but Aunt Cille, his sister, showed up soon after that. I remember her coming into the bedroom and holding me. She cried, but I didn't. I was numb.

Everyone has a different recollection of the same event. My younger sister Peggy, seven years old, was in her brownie uniform, on her way home from a meeting. Linda Pohlman, who was only a few years older than her, rode by on a bicycle. She stopped to talk. She said, "I'm sorry about your sister Jacqi." Embarrassed, indignant, Peggy said, "What are you talking about? There's nothing wrong with my sister Jacqi! What are you talking about?"

She ran home, upset. Mommy was in the bathroom crying when Peggy got there. She said, "Jacqi's gone. Dead. She's up in Heaven now." Then she sat there on the toilet and cried some more.

For the obituary see the front page of *The Mount Dora Topic*, Oct. 25, 1956. When I re-read this today, I feel some of the old rage come roiling back in my guts. The anger internalized, the beginning of the early fading. The funeral was held at the Catholic Church in Eustis. Yes, Mommy had won that last great battle for the immortal soul of my blue-eyed sister Jacqi. I guess Daddy didn't have the stomach to fight over which church would bury her. Besides that, when she had Jacqi alone with her that summer in Boston, Mommy had spent lots of time at the church. They went to services every day. Consequently, Jacqi herself expressed the wish to be Catholic in the end.

So they sent her off with the statues of the Holy Virgin looking on, in that dark place full of candles. The priest chanted in Latin and censed the coffin, swinging the smoking censer to and fro. I was there with my teary-eyed grandparents from South Carolina, Bowie Mom and Colonel Bob. I was there with my weeping sister June, with my parents, Daddy collapsing on his feet, and, once again, Mommy being "the strong one," with my little sister Peggy, who blocked the grievous business out of her young mind and has no recollection of that funeral today. All I can remember is how angry I was. At the hordes of people who came to the service, packing that small church to the gills, at my parents, at the priest, at myself, at God.

Of course I had tried everything I could think of to save her. I had prayed to the Lord, bargained in the puerile way that people often do

("Take me, not her, etc."). Nothing had worked and nobody had helped, and I hated the whole world. But I never said anything to anybody. I was a quiet person, and after Jacqi's death I just got quieter.

I missed the rest of that week at school. Sitting out on the side porch, I read my textbooks. Kept up on the assignments. There wasn't much else to do. Nobody had anything to do. Daddy took off work. We sat around, but we didn't talk much. We were not a big talking family.

We didn't have to cook. People from all over town brought casseroles, fried chicken, pies, cakes, etc., etc., etc. Of course, we had no appetite anyway. The Frenches, our next door neighbors, came over with a dish of something and got on my nerves, as usual. People would bring their food, sit around, try to say something consoling. Things that don't need saying and don't do any good. But, after all, seventy-five per cent of the words we utter to others have the same meaning as "Hello, how you doing?" Words are a way of telling your collocutor, "You're a human being and so am I and we're in this thing called the Human Condition together." She's in a better place now. God takes the best ones first. She doesn't have to suffer any more, she's sitting in the lap of the Lord.

My parents answered these comments with banalities of their own. But me, I just sat and glared. Looking back on it now, I know full well that those people were kind. There was no reason for me to be angry with anyone in Mt. Dora, Florida. But I hated them all. And myself. She was gone and we were still here. The one person I might have talked to was Prof Roseborough, but he didn't come by.

After a few days of listless sitting and reading, I went back to school. Everybody looked at me. With that same uneasy look. Nobody said anything, not Mrs. Laney, not Dan Spear, not my classmates or friends, nobody. Not even Prof. Death is an uncomfortable thing. Nobody knows what to say. Does that mean they didn't feel for me? Of course not. They felt for me. I hated them all for pretending nothing had happened. And if they had said anything, I would have hated them for what they said.

I had missed one football game, against Groveland. When I returned to school that Monday, Oct. 29, 1956, Dan Spear said, "We need you. Can you play this week against Bishop Moore?" I said "Sure." So I did, I played in a state of utter depression, until that ninety yard run lit up my spirit. I've already told you about that game on All Souls Day. I didn't know it then, but after that game Bishop Moore High School got tied into my psyche right next to my sister. Only now, while I'm writing this, do I realize why I was so happy to play B.M. a year later, on Nov. 1, 1957. It was a chance to commune, one last time, with the dear beloved dead.

Right now I'm looking at the football schedule for that 1956 season, and I don't have much recollection of the games we played toward the end. I do remember warming up out on the field, before the Umatilla game. That was on Oct. 12, ten days before she died. The Umatilla loudspeaker system was blaring out a song called "The Green Door." Something about a secret somebody was hiding behind a green door. I was tossing a football back and forth with Richard Gardner, listening to the music. Thinking, "That song is stupid. Everything and everybody is stupid. What am I doing here? I don't want to be here. I want to be nowhere."

We had a horrible record that year: 2-7. That tore you up, Dan Spear; you always hated to lose. But, frankly, I didn't care. I used to take walks at night, around the streets of Mt. Dora, in late October and early November. I would go by the school, looking at it, wishing I could break every window in every white, arcaded, Spanish-style hacienda building.

There's one funny thing about all this, Dan Spear. From the time I first started playing football for you in the ninth grade you were always trying to make me mad. You figured the best football player was an angry player. Then came Oct. 22, 1956, and shy little Bobby Bowie became the angriest player on any field anywhere. But I'm not sure you, or my team mates, ever realized that. It didn't begin immediately—the desire to hurt somebody. I was still too numb. But by the baseball season of spring, 1957, I was already a madman. I was trying to spike the legs of the players on the other team. I went into wild rages when I struck out, pounding my bat on the ground. Nobody asked what was wrong. Nobody said anything, not George Clements, the baseball coach, not my parents, not my team mates, not Prof Roseborough, who sat watching the games from his light green 1953 Chevrolet, parked out along the third base line, blowing his horn when we got a rally going.

Next fall came the 1957 football season. My leg was injured, but, if anything, that made me even angrier. I was frustrated at the injury. I played hard. I racked. Did anybody notice a difference? Doubtful. Because I didn't whoop it up or communicate with my team mates; I played in total silence. But I wanted to create havoc. I suppose the major impulse was self-destructive. If anyone at MDHS was even vaguely aware of that impulse they didn't show it. With one exception: Gary Potter. He never said anything, but I had the feeling he was trying to pull me out of the isolation. In the fall of 1957 he made a few moves to accomplish that, and I was grateful to him. Still am. Gratefulness doesn't die with the person you feel grateful to.

But I didn't want to hurt anyone in the game against Bishop Moore, not on the happiest day of my life, All Saints Day, 1957. Bishop Moore was special. That night I was laughing. Sure, I was knocking people down, running over them, around them, but I was doing it all in a spirit of pure joy. I loved Bishop Moore that night. I loved every player on their team, their fans, their cheering section, and I loved Barry Keitel.

Fourth quarter. We didn't need to hope cautiously any more. We were beyond that stage. Now we were all thinking like Lew Earle Williams, Jr. It looked like it might come down to who had the last possession. It was that kind of wild offensive game. B.M. got the ball early in the quarter and drove all the way down the field. That drive went for a total of fifty-five yards and ate up a lot of time on the clock. We couldn't stop them. We kept backing up, digging in, hanging on. But Musante and the Ellis boys were chipping away, a few yards at a time, and finally Jim Ellis scored on a one-yard plunge. They missed the kick conversion. It was 26-25. We were up by one measly point.

Then we took the kickoff and started our own drive. It bogged down around midfield, the Hornets got the ball. They started coming at us again, but we held on. The ball exchanged hands several times. After that, with about five minutes to go, we put another long drive in motion, following John Lavin's recovery of a fumble. From the B.M. thirty-two yard line Neil Stoothoff broke away again, for the third time that night. He took the ball around right end and scored. We missed the extra point, but now we were seven to the good, and that was back before the dawning of the two-point conversion. At this juncture I can imagine the benumbed B.M. fans, sitting in the grandstand on the Highland side, mumbling Hail Marys, praying for some grace. At least one person, my mother, was probably doing the same on the other side of the field.

The way things worked out, Bishop Moore had the last possession. After each team bogged down again, after several more exchanges of the ball, we had less than a minute left in the game. As Mabel Norris Reese would put it, "There was naught but sheer desperation in Hornet souls." I can conjure up Barry Keitel over there on the sidelines. Long forgotten was Dan Spear's pre-game threat to pull our team off the field and forfeit. That threat was so irrelevant now, so far distant in Barry's mind, that it might have been made ten years ago. Barry knew that this possession was the last chance his school would have to keep the undefeated season intact. Barry was chewing on the fingernails of one hand. With the other he was fingering a rosary in his pocket. He wasn't thinking "win" any more—he was praying for a tie.

Bishop Moore was no passing team. When they got the ball that one last time, they decided to go with their best. They ran John Ellis at us every play. They gave up on younger brother Jim and made a full-time blocking back out of Musante. They handed the ball to John Ellis, John Ellis, John Ellis. He was bringing it down the field, eight yards, six yards, ten yards. Now the Mt. Dora cheerleaders and fans kept up a steady, frenetic chant: "Hold that line! Hold that line!" Their voices were full of entreaty, begging us: "Hold that line!" We were trying, but we hadn't done much holding of the line all night.

All eyes kept flickering back and forth, from the field to that big score-board clock, which towered behind the Seventh Avenue goal posts, in front of the old Pohlwright stucco house. These were the days when scoreboard clocks still had a minute hand and a second hand. B.M. was trying to use time, to make it their friend, but time is nobody's friend. When they saw the minute hand begin its final revolution, they did something you can't do in life: they stopped time. But even in football you can only do this until your time outs run out.

Then Ellis again: five yards, fifteen yards, seven yards. We backed up, dug in, held on. The Mt. Dora cheerleaders had changed over to a different chorus: "Push 'em back, push 'em back, WAAAAAAY BACK!" When that one didn't work, they returned to the desperate litany called "Hold that line!" The whole Mt. Dora side of the field was booming it out, but the cheerleaders wanted more volume. They were putting mean grimaces on and shaking fists at the crowd: "Y'all aren't yelling! We want everybody yelling, EVERYBODY!... Y'all still aren't yelling! Louder! Hold that line! Hold that line!"

Then B.M. ran out of time outs. Time refused to stop any more. They stuck with Ellis. But now it was fewer yards each carry: six yards, four yards, three. The Hornet players were casting frenzied glances at the scoreboard clock. Now the minute hand had made its last turn and retired for the night, and the second hand had only one more go-round. The Mt. Dora fans and cheerleaders were on the verge of tears. They croaked out in hoarse voices: "Hold that line! Hold that line! Hold that line!"

I looked at John Ellis, and John Ellis looked tired. But he kept coming at us: four yards, two yards, one. After that one-yard gain—after Moon, Potter and McCallister unpiled from on top of him—he got up very slowly. But then he shook himself and raced back to the huddle. John Ellis was no quitter; nobody else on that B.M. team was either.

They threw a pass out of bounds, and the second hand stopped with fifteen seconds left. In those days the scoreboard clocks were inexact. Genuine game time was kept by one of the referees on the field, and now Ellis was running up to him screaming, "How much time left? How much time?" The timekeeper, who must have felt just then like God, said, "Eight seconds," and that's when I thought, "It's over."

They got off one more play. No gain. I think John Lavin made that final tackle. Or was it Earle Williams? Where was the ball when it ended? I can't remember for sure, but maybe you can, Dan Spear. On our fifteen yard line? On our eight yard line? All I know is that Ellis needed at least another twenty seconds of clock, and he had only eight. Then he had nil.

We won, 32-25. Anyone who doesn't believe it happened can turn to the sports pages of the *Orlando Sentinel*, Nov. 2, 1957. We won, and we stood there under the arc lights, dazed. We weren't laughing but we were smiling. Not slapping high fives—high fives weren't invented yet. Shaking hands with one another and smiling. As the Bishop Moore players hung their heads and trudged off toward their bus, shouting teary obscenities back our way, the Mt. Dora cheerleaders and fans broke into song: "Hurrah for Hurricanes, hurrah for Hurricanes, someone's in the crowd yelling 'Hurrah for Hurricanes!' One two three four, who you gonna yell for? Hurricanes! That's us, rah, rah, rah, hurrah for Hurricanes, hurrah for Hurricanes,..."

We stood there befuddled, grinning at each other. You mean we won? Then Coach Dan Spear came running full tilt onto the field, running as fast as he did back when he played for the University of Chattanooga. And, you know, he wasn't mad any more? He was laughing.

8

You're still the same Dan Spear/ The gallimaufry of life/ My son Jamie, who started out a runt (pediatrician telling us, "Well, no way he'll make it past five foot three"), and now he's six foot tall and getting a PhD in sociology, so there!/Conk peas, grits with cheese/ Magnolia blossoms start white, go brown/ Reading The Idiot*/ Anybody seen Creighton Snavely?/ "The country boy takes his lunch"/ A nut salesman gives me a compliment/ What I'll be like when (if) I'm 80/ Jan Potter buys drinks for Dan Spear/ I'm Leebo McCree, flooding the roast/ How to be kind to old Russian ladies/ An early end to scarfing days/ Still a star!/ /Walking the dog that bites you/ Fred Schoellhumper sticks a big toe into East Germany/ B.M. boys, reliving glory days/ "They bought the #$%%$#& referees!"/ Shards of scintillating glass/ Nightmares/ (Puny retards in orange jerseys)/ Barry smells a rat/ Dancing the Russian squat dance/ In a jock strap/ Bamboozled/ Why we won/ My loved ones live on Donnelly St./ Daddy moves to Sylvan Shores?/ "Be a good boy and say your prayers"/ Travelling thru life, "gaining geographical and economical knowledge"/ Prof/ "Don't be a slacker"/ Asphalt coalescing in the smell of jasmine/ Just like Bobby Correll/ The Walking Jesus is gone*

Post-game for me, and for you, Dan Spear, amounts to all the years
that have rolled over and played dead, like our dog Danny, since 1957. A lot
of things have happened. Billy Odom went to F.S.U. and played on the
same team as Burt Reynolds. Harry Wise, number one on the list of my
boyhood football idols, got a job selling rugs in Orlando, then died young.
They built a new Mt. Dora High, and it was integrated. You retired from
coaching, then from teaching, your wife Bert died suddenly, and you went
through God knows what else. You'll have to tell those stories yourself; my
knowledge of the high and low points in your life is limited. But I'd be
willing to bet that nothing has changed you much, that at age 77 you're the
same passionate and belligerent man you always were. The main thing is
you're still around, playing golf, digging up tree stumps, and basking in the
Mt. Dora humidity. That's an achievement, considering how many people
at that football game on All Saints Day have crossed over to what might be
a better world.

I've been telling you all along, in passing, some of the things that hap-
pened in my life. I left Mt. Dora, went to college at the University of
Florida, joined the army during the Vietnam era, studied Russian at the
Defense Language Institute in Monterey, California. I served in Germany
and England, was married, went to graduate school (Tulane, then
Vanderbilt), took a PhD in Russian literature. My life has been interesting.
Married, divorced, got three sons, and they came out great: Jamus, Robert
N., and Nathan the Grecian. Hope they read this letter some day. It might
give them an idea about what made me what I later became. I haven't
written about my marriage and my divorce, because divorce can be worse
than death and these things are too painful to air out on paper. For a few
years I was an okay husband, and I did all right at propagating the species,
but, on the whole, I wasn't too spectacular at marriage.

But since when did the Powers Above guarantee anybody a smooth
body-surf on the sea waves of life? I'm lucky to have sons. I've got a brown-

headed son, a blonde-headed son, and a red-headed son. Now how did that happen? God works in strange ways. But they're mine, all mine. Luckily, though, in some respects they take after their mother more than me. That gives them a shot at living a calmer life than the one I'm working on. So it's too bad the marriage didn't last, and there have been other problems, but then, if I were to die tomorrow, I wouldn't go whining up to Peter at the Pearly Gates (or to the Other Guy down below). No complaints, y'all! No way I intend to send it back to the Chef, the gallimaufry that He or She (my God is "equal opportunity") has dished out to me! That's a fancy word for Hungarian goulash.

To continue the food metaphor: you might ask why the cook (me) got so carried away, preparing my casserole for your tribute. Well, in the beginning I figured on making your meal out of one football game—a simple beef roast, well done. But then, in my head, I started chopping up carrots, rutabagas, okra, cabbage, tossed it all in a pot, poured in three huge bottles of tabasco, turned on the faucet. And then the faucet got stuck and the water kept running, and not only that: my knife commenced to chopping on its own, adding to the ingredients. A mess of collards, conk peas, mustard greens, grits with cheese melted in and the half-way-in-between fried and scrambled eggs that my father could fix so well, leg of lamb with mint sauce and sprinkles of parsley (lamb's an un-Southern thing, but my lips still drool when I recall the legs we Bowies feasted on, sitting at the table on the back porch of the pink house, with a magnolia blossom in a dish of water, sweet-scented and going brown at the edges of the flocculent white, the way life goes brown if you live it long enough), and, speaking of eggs, the steak and fried eggs easy over that I ate for breakfast when I lived in the dales of Yorkshire, England, at Menwith Hill with the army, after working the midnight shift in that windowless building for "spooks," surrounded by sheep grazing the resplendent green of the grass amidst a field of antennas, and then you're too exhausted to sleep, been up all night

reading Dostoevsky's *Idiot* in Russian, so after breakfast you get on the bus,
you and five others, and you ride down town, into Harrogate, just in time
for the pubs to open at 10:00 a.m., and you drink pints of bitter (Tetley's
brand is the best) all morning, then stagger back to the bus for the ride to
the barracks of Menwith and sleep till 11:00 p.m., get on the work bus, ride
down to the windowless building, baaing at the dark sheep you think you
see beside the roadway, read *The Idiot* again all night, and how, you may ask,
did you get away with reading on the job? Well, I could do the "intelligence"
part of my work in three hours, and that left me five hours of an eight-hour
shift to read Russian novels, meanwhile sergeants with deep-South faces
creeping around our "linguist" section, any foreign language Greek to those
guys, you want to freak them out just hold up a book with cyrillic writing,
they were looking for Creighton Snavely, who always slept away his midnight shift under our desk, sergeants asking, "Where's Snavely, anybody
seen Snavely? That sumbitch has disappeared again" that reminds me when
Chris Hamlet and I went to London for the weekend, we're staying in U.S.
military lodgings, wake up in the morning run into two jarheads (American
marines) who just flew in on leave from Iceland had suitcases full of nothing
but booze we start drinking at eight in the morning drank all day long doing
tours of Dickens' "Old Curiosity Shop" staying steadily happy high, until
finally their day in London is over (the marines') and we put them on a bus
for the airport, they're sunk in gloom now, grieving over going back to what
must be the worst duty station on earth, Iceland, weeping drunken tears,
embracing us (the way drunk Russians do), and Chris and I have tickets for
a play that night at the Royal Shakespeare Theatre, and we sleep through
the whole damn thing. God! Life was a ball in the army! That's where I
really learned to live laughing, of course not counting the Bishop Moore
game in 1957. Now, I wasn't drinking in fifty-seven (too young), and won't
be in ninety-seven (too old), but the army has a way of washing away your

cares in a sea of bourbon, so you might notice, Dan Spear, that my tabasco has high alcohol content,

into the pot goes Seven and Seven, I.W. Harper, Absolut (citron flavor), Amstel beer from Holland, Jack Daniels and his cousin George Dickel, Russian rotgut vodka (and I used to like the pepper flavored Stolichnaya), and, meanwhile, the faucet I turned on still running and the knife still chopping: black-eyed peas, Bermuda onions (mild! why can't you buy them in Ohio?), beet greens (my favorite greens of all), artichokes in Felippo Berio olive oil (import from Italy), when I was stationed in Monterey there were artichoke fields choking the California landscape, and me, just a hillbilly from the mountains of Central Florida, never tasted artichoke in my life, but now I have and like it, remember your lecture, Dan Spear, about the country boy and the city boy?: "City boy goes to the movies, gets bored. Country boy, when he goes to the movies, he watches the whole blessed double feature, with the newsreel and cowboy serial, twice through. The country boy takes his lunch!" Well, forty years later I'm still searching for the hidden meaning of that allegorical fable,

and still wondering just what in the hell The Walking Jesus was doing walking Mt. Dora in his white pants, chartreuse shirt, with the multicolor of translucent scarves draped around him, I saw him once when I was maybe ten, riding my bike, and he was limping on his left leg down Donnelly that day, scratching his bottom as he went, out by what is now the new W.T. Bland Library (Earle Williams and I once spent a summer pruning orange trees for W.T., "Bill," Bland), the one by the sinkhole with the goats (now what other beautiful library in the U.S.A. has a sinkhole with goats right beside it?—ah, Mt. Dora!), and as for the artichokes, I've been cutting down on olive oil recently, you get to my age and you can't metabolize any more, so I'm fasting two days a week, I'd like to keep weighing the same thing I did in 1957, and I do (almost), except it's spread now mostly over my waistline, as for women, I started late, never knew what to do with women in high school or college, or how to talk to them, pretend you're interested in the crap they're talking, but I learned all this in the army... Actually, I haven't written about women much in this story, Dan Spear, because after years of trying to figure them out, I must admit that I still don't comprehend one solitary thing about what makes a woman act like she does.

When I was at Monterey we'd go over to Carmel Beach on weekends, taking our books with us, lie on white sand studying Russian, tanning, swimming in the surf, watching the surf boarders, but mainly to scarf up women, Carmel Beach being, in my limited experience, the best scarfing grounds anywhere, we'd approach the women on their blankets and introduce ourselves, then say, "Hey, we're having a beach party tonight. Want to come?" We had other pick-up lines, but the favorite of my friend Fred Schoellhumper, a short, wide, good-natured guy from Pennsylvania, was simply "Secretaries from San Francisco?" It worked really well, since so many women on Carmel Beach on any weekend really were secretaries from San Francisco. But then one day Fred's scarfing career came to a sudden end. We're lying on our army blankets, studying our Russian, me, Ed Klebius, and Fred, and I say, "Hey, Fred, those girls over there look nice. Why don't you go see if you can't scarf them up?" So congenial, innocent Fred got up, brushed the sand off his big Pennsylvania Dutch face and his ample torso, put on his scarfing smile, and be-bopped off.

Thirty seconds later he was back. He lay down on the khaki blanket and just looked off toward Point Lobos in the distance. He didn't say anything. We (Klebius and I) said, "Well, Fred, what happened?" He didn't answer. We said, "Did you scarf them up? Are they coming to our beach party tonight?" He didn't answer. We said, "What's the matter, Fred? Huh?"

Fred didn't answer for a long time, and then he said, in this weak, hurt-little-boy voice: "Well, I walked up and spread my arms, smiling, like I always do, and I said, 'Ta-dah! Secretaries from San Francisco!' And they just stared at me for a long long time, real mean looks on their faces, and finally one of them said, 'Get lost, buster.' "

After that, we couldn't get Fred Schoellhumper to go scarfing, not ever again, and, in fact, he never did marry, and all because of one insensitive remark on a beach in 1963, which just proves that one thing women should try to be is kind.

I like foreign women best, always have, married a British woman, I like Japanese, Russian, Ugandan, etc., trouble is, I don't like them too old and this is turning into a problem, being as I'm not getting any younger. I was walking around Moscow with my Russian girlfriend Lyuda (that was in 1990), and we go by this geezer selling shelled walnuts on the square, well, we sat on a park bench for a while, this being at the Kiev train station, where the old grannies bring in their flowers on commuter trains and stand selling bouquets in their kerchiefs and the black spots where teeth are supposed to be, and speaking of teeth, it's also a big gathering spot for the infernal gypsies, who lounge around on the grass, picking their gold teeth and looking for people to rob, so we're sitting on a park bench and Lyuda decides she wants some of those walnuts, and speaking of teeth, and I should tell you in advance this is a beautiful Russian woman (Lyuda), not bragging but it's a fact, so I mosey back over to where that geezer's standing, he's got a bald head, wearing filthy clothes and his front teeth missing, and I buy some walnuts off him, and while he's measuring one cupful and pouring them into my sack, he says to me, "Say, that girl you're with, would that be your daughter?" I look insulted and I tell him, "Daughter, my ass—that's my girlfriend." (*Dochka! Yolkee-palkee, eto moya padrooshka!*) Then he sticks this really impressed look on his toothless "senior" mug and he says, "No shit? (*Neeuzhelee?*) She must be what, twenty-seven, twenty-eight?" I don't answer that one, just kind of shrug, the way Russians do, and he says, "And you, well you'll be about my age, won't you?" Then I looked at myself through his eyes and thought, "Oh my God!" (*Bozhe moj!*), because I'm looking at what he looks like and he's comparing himself to me, but I keep my cool and ask, "Well, how old are you?" He says, "Fifty-three," and I shrug again and say, "Oh, no, you're a lot older than I am. Me, I'm only fifty." And he's pouring his nuts and saying, "Wow! (*Zdoruhvuh*). And you've got a woman that looks like that! *Muhlahdyets!* (Way to go)."

So what I'm thinking is that if folks think my girlfriends are my daughters and I don't go for older women, then what's going to happen if I live to be 80? I can visualize myself sitting in a wheelchair, shrunk shanks, nothing left in the mouth but gums, spitting tobacco juice into an empty pork and beans can, like my grandfather Colonel Bob always did, brown ooze drooling down into the white stubble of his chin, and I visualize a sweet young thing pushing that wheelchair around and wiping away the drool, and she goes off to get me a Jack Daniels on the rocks, and some young twerp walking up and asking me, "Say, pops, that girl that's with you, she's a fine looking young piece, would she be your great granddaughter?" Well, I won't even answer. I'll just raise one cockeyed eyebrow and screw up my wizened prune face at this moron, and I'll spit

so like I was saying, and, oh, yeah, one more thing to be chopped up and thrown in the pot: fresh dill and cilantro, the herbs I learned to love in Russia, where I buy them from the peasant crones who squat around the metro stations, huckstering their vegetables and being cantankerous, the way all old women act in Russia, taking no guff, putting you in your place, until you make a joke, smile and kid with them and they smile back, and both of you feel the better for it, so why can't we learn to be human beings and leave the antagonism behind is something I've wondered about my own self, and about the whole world, all my life, and you may ask how come I can get young women to like an old geezer like me and the answer is that on my better days (not often, but sometimes) I remember D.D. Roseborough's advice and I put aside all the anxieties and rancor inside me and I'm *kind*.

So, to get back to the gallimaufry, maybe my sauce is a little bit too hot and maybe too much got blended into the hash I macerated up for your testimonial dinner, Dan Spear, and the faucet keeps right on running, overflowing the pot, flooding the playground, so it's like Leebo McCree and Judy Sadler out there in 1947, perched up on opposite ends of a teeter-totter and soaking their toes in a blend of white Florida sand and foaming stew, with tiny specks of garlic and kumquat floating on top, so you either put you on some high fisherman's waders there at the roast tonight, Dan Spear, or you start swimming. Maybe you better just dog paddle your way through the parts on football. Jan Potter can buy you drinks to keep you afloat. Okay, Jan?

Well, I've got a few more stories I'd like to tell, but we're almost out of time. The main thing is everything came out all right in my life, or at least as all right as anybody's life comes out. Thanks to people like you. You taught me to be tough; you taught me how to throw a side-straddle body block! So what are a few drunken Azeris, thirty years younger than me, with knives? Could I have imagined, as a boy in Mt. Dora, back in 1957, that on June 6, 1992, I'd be on a nightmare Air Azeri flight, standing up to cutthroats with Saadam Hussein mustaches, screaming hard words in their faces in the Russian language? Could anybody back in the fifties have imagined that about little Bobby Bowie?

Still a star, thirty-five years later, Dan Spear! Bobby Booby, still a hero! Thanks to you and Mt. Dora football and Bishop Moore High School. Why did I so want to be at that roast tonight, if not in person, at least in writing? The answer is obvious. It's the same answer you'll get from the ex-players who showed up, if they're honest with themselves. Of course, they, and I, want to honor you on this special occasion, pay tribute to your skills as a coach, to the way you taught us lessons about life that helped us go from boys to men. But most importantly, they, and I, want to relive the glory, to remember the "good old days," and even some that weren't so good. It's *nostalgia* that brings these people, and this, my letter, to you tonight, Coach Spear.

Funny. On the nights of insomnia Barry Keitel has really helped. I've learned to love Barry. Ever since Nov. 1, 1957, Barry Keitel and Bishop Moore football have occupied a nice warm spot in my creative imagination. For example:

It was July of 1964, and I was on guard duty overlooking the East German border, walking the dog that bit us all, carrying the M-14 rifle with no cartridges, and suddenly I started thinking of Barry Keitel. We were stationed in a wheat field, on a hill looking down on the barbed wire. This was a so-called "intelligence operation," but we weren't doing anything very intelligent. We lived TDY in huge field tents for three months. Fred Schoellhumper, who was two classes ahead of me at Monterey, ended up in that wheat field too. Good old humor-impaired Fred. He was the kind of guy who, if he said to you, "I walked home to save bus fare today," and you answered, "Well, golly, Fred, you'd have saved a lot more money by not taking a taxi," well, then Fred would say, "I told you; I didn't take a taxi—I walked home to save on bus fare." That's what I mean by "humor-impaired."

We worked in our wheat field, harvesting "intelligence," and listened to Armed Forces Radio—Mick Jagger singing "Because I Used to Love Her, But It's All Over Now." The nearest city was Helmstedt, but the only habitat anywhere near us was the village of Heidwinkle. It was boring. We used to walk down to the border sometimes, even though that was strictly against orders: the East German guards, up in their wooden watch towers, were trigger-happy, and one day they took a shot at one of our strollers. You see, the barbed wire fences were not on the actual border, but were set back a little bit, so that if you walked up to the fences, you were already in East Germany. They had mine fields on the other side of the wire, in the broad ploughed-over strips of earth.

The sergeants gave us maps showing exactly how the border ran. It zigzagged in and out, instead of going in a straight line. One night Fred Schoellhumper and I were drinking at the E.M. club in Heidwinkle. After he and I walked the mile back out to our home in the wheat field, he insisted on pulling out his map and going down to the border. We had a flashlight, and Fred staggered along, stopping periodically to consult the map. When we got to where he considered the boundary line, we may have been in East Germany already. But he was so sure this was it that he took a stick and drew a mark on the ground. Then he stood with his ample torso in what he said was West Germany and kept poking a big toe across that line, holding it in the Communist World. He yelled out insults in German (Fred was from Pennsylvania and knew German), directed at the watch towers across the way. But the border guards must have been sleeping that night; nobody took a shot at Fred's toe.

Years later, driving around in Ohio with the family, we'd see these Pennsylvania license plates with "You've Got a Friend in Pennsylvania," and I'd always say to Joan and the kids, "It's true! But how did they know it? I really do have a friend in Pennsylvania: Fred Schoellhumper." But now, even more years later, I wonder. Are you out there in life-in-the-flesh, burly, cordial, naive, humor-impaired Fred? Do I still have a friend in Pennsylvania?

Why did they send us that German shepherd dog without a handler? Because that's the army way. The dog had been trained to bite, and since there was no one to tell him not to, he proceeded to bite everybody in our wheat field. Despite that, the sergeants said he was there to protect us from the Russian tank troops who were training on the other side of the barbed wire. So we had to walk guard duty with him. They issued only that one M-14 rifle for the whole camp, and they wouldn't give us any cartridges for it. Said we "Monterey Marys" (the "linguists") might hold the gun by the wrong end and accidentally shoot ourselves. Anyway, the guy pulling guard duty got to carry an empty M-14 and lead a vicious dog. That's what I was doing, toting that gun and looking down on the fences of Communist Germany, trying to keep my distance from the dog I was walking, thinking, God, get me out of this, when suddenly Barry Keitel popped into my mind, and I started reminiscing about the glorious victory over B.M.

For treatment of depression Barry Keitel beats Prozac. When in grievous adversity conjure up Barry as you remember him (have re-created him) on Nov. 1, 1957. You reckon he's still alive today? Does he recall that game? Well, if he's alive, you can be damn sure he remembers. Paul Musante does too, and the Ellis boys. Once, around 1960, I happened to meet Jim Ellis at the University of Florida. A mutual friend, Stuart Stuart, who graduated from Bishop Moore in 1958, introduced us, and when Jim heard my name he nearly passed out on his feet. "Bowie! Oh, no. Are you the Bowie? You blankety blanked blankety blank! You ruined a whole year of my life!" I thought he was joking at first, but then, as we continued to talk, I realized that game from 1957 was still rankling in his guts. After he got started on it, we (Stuart and I) couldn't shut him up.

Now let's imagine a scene out of 1994—featuring two former B.M. players with their families on Thanksgiving Day. Let's say their hair has gone grey and they've got beer guts up front. We'll call them Billy and Bob for purposes of this fictional presentation, and we'll watch them watching Notre Dame football, drinking gin and yelling for the Irish. Their wives, former B.M. cheerleaders who got sick of football twenty-five years ago, are out in the kitchen basting up a turkey. The kids and grand kids are in the back yard, tossing a whiffle ball around. While they drink and watch, the former B.M. boys think back on the glory days of the Hornets. They get a lot of satisfaction, of course, reliving those wonderful days of yore. After all, B.M. had some great football teams, especially the fifty-seven bunch, which lost only one game. So Bobby and Billy drink and exult, and as long as they're in the euphoric stage of drinking they dwell on the victories. "We were great, you know that?" says Billy. "We were really great."

"Damn right we were," answers Bob.

But then, at a certain magic moment, their brains click over into the angry stage, and that's when All Saints Day, 1957, comes up. Bobby takes the gin bottle from the coffee table and pours himself another drink. "How, how did we do it?" he says. "How did we manage to lose that game?"

"It was the frigging officials!" answers Billy. "They were bought off!"

The boys fall silent for a moment. They sit there thinking. Bill stands up, stalks back and forth across the room, muttering under his breath. His anger builds. Now he's looking for the dog to kick, but, unfortunately, his wife Becky just let Brownie out the back door. That frustrates him even more, having no dog to kick, and Bill settles for smashing his glass against the wall. The ice and bits of glass spatter across the living room, and a thin trail of ginny water drains down onto the sofa, right where Bobby reclines. Bob doesn't react at all, just sits glaring morosely at the dribble. Then he reaches aimlessly over with his index finger and traces out three words on the wet wall: "Kilroy was here."

"Somebody bought the fucking referees!" Billy yells again.

Bob mulls it over.

"Yeah, that must have been it," he says gloomily. "We couldn't have just lost that game. There had to be a reason." Bill sits back down. He stares at the wall, where the water slowly drips. The wives come in. They've heard the sound of breaking glass. Taking one look at their grieving husbands, they understand at once what the topic of conversation is: 1957. Mt. Dora. Without a word they tiptoe back into the kitchen and check the roasting turkey.

The boys sit in silence. Billy picks up a few shards of glass from the floor, puts them on the coffee table and arranges them in various patterns.

He studies his sculptures, enchanted by the moist light shining through them. After that he goes into the kitchen and comes back with a new glass and fresh ice.

They have another shot of gin. They drink in silence. "Yeah, the god damn referees," mutters Bob.

Then comes the end stage in the drinking process—the lachrymose stage. The boys put their arms around each other, looking at the beer guts and grey hair, wondering out loud where all the years went. Tears are running down their faces, they hold each other and rock side to side, and then, finally, Bobby moans out the truth: "No, Billy, it wasn't the officials. No. We got beat. Those pathetic little hicks reamed our butts. But how, how did it happen? How could we have lost that game?"

The preceding is a totally fictitious scene, although I may have almost got it right. Then again, for all I know those boys could have become monks. They may be out in a cloister somewhere at this very moment, praying to God, saving their eternal souls. If so, they probably haven't given a thought to B.M. football in thirty years. But some nights, lying on the hard pallets that serve them as beds, in their dreams they still see a nightmare scene: a subtropical hick town, all live oaks and Spanish moss, a smell like magnolias mixed with pestilence in the air, arc lights shining on a football field, across from a stucco house with a yellow-blooming hibiscus bush, and emaciated demons in orange jerseys, grinning skeleton grins, advancing upon the boys of Bishop Moore.

It happened again in 1991. I was lying awake in the Hotel Race Horse, Moscow, USSR, the night after they kicked the shit out of my friend Volodya, and I started imagining again what went through Barry Keitel's head, before, during, and after that game. In the first place, could Barry have said to Coach John Bryan, "Now, listen, Jacko, we can't run the score up too much, 'cause Dan said he'd forfeit"? No, he wouldn't have done that. But as angry as Dan Spear was, Barry must have taken the threat seriously. And the very fact that he believed what Dan said could have had an oblique influence on the B.M. team. Even if he didn't say anything. After all, Barry Keitel was the athletic director of the high school. Psychologically, even what he was *thinking* was important!

Then, later (at least by halftime), Barry must have reached the conclusion that it was a ploy. The Mt. Dora coach had feigned anger, yelled in his face, embarrassed him. Dan Spear was a devious bastard. I can imagine Barry imagining (at some point in the second half) a scene that occurred after he babbled something incoherent and shambled his way out of the Mt. Dora gym. He imagined Dan Spear, dissolving in laughter on the floor, sitting there slapping his knees beneath the ping-pong table, while that naked kid laughed along with him. "What a riot," said Coach Spear, choking on his guffaws. "Barry swallowed it, hook, line and sinker! Hey, bob-a-ree-bah!" Then Dan got up from the floor, dusted off his hands, and said with an evil grin, "And now we're going out there on that field and rack some butt!"

Dan Spear had set him up, thought Barry. Dan knew B.M. was over-confident, and he wanted to capitalize on that. What better way than to whine and poormouth his team? "Go easy on us, dadblame it, Barry, or we'll just forfeit!"

Dan knew perfectly well, thought Barry (at some point late in the third quarter) that C.M. Jones would play that night, and play hard—though the papers said he was sidelined with a broken nose. Dan knew that the main spark plugs, Moon, Gardner, Williams, Potter, Stoothoff, were in fine playing shape and up sky high for the undefeated Hornets. Dan knew that Bowie was okay too, the Bowie who couldn't even play on offense against Groveland. Dan knew that Bowie's leg, in one short week, had made a miraculous recovery. That the pure speed was back.

Maybe even the leg wrapping was a charade, Barry was thinking (early in the fourth quarter). Dan heard that the Bishop Moore team bus had pulled in, he expected me to drop by the gym, and he made it a point to put that kid up on that ping-pong table and start wrapping his leg. Reams of tape, from hip bone to knee. He wanted to show me what a bunch of cripples he was working with! "Here's the best we've got tonight, Barry: a skinny kid with a bum leg, standing nekkid on a ping-pong table." Then, after he did that blow up act, screaming like a madman right in my face, as soon as I left, thought Barry, I can just see them yukking it up, that kid (who was it? Bowie?) climbing down from the table, Dan cutting off all the tape he'd just put around that so-called bad leg! Both of them laughing their asses off, breaking into song. Dan Spear dancing around in an Irish jig with fingers snapping, the kid (yeah, it must have been Bowie) doing the Russian squat dance in his jock strap, arms crossed over his chest, kicking out his legs. Injury. Gimpy leg. My butt! thought Barry.

I can imagine Barry Keitel when it was all over too, slouching in his seat, in that yellow school bus, with the whole team (Coach Bryan driving), on the long forlorn ride back to Orlando. He leans over to B.M. physics teacher Ignatius O'Reilly, sitting next to him, the guy who was up in the press box keeping game statistics. "How many yards rushing did Bowie have, Ignatius?" he asks.

"You don't want to know."

"I know I don't want to, but tell me anyway," says Barry. "198," says Mr. O'Reilly. "One hundred ninety-eight yards rushing."

"One ninety-eight... And how much total rushing yardage did they have?"

"Four hundred seventeen."

Barry sits there for a minute more. Then he says, "We were bamboozled." After that another pause.

"BAM BABOON BOOZLED!" he yells out, and the words reverberate all through the dead humidity and silence of the bus, blowing heavy gusts of air across the tears yet undried, on the faces of the big Irish and Italian boys.

Then the grim quiet sets back in, and Barry starts mumbling softly to himself, saying the same words over and over: "Four hundred seventeen. Four seventeen. Holy Mary, Mother of God."

But it wasn't a ploy, was it, Coach Spear? You thought you were about to see us thrashed, and you really would have pulled us off that field. You knew we had guts, but you underestimated the power of laughter. That laughter created a particular brand of adrenalin that Bishop Moore had never faced before. We were loosey goosey wild. The giddy vibes in our insides spread to our cheerleaders, and from them to our fans, wafted like the mosquito poisons, all over beautiful, subtropical Mt. Dora, Florida. That's what beat Bishop Moore that night.

Well, that plus infinite combinations of other eventualities in the minds and hearts of our players, our fans, our cheerleaders, and eons of unknown relatives. Who knows? If Dan Spear's little sister hadn't died when he was a child, we might have lost that night. Everything counts, ten million motivating circumstances determine the outcome of any one event, and then that one event adds itself to the ten billion motivations for any event that comes along later in your life. I can only speak for myself. I don't think Catholic B.M. had a prayer that night against the rosary beads of my Irish Catholic mother and the spirit of my dead Catholic sister.

I apologize to everyone in the game that night for telling it only the way I remember it. Y'all have your own personal reasons for the wild way

each of you played, and you have your own memories of the game. So take
a moment now, and tell it your way to Coach Dan Spear. That's one of the
things this roast is for. Stoothoff will remember the touchdowns he scored,
the long runs; you really were the biggest star, Rookie Stoothoff! Fiery Rick
Gardner will remember how he dug out a baseball bat in the gym after the
game and tried to go back outside and use it on those brawny B.M. players,
after they had expressed to him, with their large paws, their displeasure at
being defeated by niggling little us. The great Earle Williams will remember the punt he blocked in the first quarter and the fumble he caused,
leading to a touchdown. What do you remember, C.M. Jones, John Lavin,
Billy Moon, Gary Potter? Everybody remembers it a little bit differently,
but we all know one thing: we were great that night!

At this point I would also like to apologize to everyone on the Bishop
Moore side of this story. I know they're not at the roast tonight, but this
letter might somehow leak out and make it over to Orlando. I had to
imagine a lot of things about their view of that game. I don't really know
much about Barry Keitel, Stuart Stuart, Paul Musante, or the Ellis brothers. Only they know what they were thinking that night and what has
become of their lives forty years later. Maybe they should have a roast for
Mr. Keitel, get together the way we are tonight, talk over the memories.
One more thing: all through the writing of this business I've been trying to
remember Stuart Stuart's real last name. It was a common name, something
like "Miller." I met Stuart as a freshman at The University of Florida, and
we reminisced over old sports glories, talked about the Bishop Moore-Mt.
Dora football games. He was a large amiable guy with a big nose and a
spastic huh-huh-huh of a laugh. A really fine human being, excellent
student, whose shoulders had this hunched up way of jiggling when he
heard something funny. For the life of me, I can't remember your last name,

so I've just been calling you "Stuart Stuart" all the time. Sorry, Stuart. But you know who you are.

Anyway, my story is about a competition, so it has to have "good guys" and "bad guys." The bad guys are, of course, the B.M. folks and the good guys are us. But now really, anyone knows that life is never that clearly defined. Barry Keitel and Stuart, Bernie Bauman, Mike DeVoe and Ignatius O'Reilly, Johnny and Jim Ellis, and the rest of the gang from Orlando are not bad guys. Like all of us, they've got their humanities. At any rate, you of the splendrous black and gold, I hope you're thriving today, and I hope that the world has been kind to you, and may all the "football seasons" of the rest of your lives be undefeated!

Wait! Wait! Baker! I think his name was Stuart Baker!

As for the stuff about Catholicism, I hope nobody at B.M. gets offended if it seems like I don't love the Pope. I already told you that I owe a lot to the Pope. It's just that I used to be pretty mad at Catholics (and Protestants), and my story reflects the old anger. But I'm not mad anymore, and, with regard to any and all world religions, all I can say is what another Catholic once said: whatever helps you make it through the night is fine with me.

We didn't lose another game that year; we beat Eustis the very next week. Our record turned out 8-1. That was the best record at MDHS in a long time. Not the best team, maybe, but the best record.

So that's it, Dan Spear; that's the end of my story. Sorry I couldn't be there for the roast. I don't get back to Mt. Dora much these days. My only relatives left in town are now residing in a limited space at the far end of Donnelly Street: my grandparents, Aunt Cille, my mother, my daddy, Jacqi.

My mother died in 1975, of a blood and bone marrow disease. She had aplastic anemia. She found it ironic that at one point she was on some of the same medicine that Jacqi had taken. The last thing my mother said to me, in the intensive care ward at Shands Hospital in Gainesville, was "Go." She didn't actually say it, she mouthed it. She couldn't talk by that point, and I suppose she felt awkward, having loved ones sit there watching her die. Dying must be an embarrassing thing to do, especially when people are watching. She passed away at sixty-three, never having made the friends she wanted to make, never having taken the European trip she always wanted to take, and never having set foot in the state of Nebraska.

Myrtle H. Bowie was always good with kids. She was a lonely person, and I think that being with kids made her feel a little less so. Maybe not as much with her own kids though. It always seemed like she still felt lonely with me, and I felt lonely with her too. That's one of the mysteries, and also one of the great sadnesses of my life—the loneliness that stood there between me and my mother.

She was a telephone operator in New Jersey when she met Daddy, but she never worked a job during the whole of her life in Florida. She was what then was (and what now should still be) a perfectly respectable thing for a woman to be—a housewife. She volunteered for a lot of things connected with the schools, arbor days, girl scouts. The last thing I can remember her working on was the Head Start program in East Town. She told me about a five-year-old black kid she was reading stories to, and one day that boy said, "You know, I hate white folks. I believe white folks is the Devil." And Mommy said, "Well, look at me. I'm white. Isn't that so?" And he looked at her, bewildered, and he opened his mouth, and he finally said, "Aww-haw." And she said, "Now, you don't hate me, do you?" And he looked at her again with his mouth open, and he said, finally, "No, ma'm." I hope he's still circulating around somewhere in life today, not hating anyone, because toning down the hatred that roils inside our emotional selves is the only shot we people, black and white and all other races, have at becoming human beings.

Daddy remarried after a few years, to Bettye Ray. He sold the pink house, moved in with her, and lived out his life on the banks of Lake Gertrude. Who would have thought it? My daddy out with the rich folks, in Sylvan Shores. Robert N. Bowie, scraped out of the red clay of South Carolina, certainly never was a Sylvan Shores type. He and Bettye lived together ten years, and it seemed like a good marriage. Bettye did a fine job of taking care of him, right to the end of the Alzheimer's, and we're grateful to her for that.

I was there for the celebration of his seventy-fifth birthday, in March of 1987. I flew down from Ohio, and my sisters came with their families. The star attraction of the party was my nephew Jeff, June's son, who roared into Sylvan Shores on his Harley, in full biker regalia, accompanied by a motorcycle buddy, Mike. Jeff and Mike had spent the previous evening wrecking a bar down in Brevard County. They had, in fact, been run out of Brevard and given a police escort to the county line. Now they were on the way back to their gangland home in Louisiana, but they stopped off in honor of Daddy, whom Jeff loved like the father he never had. What a sight that was, Harley Davidson bikers, black leather jackets and tattooed arms, in lovely, subtropical, moss-draped, snooty Sylvan Shores, Florida.

Just think, we might have been high class too, since in America money is all that makes for class distinctions, and Daddy could have got rich. Back in the fifties, when he was doing very well at selling life insurance, he was offered a chance to buy lakefront property out on Lake Johanna. He had the money but he was too conservative to make investments. Embedded deeply in his mind was that scene from 1917, in South Carolina, when he, a five-year-old boy, had to watch his family pile what they could salvage on a horse-drawn wagon and drive away from the unpaid mortgage on the family farm. But if only he'd have bought that land! I could be living in a big lakefront house! I'd be as successful as the Potter brothers—Del Gene, with his mansion on Lake Gertrude, or Jan, with that wonderful place out on Lake Ola!

Instead I ended up teaching Russian literature and telling stories, like the one I'm telling you now. They don't pay much for that sort of thing, but it's interesting. Maybe I got my inspiration from Mt. Dora's own Pat Frank. Now there's a fellow who really did make some money. Back when Daddy and I used to fish on Lake Beauclaire, trolling for bass, we'd go puttering with our five-horse Johnson outboard motor down the lakefront, and Daddy would point out where Pat Frank lived, author of *Adam's Rib* (they made a movie out of that one) and *Alas, Babylon*.

Starting in his early fifties, my father developed angina pectoris, and then more cardiovascular problems. But his heart held out for another twenty-five years. What finally got him was Alzheimer's. When I visited him for the last time, in Oct., 1992, his mind was pretty far gone. His parting words to me were these: "Now, you be a good boy, you hear? You be a good boy and say your prayers at night, and when you die you'll go to Heaven."

Here's the conclusion to his travel memoir, written in 1931, age nineteen:

Since we had left home the past February we had covered almost ten thousand miles. It had cost us but approximately fifty dollars each. We had passed thru thirty states, had seen the most worthy scenes of our country, had swam in both oceans and most of the large inland bodies of water, passed through most of the large cities of the U.S. And above all had gained much geographical as well as economical knowledge. The trip was made in about two months traveling time and could have been made quicker if we had not delayed many times at the important historical and

natural scenes. We think, in conclusion, that every healthy American boy
between the ages of seventeen and twenty-one should enjoy the experience of adventure.

The End

I happened to be in Mt. Dora for a visit when Prof Roseborough died.
I was privileged to talk to him on the last day of his life. That must have
been some time in the early eighties. I heard he had had another stroke, and
I walked up the street from our pink house to see him. Precious greeted me
at the door of the long-time Roseborough residence on Clayton St., beside
the playground, and ushered me into the bedroom, where Prof was sitting
up, wearing a gown. As always, he was happy to see me. He gave me his left
hand to shake, since the right arm didn't function any more. He still had
that white shock of hair, the bright grey eyes behind the rimless eyeglasses.
He smiled his Prof smile and chuckled his Prof chuckle. Don't remember
what we talked about, but I left with a good feeling. Why was that? It was
something Prof could always do for me: leave me feeling good. The next
morning, when I got up, they told me somebody just called; Prof
Roseborough had died in his sleep that night.

So I don't get back to Mt. Dora much, Coach Spear, but I do go home
a lot in my dreams. Funny how you're not living in a place for forty years,
but the dream producers still keep using it as a setting for the skewed
dramas they stage in your mind. When I'm asleep I see the view of Lake
Dora from the hill where The Castle used to stand, or from what used to be
the porches on the old Grandview Hotel. I see the hibiscus bushes, the
lantana, poinsettias, azaleas, the luxuriant red-blooming bougainvillaea
growing up the back of the pink house. I watch the ear trees straining to

hear the sounds, among them all the familiar ones: my mother's cackling laugh, my daddy's way of saying so long ("Abyssinia," meaning "I'll be seeing you"), Prof Roseborough's chuckling admonitions ("Bowie, huh, huh. Bowie, son. Don't be a slacker, now, Bowie. You hear?"), the lugubrious coos of the mourning doves. I smell the asphalt coalescing in the cool of the evening, the orange blossoms and the night blooming jasmine. I see The Walking Jesus ambling off down that clay road between chinaberry trees, "Yea, though I walk through the Valley," evaporating into mist.

In closing, let me say, thank you, Dan Spear, for all the wonderful memories that came out of my years playing football for you. Thanks for the coaching. Thanks for the plays. Thanks for wrapping the leg and making it last through the fifty-seven season. When I think back on it all, it really was a glorious time, and you were a great coach. I wrote about the Bishop Moore game, because for me that was the high point of all the glory. I mean, when in my life have I ever been so purely happy? When, before or since, have I had such sheer crazy fun? You know, we ran wild that night, Dan Spear, and we *racked!* We knocked a lot of people down, and if they got up, we knocked them down again, and if they got up *again*, well, we knocked them down *again!*

Just like Bobby Co-ral.

The Documentary Evidence–1

Orlando Sentinel, Nov. 3, 1956

Bishop Moore Nips Mount Dora, 13-12

By BOB PRICE
Staff Writer

The Bishop Moore Hornets gained 257 yards on the ground at Harper-Shepherd Field last night, but had to settle for a 13-12 triumph over the Mount Dora Hurricanes.

Mount Dora could penetrate

THE YARDSTICK		
Mount Dora		Bishop Moore
10	First downs	21
139	Rushing yardage	257
16	Passing yardage	41
2-3	Passes attempted	6-12
1	Passes intercepted	1
3-31	Punts	1-42
2	Fumbles lost	0
60	Yards penalized	50

Individual yardage:
Mount Dora—Gardner 63; Simpson 31; Lane 9; Bowie 30.
Bishop Moore—DeVoe -16; Ellis 90; Musante 72; Baccarney 85.

the Hornet line for only 139 yards and got only 16 more through the air. Bishop Moore's air game collected 41 yards.

BOB BOWIE, a jet-propelled 155-pounder, was the individual star of the night, getting two Mount Dora touchdowns. Bowie moved over from the 14 for his first score and then intercepted a Bishop Moore pass on his own 10 and rambled 90 yards for the other.

Bishop Moore's better balance paid off. The Hornets, with John Ellis, Paul Musante and Paul Baccarney sharing the ball toting chores, controlled the ball for most of the game. Ellis was the top gainer with 90 yards in 15 carries. Baccarney had 85 in 13 attempts.

JOHN HORMUTH, Dick Beausejour, Bernie Bauman and James Lane were the reasons why Mount Dora could get only 139 yards.

The Hornets scored midway in the opening period on a drive of 60 yards that needed 13 plays to complete. Musante went the last yard through right guard. Mike DeVoe's kick was good and it turned out to be the winning margin.

Bishop Moore counted again in the third period with Baccarney going the final three yards of a 55-yard march. He had started the drive by intercepting a Mount Dora pass on his own 35 and returning to the 45.

Mount Dora got both of its TDs in the last period and Bowie completed a 58 yard drive for the first one. The Mount Dora speedster had a bit of luck on his interception TD, as the ball bounced off the knee of Ellis and into Bowie's arms. But after that it was Bowie, all the way. He seemed to gain speed as he went along and never was touched by the Hornets. He was 10 yards in front of the nearest man as he crossed the double stripe.

Score by periods:				
Mount Dora	0	0	0	12—12
Bishop Moore	7	0	6	0—13

Mount Dora scoring — Touchdowns—Bowie (14, run; 90, intercepted pass and run).
Bishop Moore scoring — Touchdowns—Musante (1, plunge); Baccarney (0 plunge). Conversions — DeVoe.

The Documentary Evidence–2
Orlando Sentinel, Nov. 2, 1957

At Mount Dora

BM-Upset, 32-25

By FRED SANWALD

MOUNT DORA — The Golden Hurricanes of Mount Dora blew the Hornets of Bishop Moore off the field here last night and handed Bishop Moore its first defeat of the season, 32-24.

The highly touted Hornets ran into a fired-up Mount

```
             THE YARDSTICK
Bishop Moore              , Mount Dora
13 ------- First Downs ------- 10
367 ----- Rushing Yardage ----- 417
16 ----- Passing Yardage ----- 25
8-12 --------- Passes --------- 1-3
1 -- Passes intercepted by -- 0
8-36 --------- Punts --------- 2-50
2 ------ Fumbles Lost ------ 2
20 ----- Yards penalized ----- 60
Individual yardage:
Bishop Moore: John Ellis 204, Jim Ellis
56, Musante 101, Pierson -10, Bauman
-21.
Mount Dora: Stoothoff 155, Bowie 198,
Gardner 57, Drake 7.
```

Dora team that was forced to play the game with six of the first string players sitting in the grandstand instead of on the bench or on the field.

This was the team that lost to Groveland last week, 40-0.

BISHOP MOORE sent the Ellis brothers — Jim and John — into action in the first period and the Hornets scored first as Jim Ellis cracked the line with a two-yard plunge to finish off a 45-yard drive.

Early in the second period Mount Dora began its scoring drive when Bob Bowie went off left tackle for a 10-yard score

after the Hurricanes had blocked a Hornet punt. The conversion failed and the score of 6-6 put the game on an even basis again.

AS SOON as the Hurricanes got their hands on the ball again in the second period. Richard Gardner grabbed a short flat pass from Neil Stoothoff and weaved his way for the remaining 25 yards to send the Dorans into the lead at the half, 13-6.

Stoothoff claimed the scoring honors in the third quarter for the Hurricanes, reeling off scoring runs of 45 and 26 yards, putting Mount Dora well ahead, 26-6.

AT THIS point, the Hornets' Ellis brothers came back into the spotlight as John went around right end for 40 yards and a score. Jim climaxed a 55-yard drive with a one-yard plunge to bring the Hornets to within seven points of the Hurricanes.

Stoothoff scored the last TD of the game late in the final period when he scampered 32 yards around right end to hang up the last tally in the free scoring tilt.

```
Score by periods:
Bishop Moore --------- 6  0 13  6—25
Mount Dora  --------- 0 13 13  6—32
   Bishop Moore scoring — Touchdowns:
Jim Ellis (2, rush:1, rush): John Ellis
(40, run: 1, rush). Conversions: Jim
Ellis (rush).
   Mount Dora scoring — Touchdowns:
Bowie (10, run): Gardner (25, pass from
Stoothoff): Stoothoff (45, run: 26, run:
32, run). Conversions: Dake (kick):
Gardner (kick).
```

Postscriptum:

A Letter from Dan Spear

Sat., May 21, 1994

Bob,

Thanks for the nice letter. It stole the show at the roast. Of course they didn't read the whole thing. You certainly have a good memory, but you always did have a good mind.

If you, Kinsey, Gardner, and Sadler had played on the same team as Odom, Wise, and Dake, you all would have been just as great. It's good to be at the right place at the right time.

Yes, I remember the "57" team. It was one of my best teams. I remember the team being sick with the Asiatic flu and Gary Potter getting out of bed to play in that Groveland game. I'm sure you remember him vomiting on the field. If I remember right, it seems we had to play a postponed game on the Monday before we played Groveland on Friday. That didn't help any.

By the way, Earle Williams was there at the "roast." I didn't expect him to be there. I haven't seen him since he graduated.

Yes, we still play Eustis. We beat them last fall 9-6 or 9-0 on 3 field goals of 35, 41, and 42 yds. out. We have a great field goal kicker.

I agree with you. I believe beating Bishop Moore, under the circumstances, was one of Mt. Dora's greatest victories. That proves what adrenalin will do when you are desperate.

I didn't realize that anyone heard me telling Keitel about the condition of our team.

Prof was one of the finest men that ever lived. He was good to me.

Mr. Sutley is still around. He always comes to the class reunions. The kids all had a great respect for him. He was a good teacher.

I didn't know your dog was named Danny, but I remember all the things you mentioned. I also remember Jacqi. The whole town mourned her death. I had her in my swimming class. I always kidded her and she always had that pleasant smile. I also lost a sister when she was very young and it still hurts.

You are right, I didn't think we had a chance against Bishop Moore with 6 starters sitting in the stands. I knew we had some tough kids with guts to spare, but I didn't think that would be enough. Moon and Gardner had guts to spare and I think they inspired the rest of the team.

Never underestimate your opponent. This is why I never liked to play a weak team. If you are not mentally prepared before the game, you can not pick up after the game starts. Adrenalin is the great equalizer. That's why we have upsets, but I'm sure you know this.

Thank you again for taking the time to write the letter. Everyone enjoyed it.

Sincerely,

Dan

P.s. next page

I saw your dad at a party at the yacht club before he passed away. I told him who I was and we talked briefly. I'm not certain that he knew who I was, but I thought I should speak to him. Betty said he probably wouldn't know me.

In case you didn't know, my wife Bert passed away Dec. 21, 1980. She had a rare form of leukemia that is fatal in 4 days in her case. It is

....

called myleomonocytic leukemia. Doc Montgomery said he never heard of it, but a man in Cleveland, Ohio, died of it the following week.

I've been to your college town once. It seemed like a pretty town.

I hope you get back to Mt. Dora some time. If and when you do, please look me up. If I'm not home, check with the golf club on Highland.

Dan

(over)

P.s. 2

I see Lavonia at the class reunions, but where are June and Peggy? I know June married a boy from Eustis and then divorced him. I lost track of her after that.

Bobby Correll passed away last May. He came to the reunion of the "51" team which was undefeated and untied. That was the fall of "86." We had a cocktail party at my house and then went to the ball game and were introduced to the crowd at half-time. After the game we went to the Lampost for dinner (Lampost is above Charlie's Place—across from Donnelly Park).

He died of cancer. We spread his ashes over Lake Dora, as he had requested.

ORDER FORM

A Roast for Coach Dan Spear is available in select book stores and other sales outlets. It may be mail ordered from the following address:

Ogee Zakamora Publications
P.O. Box 7207
Hamilton, OH 45013

Name:_____

Address:_____

City:_____

Telephone:_____

Price: $12.95

Please add $3.00 for handling and shipping of the first book; additional books shipped for 1.50 apiece.

Sales tax: For books shipped to Ohio addresses, add 5.5%.